**Formal Approaches to Computing and
Information Technology**

Springer
*London
Berlin
Heidelberg
New York
Barcelona
Budapest
Hong Kong
Milan
Paris
Santa Clara
Singapore
Tokyo*

J.C. Bicarregui (Ed.)

Proof in VDM: Case Studies

With 33 Figures

With contributions from:

Sten Agerholm
Bart Van Assche
John Fitzgerald
Jacob Frost
Albert Hoogewijs
Cliff Jones

Peter Lindsay
Savi Maharaj
Brian Matthews
Paul Mukherjee
Noemie Slaats

 Springer

J.C. Bicarregui, BSc, MSc, PhD
Department of Computing, Imperial College of Science, Technology and Medicine
180 Queen's Gate, London SW7 2BZ, UK
and
Computing and Information Systems Department, Rutherford Appleton Laboratory,
Chilton, Didcot, Oxfordshire OX11 0QX, UK

Series Editor
S.A. Schuman, BSc, DEA, CEng
Department of Mathematical and Computing Sciences
University of Surrey, Guildford, Surrey GU2 5XH, UK

ISBN-13:978-3-540-76186-0

British Library Cataloguing in Publication Data
Proof in VDM : case studies. - (Formal approaches to
    computing and information technology)
    1.Proof theory - Case studies 2.Computer software - Development
    I.Bicarregui, Juan C.
    005.1
    ISBN-13:978-3-540-76186-0

Library of Congress Cataloging-in-Publication Data
Proof in VDM : case studies / J.C. Bicarregui (ed.).
    p.   cm. -- (Formal approaches to computing amd information technology)
    Includes index
    ISBN-13:978-3-540-76186-0   e-ISBN-13:978-1-4471-1532-8
    DOI: 10.1007/978-1-4471-1532-8

    1. Computer software--Development--Case studies. 2. Automatic theorem proving.
    I. Bicarregui, J.C. (Juan Carlos), 1962-   II. Series.
    QA76.76.D47P775   1997
    005.1'4--dc21   97-29213
                                                                              CIP

Typesetting: Camera ready by editor

34/3830-543210 Printed on acid-free paper

Preface

Not so many years ago, it would have been difficult to find more than a handful of examples of the use of formal methods in industry. Today however, the industrial application of formal methods is becoming increasingly common in a variety of application areas, particularly those with a safety, security or financially critical aspects. Furthermore, in situations where a particularly high level of assurance is required, formal proof is broadly accepted as being of value.

Perhaps the major benefit of formalisation is that it enables formal symbolic manipulation of elements of a design and hence can provide developers with a variety of analyses which facilitate the detection of faults. Proof is just one of these possible formal activities, others, such as test case generation and animation, have also been shown to be effective bug finders. Proof can be used for both validation and verification. Validation of a specification can be achieved by proving formal statements conjectured about the required behaviours of the system. Verification of the correctness of successive designs can be achieved by proof of a prescribed set of proof obligations generated from the specifications.

The development of accurate formal specifications is clearly a difficult, time consuming and error prone task. Constructing proofs - typically several times larger than the software they are concerned with - is no simpler, but its value comes not only from of the degree of assurance given by proof, but also from the process of proof itself. Often, attempting a proof, that may well be impossible because of some mistake in the informal reasoning that led to the design, will uncover the precise nature of the fault and indicate the required correction. Other times, even though a design may be correct, the proof activity may lead us to a clearer, more elegant specification, which will in turn lead to higher quality software.

The automatic checking of the correctness of a completed fully formal proof is a relatively straightforward task which can be performed by a simple program that it is possible to trust. However, the construction of such proofs is at best computationally complex and, in general, impossible to automate. In some circumstances, it may be possible to lessen the cost of proof development by allowing rigorous rather than fully formal proof, but this increases the complexity of proof checking and hence reintroduces the possibility of acceptance of an incorrect proof. Unlike mathematical proofs which are repeatedly studied by successive generations of scholars, proofs of software are unlikely to be of interest outside the development team, unless such inspections are built into the development process.

This book describes a collection of case studies in the use of formal and rigorous proof in the validation and verification formal specifications mostly in safety- or security-critical application areas. In an earlier book in this series, "Proof in VDM: A Practitioner's Guide", the editor and several contributors explained the basic principles of proof and illustrated how it can be used in practice in VDM. This book is in many ways a companion to that text, presenting the use those techniques in a range of actual applications. Again, attention is focused on VDM-SL because of its ISO standardisation and because it has a well-documented and well-developed proof theory.

The case studies illustrate different aspects of the use of proof in formal development covering the validation of security and safety properties and the verification of formal refinement. The first four chapters describe case studies in which the proofs were developed by hand. These proofs are presented in considerable detail although not fully formally. The remaining chapters deal with machine supported, fully formal proof, employing a variety of support tools. The tools described are Mural, PVS and Isabelle.

The first case study describes *a formal model of a nuclear process tracking system* which was developed for the UK Health and Safety Executive. It presents the formal model itself, the elicitation and formalisation of safety properties from the model, and the proof that the model is consistent with respect to these properties. The study illustrates issues in the modular structuring of specifications and proofs as well as questions of methodology and specification style.

The second case study describes *the validation of an explosives store* against informally expressed requirements. This chapter uses an existing specification of UN regulations for safe storage of explosives to illustrate and compare a range of validation techniques available to the developer. Issues considered include levels of type checking, testing of executable specifications, and proof.

The third chapter describes *the specification and validation of a security policy model* for a network handling sensitive and classified material. The security policy model is specified and validated by showing that it is mathematically consistent and satisfies certain security properties. Some new techniques concerning proof obligations for exception conditions in VDM-SL are described.

The fourth chapter describes *the specification and proof of an EXPRESS to SQL compiler*. An abstract specification of an EXPRESS database is given and then refined by an implementation on top of a SQL relational database. The compiler is thus formalised as a refinement and the equivalence of the abstract and concrete specifications becomes the justification of its correctness.

The fifth chapter presents *a unified formalisation of shared memory models* for explicitly parallel programs, giving the semantics of the memory access and synchronisation instructions. It describes how the Mural tool was used in writing the VDM specification, generating the corresponding formal theory and constructing some fully formal proofs of basic properties of the model.

The sixth chapter describes *the use of the PVS system to support proof in VDM.*

It presents an easy and direct translation from VDM-SL into the PVS specification language and describes the use of PVS for typechecking and verifying properties of VDM-SL specifications and refinements. The translation and possibilities for proof arising from it are illustrated through a number of small examples and one larger case study of a protocol for inter-processor communications used in distributed, microprocessor-based nuclear safety systems.

The last chapter describes the instantiation of *Isabelle as a theorem proving component for VDM-SL*. The instantiation supports proof in VDM including handling difficult constructs such as patterns and cases expressions in a novel way using reversible transformations. The chapter illustrates the use of the theorem prover on two examples which demonstrate the handling of the three-valued Logic of Partial Functions underlying VDM-SL.

Together these case studies cover a broad range of issues in the use of proof in formal software development in many critical application areas. The book as a whole will be of value primarily to practitioners of formal methods who have experience of writing formal specifications and who need to construct proofs about them. This particularly applies to those seeking conformance with the higher levels of systems development standards, such as U.K. Defence Standard 00-55, the CEC's Information Technology Security Evaluation Criteria, U.S. Department of Defense Standard 5200.28-STD. Secondly, the book should be of use to potential users of formal methods seeking knowledge of existing experience in the application of formal methods and proof. Thirdly, it will be of interest to students of formal methods requiring a more detailed introduction to the practicalities of proof than that provided by the standard tutorial texts and researchers interested in the role of theorem proving in formal development and relevant tool support.

The editor would like to thank the contributors and publisher for their patience and his colleagues, in particular, Brian Ritchie, Stuart Robinson, Kevin Lano and Tom Maibaum, for their support during its preparation.

Contents

Contributors

Sten Agerholm
Institute of Applied Computer Science,
(IFAD)
Forskerparken 10,
DK-5230, Odense M, Denmark.
sten@ifad.dk

Juan Bicarregui
Rutherford Appleton Laboratory,
Chilton, Didcot, Oxon OX11 OQX, UK.
j.c.bicarregui@rl.ac.uk

John Fitzgerald
Centre for Software Reliability,
University of Newcastle upon Tyne,
Newcastle NE1 7RU, UK.
John.Fitzgerald@ncl.ac.uk

Jakob Frost
Department of Information Technology,
Technical University of Denmark,
DK-2800 Lyngby, Denmark.

Albert Hoogewijs
Department of Pure Mathematics and
Computer Algebra, University of Gent,
Galglaan 2, 9000 Gent, Belgium.

Cliff Jones
Harlequin plc,
Queens Court,
Wilmslow Road,
Cheshire, SK9 7QD, UK.

Peter Lindsay
Software Verification Research Centre,
School of Information Technology,
University of Queensland,
Brisbane, Qld 4072, Australia
pal@it.uq.edu.au

Savitri Maharaj
Department of Computing Science and
Mathematics, University of Stirling,
Stirling FK9 4LA, UK.
savi@cs.stir.ac.uk

Brian Matthews
Rutherford Appleton Laboratory,
Chilton, Didcot, Oxon OX11 OQX, UK.
b.m.matthews@rl.ac.uk

Paul Mukherjee
School of Computer Studies,
University of Leeds, Leeds LS2 9JT, UK.
paulm@scs.leeds.ac.uk

Noemie Slaats
Department of Pure Mathematics and
Computer Algebra, University of Gent,
Galglaan 2, 9000 Gent, Belgium
ns@cage.rug.ac.be

Bart Van Assche
Department of Pure Mathematics and
Computer Algebra, University of Gent,
Galglaan 2, 9000 Gent, Belgium

Chapter 1

Proof in the Analysis of a Model of a Tracking System

John Fitzgerald and Cliff Jones

Summary

Fully formal proof is not always possible within the financial and labour constraints of a commercial project. This chapter shows how knowledge of the structure of a proof can guide inspections and reviews, even when the proof itself is not to be derived. The study illustrates, on a reduced example, the main issues which arose as part of the proof-based analysis of a specification of a tracking mechanism for a nuclear plant.

1.1 Introduction

Many of the benefits of formal techniques in software development result from the ability to model a system at a level of abstraction which may not have been possible hitherto. To some extent, this is independent of the formality of the modelling language. The particular contribution of formality lies in the high degree of rigour which is available to the developer in analysing the model. Apart from syntax- and type-checking, and testing executable parts of models, the opportunity exists to use mathematical proof to increase confidence in a model.

Because of the effort (in training and application) involved, proof is often seen as a technique to be applied only when mandated. However, proofs can be conducted at various levels of detail, each with different levels of cost and benefit. This chapter discusses the application of proof at various levels of rigour in the analysis of a substantial formal model developed as part of an industrial project. Experience on the project emphasised proof, not as a machine-based activity which produces an inscrutable script, but as a technique for structuring the arguments which should take place in reviewing a formal model.

The particular application on which this chapter is based is a demonstrator system for tracking the movement of nuclear material through the phases of re-processing in an industrial plant. Section 1.2 gives the background to the project in more detail, while Section 1.3 introduces a concise formal model derived from the model developed in the project but reduced in scope for the purposes of this chapter. The reduced model nevertheless shares many of the characteristics of its larger-scale sibling. Section 1.4 contains two illustrations of the rôle of proof in validating and revising the formal model of the demonstrator. A number of issues were raised by the proof activity concerning such matters as the careful delineation of system boundaries, the use of proof in the review cycle, the degree of genericity in the specification and alternative models which might have been more appropriate for the validation task. These are discussed in Section 1.5.

1.2   Context of the Study

This chapter concerns work carried out with British Nuclear Fuels (Engineering) on the tracking of nuclear material as it passes through the various stages of industrial re-processing. For reasons of safety and security, as well as efficiency, it is necessary to track the movement of material through the reprocessing plant to ensure, for example, that there is not a build-up of fissile material in one stage of processing, and that all material is accounted for. Typically, the information about the movement of materials is distributed among the computers associated with each processing stage. A new approach to tracking was proposed, based on an architecture of *tracking managers*. Each tracking manager is responsible for monitoring, recording and permitting the movement of material through part of the plant.

The study reported here investigated the use of formal modelling in clarifying the requirements for a tracking manager architecture and validating its safety properties. Informal requirements for a *demonstrator plant* illustrating the use of the tracking manager architecture were determined in collaboration with domain experts at British Nuclear Fuels (Engineering) Ltd (BNFL). Certain properties of the system were felt to be related to the safe operation of the plant. These properties, which were expected to hold in the demonstrator plant, were stated informally. A formal model of the demonstrator plant in VDM-SL [1] was developed using SpecBox [3] and the IFAD VDM-SL Toolbox [8]. The model was syntax- and type-checked using the tools, but was not exercised (the Toolbox has extensive animation facilities). As a validation exercise, two formal reviews were conducted and an investigation of the use of proof in discharging proof obligations and validation conjectures (including safety properties) took place. The rest of this chapter concentrates on the proof activity.

1.3 A Formal Model of a Tracking System

Consider a simplified waste processing plant. Material arrives in a number of *packages* stored in a *crate*. The crate and packages are opened and the contents distributed among a number of *liners*, each of which contains material of just one type (examples of material types are *glass*, *metal*, *plastic* and *liquor*). Liners are assayed to determine their fissile material content and sent to the next phase, product treatment. When liners arrive at the next phase, they may be sent to a compaction device to be crushed. A crushed liner is called a *puck*. Pucks and non-compacted liners are stored in *drums* before being passed to a storage phase. The storage phase contains sub-phases to deal with the allocation of drums to locations in a store.

In the tracking manager project, the plant described was modelled in some detail, with additional models of the tracking managers themselves and the history of movements of containers around the plant. Here consideration is confined to modelling the containers in the plant and their movement. The plant modelled here follows much the same process as that described in the example above, with five principal phases: unpacking crates, sorting contents, assaying materials, compacting materials and exporting from the plant.

The two main components of the system state are shown below:

> state *System* of
>   *phases* : *PhaseId* $\xrightarrow{m}$ *Phase*
>   *containers* : *ContainerId* $\xrightarrow{m}$ *Container*
>
>   inv mk-*System* (*phases*, *containers*) $\triangleq$
>   . . .
>
>   init *sys* $\triangleq$ . . .
> end

The *phases* component models the current status of the plant, indicating which containers are in processing in each phase. The *containers* component records all the current information about each container. In the remainder of this section, the details of the model are supplied. In many cases, these details have been added to illustrate characteristics of the larger formal model derived in the tracking manager project, and the model derived here should be viewed in that light.

Data Model

First, consider the models of containers and the materials they contain. Materials and types of container are modelled as enumerated types:

> *Material* = GLASS | PLASTIC | METAL | LIQUOR;

> *ContainerType* = CRATE | PACKAGE | LINER | PUCK | DRUM;

A container has a certain type. From the system description, it is apparent that containers may contain either "raw material" or other containers. This is modelled using optional types. In addition, each container has some associated assay data relating to the fissile material in it:

$$Container :: type : ContainerType$$
$$material : [Material]$$
$$contents : [ContainerId\text{-set}]$$
$$data : [AssayData]$$

A container may contain either raw material or other containers, but not both, so an invariant is added to record the restriction that exactly one of the *material* and *contents* fields must be nil :

$$\text{inv } c \triangleq$$
$$c.material = \text{nil} \quad \Leftrightarrow \quad c.contents \neq \text{nil}$$

The *data* field is permitted to be nil when no assay data has yet been assigned to the container. The representation of assay data is immaterial to the study, so the type *AssayData* can be represented as token:

$$AssayData = \text{token}$$

Now it is possible to consider the phases of the plant. Each phase has an associated input buffer and output buffer[1], each with a maximum capacity. Each phase expects a certain kind of container at its input and produces a certain kind of container at its output. No ordering among the elements of each buffer is used in the study and so each buffer is modelled as a set of container identifiers:

$$Phase :: input\text{-}capacity : \mathbf{N}$$
$$input\text{-}type : ContainerType$$
$$current\text{-}input : ContainerId\text{-set}$$
$$output\text{-}capacity : \mathbf{N}$$
$$output\text{-}type : ContainerType$$
$$current\text{-}output : ContainerId\text{-set}$$

Container identifiers can be modelled as token, as their representation is immaterial:

$$ContainerId = \text{token}$$

It is expected that the capacities of the input and output buffers of a phase will be respected. In fact, preventing the build-up of hazardous materials in one area may be a safety issue for a plant such as this. An invariant records the restriction that the cardinalities of the buffers do not exceed the limits. An additional restriction is that no container can appear in both buffers simultaneously:

---

[1]In practice, these are often rail sidings in which materials, having been moved about the plant by rail, await treatment or further movement.

inv p $\triangleq$
  card $p.current\text{-}input \leq p.input\text{-}capacity$ $\wedge$
  card $p.current\text{-}output \leq p.output\text{-}capacity$ $\wedge$
  $p.current\text{-}input \cap p.current\text{-}output = \{\}$

State Invariant

Now it is possible to complete the overall data model of the plant. The state consists of mappings relating the identifiers to descriptions of phases and containers:

state *System* of
  phases : *PhaseId* $\xrightarrow{m}$ *Phase*
  containers : *ContainerId* $\xrightarrow{m}$ *Container*
end

In previous projects, the BNFL participants had remarked on the value of invariants as a means of recording restrictions on systems which would otherwise be tacitly assumed. In this project, the state invariant was used to record three main kinds of restriction:

- Consistency between state components. For example, all the containers in phases should be known in the container mapping.

- Additional constraints required for system safety. For example, that the total fissile mass of containers in a phase should not exceed a certain value.

- Consistency properties on the containers in the plant. These mainly took the form of *containment laws*: regulations regarding the materials and containers which each kind of container may hold.

Each kind of restriction can be illustrated in the small model presented so far. The property that all containers in *phases* must be known in the *containers* mapping is recorded as:

inv mk-*System* (*phases*, *containers*) $\triangleq$
  $\bigcup \{p.current\text{-}input \cup p.current\text{-}output \mid p \in$ rng *phases*$\} \subseteq$
  dom *containers*

An additional requirement is that a container should not appear in more than one phase:

inv mk-$System$ ($phases, containers$) $\triangleq$
   . . . $\wedge$

($\forall\, p1, p2 \in$ dom $phases \cdot p1 \neq p2 \;\Rightarrow$
                ($phases\,(p1).current\text{-}input \cup$
                $phases\,(p1).current\text{-}output$)
                $\cap$
                ($phases\,(p2).current\text{-}input \cup$
                $phases\,(p2).current\text{-}output$)
                $= \{\}$)$\cdot$

It is a safety requirement that the containers in each phase should be of the type expected for the phase:

inv mk-$System$ ($phases, containers$) $\triangleq$
   . . . $\wedge$

($\forall\, p \in$ rng $phases \cdot$
     $\forall\, c \in p.current\text{-}input \cdot containers\,(c).type = p.input\text{-}type \wedge$
     $\forall\, c \in p.current\text{-}output \cdot containers\,(c).type = p.output\text{-}type$)

The containment laws are summarised as follows:

1. The contents of any container must be known.

2. Crates contain only packages.

3. Packages contain only raw material.

4. Liners contain only packages.

5. Drums contain only pucks and liners.

6. Pucks contain only one liner of non-liquor material.

These are formalised as conjuncts of the invariant, giving the complete invariant shown in Figure 1.1.

Initialisation Clause

A characteristic of the formal model developed on project was that it described a particular "demonstrator" plant with a certain structure and series of processing phases. Despite this, the basic data type definitions in the model were not specific to a given phase structure. The particular structure was fixed in the state initialisation clause. In the smaller example developed in this chapter, the plant is initialised to five phases with different kinds of expected container and different buffer capacities:

state *System* of
  phases : *PhaseId* $\xrightarrow{m}$ *Phase*
  containers : *ContainerId* $\xrightarrow{m}$ *Container*

  inv mk-*System* (*phases*, *containers*) $\triangleq$
    $\bigcup \{p.current\text{-}input \cup p.current\text{-}output \mid p \in$ rng *phases*$\} \subseteq$
    dom *containers* $\wedge$
    $(\forall p1, p2 \in$ dom *phases* ·
        $p1 \neq p2 \Rightarrow$
        $(phases\,(p1).current\text{-}input \cup phases\,(p1).current\text{-}output)$
        $\cap$
        $(phases\,(p2).current\text{-}input \cup phases\,(p2).current\text{-}output)$
        $= \{\}) \wedge$
    $(\forall p \in$ rng *phases* ·
        $(\forall c \in p.current\text{-}input ·$
            $containers\,(c).type = p.input\text{-}type) \wedge$
        $(\forall c \in p.current\text{-}output ·$
            $containers\,(c).type = p.output\text{-}type)) \wedge$
    $\forall c \in$ dom *containers* ·
        let mk-*Container* (*type*, *material*, *contents*, -) =
            containers (*c*) in
        $(contents \neq$ nil $\Rightarrow contents \subseteq$ dom *containers*$) \wedge$
        $(type = \text{CRATE} \Rightarrow$
        $contents \neq$ nil $\wedge$
        $\forall p \in contents · containers\,(p).type = \text{PACKAGE}) \wedge$
        $(type = \text{PACKAGE} \Rightarrow material \neq$ nil $) \wedge$
        $(type = \text{LINER} \Rightarrow$
        $contents \neq$ nil $\wedge$
        $\forall c1 \in contents · containers\,(c1).type = \text{PACKAGE}) \wedge$
        $(type = \text{DRUM} \Rightarrow$
        $contents \neq$ nil $\wedge$
        $(\forall c1 \in contents · containers\,(c1).type = \text{PUCK} \vee$
                            $containers\,(c1).type = \text{LINER})) \wedge$
        $(type = \text{PUCK} \Rightarrow$
        $contents \neq$ nil $\wedge$ card *contents* $= 1 \wedge$
        let $\{l\} = contents$ in
        $containers\,(l).type = \text{LINER} \wedge$
        $\forall p \in containers\,(l).contents ·$
            $containers\,(p).material \neq \text{LIQUOR})$

end

Figure 1.1: State Invariant for the Plant

init $sys \triangleq sys =$ mk-$System$
$\qquad$(
$\qquad$ {UNPACK $\mapsto$
$\qquad\qquad$ mk-$Phase$ $(10, \mathrm{CRATE}, \{\}, 1000, \mathrm{PACKAGE}, \{\})$,
$\qquad\quad$ SORT $\mapsto$
$\qquad\qquad$ mk-$Phase$ $(500, \mathrm{PACKAGE}, \{\}, 100, \mathrm{LINER}, \{\})$,
$\qquad\quad$ ASSAY $\mapsto$
$\qquad\qquad$ mk-$Phase$ $(1000, \mathrm{LINER}, \{\}, 1000, \mathrm{LINER}, \{\})$,
$\qquad\quad$ COMPACTION $\mapsto$
$\qquad\qquad$ mk-$Phase$ $(1000, \mathrm{LINER}, \{\}, 1000, \mathrm{PUCK}, \{\})$,
$\qquad\quad$ EXPORT $\mapsto$
$\qquad\qquad$ mk-$Phase$ $(100, \mathrm{PUCK}, \{\}, 250, \mathrm{DRUM}, \{\})\}$,
$\qquad$ $\{\mapsto\})$

The *containers* state component is initially empty.

Example Operations

The model developed in the project described the behaviour of the demonstrator plant by means of operations. Here too, there was a mixture between the generic and the particular. Most operations were specific to each phase, for example describing the effects of assaying a container on the record maintained about that container in the system state. It was observed that some actions recurred frequently throughout the system. For example, most phases involve packing a new container at some point, filling it with a volume of material or a number of other containers. A number of generic operations were defined to describe these actions and these were then used in the phase-specific operations by quoting their post-conditions.

As an example, consider the operation describing part of the sorting process which follows the unpacking phase. Packages are placed in liners according to the kind of material they contain. The process of moving a set of packages into a liner is described by the operation given below:

$\qquad$ $SORT$ $(new : ContainerId, mat : Material, packs : ContainerId$-set$)$
$\quad$ ext wr $phases : PhaseId \xrightarrow{m} Phase$
$\qquad$ wr $containers : ContainerId \xrightarrow{m} Container$
$\quad$ pre let $p = phases$ (SORT) in
$\qquad$ $packs \subseteq p.current\text{-}input \wedge$
$\qquad$ $(\forall\, p \in packs \cdot containers\,(p).material = mat) \wedge$
$\qquad$ card $p.current\text{-}output < p.output\text{-}capacity \wedge$
$\qquad$ pre-$PACK$ $(new, \mathrm{LINER}, $ nil $, packs,$ mk-$System\,(phases, containers))$

post let $p = \overset{\frown}{phases}$ (SORT) in

$phases = \overset{\frown}{phases}$ †
$\{$SORT $\mapsto \mu\,(p, current\text{-}input \mapsto p.current\text{-}input \setminus packs,$
$\quad current\text{-}output \mapsto p.current\text{-}output \cup \{new\})\} \wedge$
post-$PACK\,(new, \text{LINER}, \text{nil}, packs,$
$\qquad\qquad \text{mk-}System\,(\overset{\frown}{phases}, \overset{\frown}{containers}),$
$\qquad\qquad \text{mk-}System\,(phases, containers))$

The operation takes as input the identifier of a container which will hold the sorted packages, the kind of material contained in all the packages and the set of identifiers of the packages to be sorted. The precondition ensures that the packages to be sorted are all in the input buffer of the phase, that they share a common material and that there is room for the new container in the output buffer. The postcondition requires that the state be updated with the packages removed from the phase input and packed into a container which is added to the phase output.

The pre- and postconditions of another operation, *PACK*, are quoted in the *SORT* operation. This more generic operation is used in the operations which are specific to particular phases in the plant. It specifies the process of putting arbitrary contents into a given container, updating the *containers* state component accordingly. The *PACK* operation is studied in more detail in Section 1.4 below. However, it can be presented here:

$PACK\,(cid: ContainerId, ctype: ContainerType,$
$\qquad cmaterial: [Material], ccontents: [ContainerId\text{-set}])$
ext wr $containers: ContainerId \xrightarrow{m} Container$

pre $cid \notin \text{dom } containers \wedge$
$\quad (ccontents \neq \text{nil} \;\Rightarrow\; ccontents \subseteq \text{dom } containers)$

post $containers = \overset{\frown}{containers}$ †
$\quad \{cid \mapsto \text{mk-}Container\,(ctype, cmaterial, ccontents, \text{nil})\}$

The container identified by *cid* is to be created containing the given *ctype*, *cmaterial* and *ccontents*. The precondition states that, for container packing to be applied correctly, the new container should not already exist (i.e. it should not be in the domain of the *containers* state component) and if it is to contain other containers, these other containers should be known. If this condition holds, the *containers* state component is updated with the new container.

The Formal Model

This concludes the introduction to the formal model. The characteristics of the model of special note are:

1. the use of the state invariant to record properties derived from the safety analysis of the plant;

2. the mixture of generic data types, which could be applied in a model of any plant (e.g. *Phase*) with types specific to the demonstrator plant (e.g. *Material*);

3. the use of the initialisation clause to fix the structure of the plant;

4. the mixture of generic operations (e.g. *PACK*) with operations specific to particular phases (e.g. *SORT*).

The full model developed in the project was much more complex in a number of respects. Additional state components were needed to record histories of container movement and the mechanism for granting permission for container movement. In addition, the plant structure itself was hierarchical, with phases divided into sub-phases.

The reader may have already identified deficiencies in the model presented so far. It should be stressed that the model presented here is being shown "warts and all". The main purpose of this chapter is to show how a knowledge of proof assists in improving such a model. In fact, a fully-reviewed model of the demonstrator plant could look significantly different. In the following section, the review process applied in the project is illustrated on some examples of safety-related properties.

1.4 Analysing the Model with Proof

One aim of the tracking manager project was to see if a formal model of the plant could be useful in analysing the safety features which the proposed tacking manager architecture would have to maintain. It is in the validation of the formal model that this checking is carried out. In this section, some of the techniques employed to analyse the model in the project are illustrated on the reduced model developed above. First, two conjectures which arose in the project are introduced. The proofs of these conjectures are discussed: one involving rigorous reasoning guided by the structure of a formal proof; the second containing a fully formal element. In each case, deficiencies in the formal model are highlighted and discussed.

In VDM-SL, specifications consist of a state definition in terms of some defined data types, along with specifications of operations which can be invoked to change the system state. Typically, the state definition contains a number of state variables whose values are constrained by an invariant. Most important for this study, many of the constraints necessary to avoid hazards arising were added to the invariant: for example, the requirement that liners must contain packages of a single type. The specified operations on the system must never lead to a state which violates the invariant. It is therefore necessary to check the operation specifications to ensure that this is indeed the case

Each operation is specified in terms of a *precondition* and *postcondition*. The precondition records assumptions about the state and input parameters, while the postcondition indicates how the state may be modified and what result is returned.

There is an obligation on the author of the specification to show that the precondition and postcondition are consistent in the sense that every combination of system state and inputs satisfying the precondition has a corresponding state and output combination satisfying both the invariant and the postcondition. This is termed the *satisfiability proof obligation* [8]. In discharging the satisfiability obligation, one shows that the operation respects the invariant, and consequently for the tracking manager specification, respects the safety properties.

The formal model used in the BNFL project was too large (2500 lines approx.) to permit the proof that all the safety properties are respected by all the operations within the resources of the project. Instead, three typical safety-related conjectures, including one satisfiability proof obligation, were chosen. They concentrated on areas of the specification which its authors felt were the most susceptible to error and were representative of other proofs which could be undertaken.

The following section introduces three levels of rigour at which proofs may be constructed, and indicates the trade-offs between them. Section 1.4.2 describes the particular conjectures chosen for the tracking manager study.

1.4.1 Levels of Rigour in Proof

A proof based on a formal specification can be carried out at various levels of rigour. The three identified here are:

"Textbook" proof: This is the level of rigour found in most general mathematics texts. The argument is made in English, supported by formulae. Justifications for steps in the reasoning often appeal to human insight. This is the easiest of the three styles of proof to read, but the reliance on intuition means that such proofs can only be checked by other human beings.

Fully formal proof: At the other extreme, a fully formal proof (of the kind discussed in [2]) is a highly structured sequence of assertions in a well-defined formal language. Each step is justified by appealing to a formally-stated rule of inference. A formal proof is so detailed that it can be checked mechanically. It is possible to have a high degree of confidence in such a proof, but construction of the proof is very laborious, even with such machine assistance as is currently available. Formal proof is most frequently employed in highly critical applications.

Rigorous proof: This refers to a proof which borrows the ideas of careful structuring and line-by-line justification from the formal proof, but relaxes some of the strictures which make the production of a formal proof so costly. Obvious typing hypotheses may be omitted, abbreviations may be used, justifications may appeal to general theories rather than to specific rules of inference.

When executed carefully, "textbook", and even rigorous, proofs should provide a structure on which a fully formal proof could subsequently be based. All three levels of rigour were viable options for proofs of safety properties in the demonstrator plant model.

1.4.2   Validation Conjectures

This section introduces two conjectures considered in the analysis of the model of the demonstrator architecture. The conjectures are based on the following questions and observations:

- The operation for packing a container is generic. Could it violate the containment clauses, i.e. is it possible to pack something into a container which is not allowed to contain it?

- It should not be possible to compact liquor.

Although one might state conjectures in this informal way in a normal development process, the aim of verifying them against a formal specification requires greater precision in their formulation. For example, the second conjecture fails to draw a clear distinction between the specification of the system and the physical system of which the specification is merely a model. The formal model can not itself prevent compaction of liquor, but the model can be analysed to see if the specified compaction operation can be applied to liners containing any containers which contain liquor.

1.4.3   Container Packing

The first conjecture is that the container packing operation respects the containment laws. When the model was introduced above, the containment laws were stated as part of the invariant on the overall state. It would be expected that the proof of preservation of the state invariant would form a part of the satisfiability proof of the *PACK* operation, so this is where an examination of the model should begin. Indeed, it is noted in the "Proof in VDM" book [2] that the bulk of the work associated with showing satisfiability is in showing invariant preservation.

In the BNFL project, a preliminary examination of the satisfiability proof obligation suggested modifications to the model. A systematic attempt to show satisfiability at the "mathematical textbook" level then pointed to a number of more subtle errors which could otherwise have escaped detection until later in the development.

Following the formalism laid down in [2] (page 177), an operation specification

$$Op\,(x:X)\;y:Y$$
$$\textsf{ext rd}\;\;r:R$$
$$\textsf{wr}\;\;w:W$$
$$\textsf{pre}\;\;Pr(r,w)$$
$$\textsf{post}\;\;Po(r,\overleftarrow{w},w)$$

operating on a state

> state Σ of
> $r : R$
> $w : W$
> $u : U$
> end

has satisfiability obligation

$$\boxed{\text{Op-sat}} \quad \frac{x : X;\, mk\text{-}\Sigma(\overleftarrow{r},\overleftarrow{w},\overleftarrow{u}) : \Sigma;\, pre\text{-}Op(\overleftarrow{r},\overleftarrow{w});}{\exists\, y : Y,\, mk\text{-}\Sigma(r, w, u) : \Sigma \cdot}$$
$$post\text{-}Op(x, y, r, \overleftarrow{w}, w) \wedge r = \overleftarrow{r} \wedge u = \overleftarrow{u}$$

Note that the "framing" constraints given by the operation's externals clause must be carefully handled.

Stated formally, the satisfiability obligation for *PACK* is as follows:

> $cid : ContainerId;$
> $ctype : ContainerType;$
> $cmat : [Material];$
> $ccnts : [ContainerId\text{-set}];$
> $mk\text{-}System(\overleftarrow{phases}, \overleftarrow{containers}) : System$

$$\boxed{\text{PACK-sat}} \quad \frac{pre\text{-}PACK(cid, ctype, cmat, ccnts, \overleftarrow{containers})}{\exists\, mk\text{-}System(phases, containers) : System \cdot}$$
$$post\text{-}PACK(cid, ctype, cmat, ccnts, \overleftarrow{containers}, containers)$$

Before embarking on a proof, time spent trying to construct a counter-example to the conjecture can be rewarding. If a counter-example can be found easily, it is as well to consider modification of the specification before proceeding further. Knowing that the proof of *PACK-sat* would concentrate on showing that the containment laws are respected, the reviewers of the specification tried to construct a counter-example, and one was forthcoming. The reader might wish to treat this as an exercise before reading on.

Consider invoking *PACK* on a liner *l*, wanting to pack inside it a crate *c*. The precondition evaluates to true, so the satisfiability obligation requires that a state be found to satisfy the post-condition. The post-condition requires that

$$containers = \overleftarrow{containers} \dagger \{l \mapsto mk\text{-}Container\,(\text{LINER}, \text{nil}, \{d\}, \text{nil})\}$$

but this contradicts the clause in the state invariant which states that liners in the *containers* mapping may only contain packages:

$(type = \text{LINER} \Rightarrow$
$contents \neq \text{nil} \wedge$
$\forall c1 \in contents \cdot$
$\qquad containers\,(c1).type = \text{PACKAGE} \wedge \dots)$

It was not therefore possible to show that the containment laws would be respected for all valid inputs to *PACK*, and so a number of alternative strategies for overcoming this were considered. The precondition of *PACK* could be modified to reflect all the containment laws. However, this would make the precondition rather large and unwieldy, certainly in a proof. It would be more practical to record the containment laws as a separate auxiliary function. However, it was also noted that the containment laws and some other conjuncts in the invariant relate solely to the *containers* state component and do not relate it to the *phases* component, so the preferred solution was to define a new type *ContainerMap* which has an invariant recording all the restrictions relating solely to containers, including the laws. This type definition is given in Figure 1.2. The state definition now uses the new type

$ContainerMap = ContainerId \xrightarrow{m} Container$

inv *containers* $\triangleq$
$\quad \forall c \in \text{dom } containers \cdot$
$\qquad$ let mk-*Container* $(type, material, contents, \text{-}) =$
$\qquad\qquad containers\,(c)$ in
$\qquad (contents \neq \text{nil} \quad \Rightarrow \quad contents \subseteq \text{dom } containers) \wedge$
$\qquad (type = \text{PACKAGE} \quad \Rightarrow \quad material \neq \text{nil} \,) \wedge$
$\qquad (type = \text{LINER} \Rightarrow$
$\qquad contents \neq \text{nil} \wedge$
$\qquad \forall c1 \in contents \cdot containers\,(c1).type = \text{PACKAGE}) \wedge$
$\qquad (type = \text{DRUM} \Rightarrow$
$\qquad contents \neq \text{nil} \wedge$
$\qquad (\forall c1 \in contents \cdot containers\,(c1).type = \text{PUCK} \vee$
$\qquad\qquad\qquad\qquad\qquad containers\,(c1).type = \text{LINER})) \wedge$
$\qquad (type = \text{PUCK} \Rightarrow$
$\qquad contents \neq \text{nil} \wedge$
$\qquad$ card $contents = 1 \wedge$
$\qquad$ let $\{l\} = contents$ in
$\qquad containers\,(l).type = \text{LINER} \wedge$
$\qquad \forall p \in containers\,(l).contents \cdot$
$\qquad\qquad containers\,(p).material \neq \text{LIQUOR})$

Figure 1.2: New *ContainerMap* type incorporating containment laws

and the containment laws can be omitted from the state invariant. The modified state definition is given in Figure 1.3. Now the *PACK* operation can be modified

state *System* of
 phases : *PhaseId* $\xrightarrow{m}$ *Phase*
 containers : *ContainerMap*

 inv mk-*System* (*phases*, *containers*) $\triangleq$
  $\bigcup$ {*p.current-input* $\cup$ *p.current-output* | *p* $\in$ rng *phases*} $\subseteq$
  dom *containers* $\wedge$
  ($\forall$ *p*1, *p*2 $\in$ dom *phases* ·
   *p*1 $\neq$ *p*2 $\Rightarrow$
   (*phases* (*p*1).*current-input* $\cup$ *phases* (*p*1).*current-output*) $\cap$
   (*phases* (*p*2).*current-input* $\cup$ *phases* (*p*2).*current-output*)
   = {}) $\wedge$
  ($\forall$ *p* $\in$ rng *phases* ·
   $\forall$ *c* $\in$ *p.current-input* ·
    containers (*c*).*type* = *p.input-type* $\wedge$
   $\forall$ *c* $\in$ *p.current-output* ·
    containers (*c*).*type* = *p.output-type*)
 init *sys* $\triangleq$ *sys* = ...
end

Figure 1.3: State after introducing *ContainerMap*

by quoting the *ContainerMap* invariant in the precondition to ensure that the new *containers* state component to be constructed will respect the laws:

PACK 2 (*cid* : *ContainerId*, *ctype* : *ContainerType*, *cmaterial* : [*Material*],
   ccontents : [*ContainerId*-set])
ext wr *containers* : *ContainerMap*
pre inv-*ContainerMap* (*containers* †
      {*cid* $\mapsto$ mk-*Container* (*ctype*, *cmaterial*,
          ccontents, nil)}) $\wedge$
 inv-*Container* (mk-*Container* (*ctype*, *cmaterial*, *ccontents*, nil)) $\wedge$
 cid $\notin$ dom *containers* $\wedge$
 (*ccontents* $\neq$ nil $\Rightarrow$ *ccontents* $\subseteq$ dom *containers*)
post *containers* = $\overleftarrow{\text{containers}}$ †
  {*cid* $\mapsto$ mk-*Container* (*ctype*, *cmaterial*, *ccontents*, nil)}

The satisfiability proof obligation can now be revisited with a view to constructing a "textbook" proof. The conclusion of the conjecture is an existential expression. A common strategy for demonstrating the existence of a value satisfying some condition is actually to construct such a value which stands as a witness to the truth of the existential expression (Section 3.3.1 of [2]). In this case, the proof must conclude

that there exists a system satisfying the post-condition. The post-condition suggests
a suitable witness value: it states that the *containers* component of the system is
updated to include the new *cid* and the *Container* it points to, and the other state
component remains unchanged. The witness value is therefore

$$\text{mk-}System\,(\overleftarrow{phases},\,containers)$$

where

$$containers = \overleftarrow{containers} \dagger$$
$$\{\,cid \mapsto \text{mk-}Container\,(ctype, cmaterial, ccontents, \text{nil}\,)\}$$

Call this witness value σ. To discharge the proof obligation, it is necessary to show
three sub-obligations:

- that σ has the correct basic type (*System*);

- that σ satisfies *post-PACK2*;

- that σ satisfies inv-*System*.

The first sub-obligation is straightforward. For σ to be a system, its components
must all be of the correct type. The unchanged components were drawn from a
System ($\overleftarrow{\sigma}$) and so are still of the correct type. For the new *containers* component
to be a *ContainerMap* it must

- be a mapping from *ContainerId* to *Container*; and

- satisfy inv-*ContainerMap*.

The constructed system σ is certainly a mapping between the correct types. It
is also known to satisfy inv-*ContainerMap* because this is now guaranteed by the
hypothesis *pre-PACK2* in the conjecture.

The second sub-obligation is also straightforward: σ satisfies *post-PACK2* by construction.

It remains to show that σ is indeed a well-formed *System*, satisfying the invariant. The approach employed when reviewing the demonstrator plant model was
to consider each conjunct of the invariant in turn to see if it could fail. Although
one problem was spotted and remedied before a detailed proof was considered by
the definition and use of inv-*ContainerMap* in the precondition, the clause-by-clause
examination of inv-*System* revealed several cases in which satisfiability was still not
guaranteed. Three examples are considered below:

1. $\bigcup\{p.current\text{-}input \cup p.current\text{-}output \mid p \in \text{rng } phases\}$
       $\subseteq \text{dom } containers$

This clause asserts that all the containers in the buffers of all phases are known in the *containers* mapping. The new state σ adds a new identifier *cid* to the domain of *containers* (the fact that *cid* is new is guaranteed by the hypothesis *pre-PACK*) and does not change any other part of the *containers* mapping so all the containers known before the *PACK* operation are still known afterwards. This conjunct is therefore preserved.

2.   ($\forall\, p1, p2 \in$ dom *phases* ·

       $p1 \neq p2 \Rightarrow$

       (*phases* ($p1$).*current-input* $\cup$ *phases* ($p1$).*current-output*) $\cap$

       (*phases* ($p2$).*current-input* $\cup$ *phases* ($p2$).*current-output*) = {})

This conjunct describes the requirement that no two phases should have any containers in common. This is unaffected by any change in the *containers* mapping, and so still holds after *PACK* has been applied.

3. $\forall\, p \in$ rng *phases* ·

       ($\forall\, c \in p.current\text{-}input$ · *containers* (c).*type* $= p.input\text{-}type$) $\wedge$

       ($\forall\, c \in p.current\text{-}output$ · *containers* (c).*type* $= p.output\text{-}type$)

This conjunct asserts that containers respect the container types expected for each buffer. The *phases* state component is not affected by *PACK* and, as already argued, the *containers* mapping is added to and not otherwise changed, so this conjunct is again regarded as preserved.

Depending on the level of level of confidence one has in an argument of this form, it would be possible to stop here or to go further and formalise each of the three sub-obligations as lemmas which contribute to a formal overall proof of satisfiability.

In the demonstrator plant specification, some 21 conjuncts of the invariant were affected by *PACK*. Examination in this structured but informal way revealed a number of errors which might otherwise have gone undetected.

1.4.4   Safety of Compaction

The second conjecture considered was that it should be "impossible to compact liquor". This conjecture is slightly more difficult to formulate than satisfiability of *PACK*. However, after consultation with domain experts, it became clear that the operation describing the compaction phase should be protected by its precondition from operating on containers with liquor in them. The specification of the compaction operation is given in Figure 1.4. The compaction operation updates the *phases* mapping by removing a container from the input buffer and generating a puck containing only the compressed container in the output buffer. The precondition is of more interest for the conjecture proposed. It states that the compacted container is known and that there is capacity for the puck in the output buffer of the compaction phase. The precondition of *PACK2* is established. The last two

$COMPACTION\,(cid : ContainerId, new : ContainerId)$
ext wr $phases : PhaseId \xrightarrow{m} Phase$
   wr $containers : ContainerMap$
pre let $p = phases\,(\text{COMPACTION})$ in
    $cid \in p.current\text{-}input \wedge$
    card $p.current\text{-}output < p.output\text{-}capacity \wedge$
    pre-$PACK2\,(new, \text{PUCK}, \text{nil}, \{cid\},$
                mk-$System\,(phases, containers)) \wedge$
    $containers\,(cid).contents \neq \text{nil} \wedge$
    $\forall\, c' \in containers\,(cid).contents \cdot$
        $containers\,(c').material \neq \text{LIQUOR}$
post let $p = \overleftarrow{phases}\,(\text{COMPACTION})$ in
    $phases = \overleftarrow{phases} \dagger \{\text{COMPACTION} \mapsto$
      $\mu\,(p, current\text{-}input \mapsto p.current\text{-}input \setminus \{cid\},$
        $current\text{-}output \mapsto p.current\text{-}output \cup \{new\})\} \wedge$
    post-$PACK2\,(new, \text{PUCK}, \text{nil}, \{cid\},$
               mk-$System\,(\overleftarrow{phases}, \overleftarrow{containers}),$
               mk-$System\,(phases, containers))$;

Figure 1.4: Compaction operation

conjuncts of the precondition were intended to ensure that the liner arriving for compaction does not contain any packages of liquor.

The conjecture should, roughly, take the following form:

$cid : ContainerId;$
$new : ContainerId;$
$mk\text{-}System(phases, containers) : System;$
Compaction $\dfrac{pre\text{-}COMPACTION(cid, new, containers, phases)}{\text{Liquor not in } cid}$

How should the "Liquor not in cid" condition be expressed? The containment rules give a hierarchy of possible containments. Given a $ContainerMap$ and a $ContainerId$, it should be possible to define a recursive function which gathers all the material types in a container and its sub-containers:

$gather : ContainerMap \times ContainerId \to Material\text{-set}$

$gather\,(m, c) \triangleq$
  if $m\,(c).material \neq \text{nil}$
  then $\{m\,(c).material\}$
  else $\bigcup \{gather\,(m, c') \mid c' \in m\,(c).contents\}$
pre $c \in \text{dom } m$

Thus the formal conjecture should be:

$$cid : ContainerId;$$
$$new : ContainerId;$$
$$mk\text{-}System(phases, containers) : System;$$
$$cid \in \mathsf{dom}\ containers;$$

$$\boxed{\text{Compaction}}\ \frac{pre\text{-}COMPACTION(cid, new, containers, phases)}{\text{LIQUOR} \notin gather(containers, cid)}$$

The *gather* function was drafted purely to assist in the proof process: it was not part of the model of the plant. However, it was apparent that the *COMPACTION* function did not make use of the same kind of recursive accumulation function. Did another part of the precondition ensure that the compaction operation was only applied to containers nested one deep, or did this hint at a counter-example?

In fact, it was possible to construct a counter-example to the conjecture. Consider a drum d which contains one liner l which contains a package p which contains liquor. In this case, the precondition of *COMPACTION* is satisfied, because all the containers in d have the *material* component set to nil. However, the *gather* function would discover the liquor "hiding" in the package p.

It was clear that the compaction operation somehow relied on the input being a liner, so the precondition was modified to include an explicit check to this effect. A further discussion of the flaw in the operation specification and this resolution follows at the end of this section.

The modified compaction operation is:

$COMPACTION2\,(cid : ContainerId, new : ContainerId)$
ext wr $phases : PhaseId \xrightarrow{m} Phase$
    wr $containers : ContainerMap$
pre let $p = phases\,(\text{COMPACTION})$ in
    $cid \in p.current\text{-}input\ \wedge$
    card $p.current\text{-}output < p.output\text{-}capacity\ \wedge$
    $new \notin \mathsf{dom}\ containers\ \wedge$
    pre-$PACK2\,(new, \text{PUCK}, \text{nil}\,, \{cid\},$
               $mk\text{-}System\,(phases, containers))\ \wedge$
    $containers\,(cid).contents \neq \text{nil}\ \wedge$
    $\forall\, c' \in containers\,(cid).contents\ \cdot$
        $containers\,(c').material \in safe\text{-}materials$
post $\ldots$

Having modified the specification, the reviewers were not sufficiently confident about the correction to accept a "textbook" argument. Instead a rigorous proof of the conjecture was undertaken. The proof process begins by setting out the hypotheses and conclusion:

from cid : $ContainerId$;
    new : $ContainerId$;
    $mk\text{-}System(phases, containers)$: $System$;
    $cid \in$ dom $containers$;
    $pre\text{-}COMPACTION(cid, new, containers, phases)$
    $\vdots$
infer $LIQUOR \notin gather(containers, cid)$

The proof's structure can be predicted by considering the informal argument. One can begin by working backwards from the conclusion, expanding the definition of *gather*. It will be necessary to show that none of the packages in the container identified by *cid* contain liquor. In order to do this, we can reason forwards from the hypotheses: the (modified) precondition ensures that *cid* identifies a liner, which must (by the containment laws) contain only packages. It will be necessary to show that the none of the packages contain liquor. This ought to follow from the last conjunct of *pre-COMPACTION*. If none of the packages contain liquor, it should be possible to show that *gather(containers, cid)* does not contain liquor.

The central point of the proof, therefore, is going to be an assertion of the form:

$$\forall c' \in container(cid).contents \cdot LIQUOR \notin gather(containers, c')$$

Call this crucial line α. The proof is of the form:

from cid : $ContainerId$;
    new : $ContainerId$;
    $mk\text{-}System(phases, containers)$: $System$;
    $cid \in$ dom $containers$;
    $pre\text{-}COMPACTION(cid, new, containers, phases)$
    $\vdots$
α $\forall c' \in container(cid).contents \cdot LIQUOR \notin gather(containers, c')$
    $\vdots$
infer $LIQUOR \notin gather(containers, cid)$

To obtain α, a $\forall$-introduction rule ([2], pg. 45) is appropriate. Applying this backwards opens a subproof β:

from *hypotheses*

   $\vdots$

β from $c' \in container(cid).contents$

      $\vdots$

      infer $LIQUOR \notin gather(containers, c')$

α $\forall c' \in container(cid).contents \cdot LIQUOR \notin gather(containers, c')$

                                            $\forall\text{-I}, \beta$

   $\vdots$

infer $LIQUOR \notin gather(containers, cid)$

Notice that line α is not exactly justified by the $\forall$-I rule, which requires a typing rather than set membership hypothesis on the subproof. Such compromises make the argument rigorous rather than fully formal.

The subproof β contains the bulk of the argument for this conjecture. Working backwards from its conclusion, it is possible to see from the definition of *gather* that

$$gather(containers, c') = \{containers(c').material\}$$

From the last conjunct of *pre-COMPACTION*, it should also be possible to infer that

$$containers(c').material \neq LIQUOR$$

and hence the conclusion. Updating the proof with this line of reasoning:

from *hypotheses*

   $\vdots$

β from $c' \in container(cid).contents$

      $\vdots$

a $gather(containers, c') = \{containers(c').material\}$

b $containers(c').material \neq LIQUOR$

      infer $LIQUOR \notin gather(containers, c')$ Lemma1, a, b

α $\forall c' \in container(cid).contents \cdot LIQUOR \notin gather(containers, c')$

                                            $\forall\text{-I}, \beta$

   $\vdots$

infer $LIQUOR \notin gather(containers, cid)$

Lemma 1 is used to justify the subproof's conclusion, along with rules for the substitution of equal values:

$$\boxed{\text{Lemma1}} \; \frac{m, n : A; \; m \neq n;}{n \notin \{m\}}$$

We need to show that line a holds, by appealing to the definition of *gather*. This function is based on a conditional (if ... then ... else ...), so it is necessary to show which arm of the conditional applies. In a formal proof it would also be necessary to show that the condition itself is defined. In this case, the first arm of the conditional is taken, because

$$containers(c').material \neq \text{nil}$$

and this is known because c' must refer to a package. This is in turn known because c' is in the *contents* component of the container identified by *cid*, and *cid* must refer to a liner. The containment laws state that liners may only contain packages. Adding this chain of backwards reasoning to the proof, we have:

from *hypotheses*

   $\vdots$

β from $c' \in containers(cid).contents$

      $\vdots$

k	$container(cid).type = \text{LINER}$	???
j	$cid \in \text{dom } containers$	???
i	$container(cid).type = \text{LINER} \Rightarrow$	
	$\quad containers(cid).contents \neq \text{nil } \wedge$	
	$\quad \forall c1 \in containers(cid).contents \cdot$	
	$\quad containers(c1).type = \text{PACKAGE}$	
		$\wedge\text{-E}, \forall\text{-E inv-}ContainerMap, \text{ j}$
g	$\forall c1 \in containers(cid).contents \cdot$	
	$\quad containers(c1).type = \text{PACKAGE}$	$\Rightarrow\text{-E-left, i, k}$
f	$containers(c').type = \text{PACKAGE}$	$\forall\text{-E, g}$
e	$c' \in \text{dom } containers$	???
d	$containers(c').type = \text{PACKAGE} \Rightarrow$	
	$\quad containers(c').material \neq \text{nil}$	$\wedge\text{-E}, \forall\text{-E inv-}ContainerMap, \text{ e}$
c	$containers(c').material \neq \text{nil}$	$\Rightarrow\text{-E-left, d, f}$
a	$gather(containers, c') = \{containers(c').material\}$	defn of *gather*
b	$containers(c').material \neq \text{LIQUOR}$	???
	infer $\text{LIQUOR} \notin gather(containers, c')$	Lemma1, a, b
α	$\forall c' \in container(cid).contents \cdot \text{LIQUOR} \notin gather(containers, c')$	
		$\forall\text{-I}, \beta$

   $\vdots$

infer $\text{LIQUOR} \notin gather(containers, cid)$

The fact that *cid* indicates a liner is guaranteed by the modified precondition which is a hypothesis of the conjecture. It remains to establish that *cid* and *c′* are both in the domain of the *containers* mapping. In the case of *cid*, this is guaranteed by the fourth hypothesis of conjecture. In the case of *c′* it is guaranteed by the the invariant on *containers*, because *c′* is contained in the container identified by *cid*.

Finally, the last conjunct of *pre-COMPACTION* ensures that packages do not contain liquor. This allows completion of the subproof (and numbering of the lines) as follows:

from *hypotheses*

$\vdots$

β from $c' \in containers(cid).contents$

$\beta.1$ $container(cid).contents \neq$ nil $\Rightarrow$

           $containers(cid).contents \subseteq$ **dom** $containers$

                              $\wedge$-E, $\forall$-E inv-*ContainerMap*, h4

$\beta.2$ $containers(cid).contents \subseteq$ **dom** $containers$

                             $\Rightarrow$ -E-left, $\beta.1$, *pre-COMPACTION*

$\beta.3$ $container(cid).type = $ LINER $\wedge$-E, *pre-COMPACTION*

$\beta.4$ $container(cid).type = $ LINER $\Rightarrow$

           $containers(cid).contents \neq$ nil $\wedge$

           $\forall\, c1 \in containers(cid).contents \cdot$

           $containers(c1).type = $ PACKAGE

                              $\wedge$-E, $\forall$-E inv-*ContainerMap*, h4

$\beta.5$ $\forall\, c1 \in containers(cid).contents \cdot$

           $containers(c1).type = $ PACKAGE $\Rightarrow$ -E-left, $\beta.4$, $\beta.3$

$\beta.6$ $containers(c').type = $ PACKAGE $\forall$-E, $\beta.5$

$\beta.7$ $c' \in$ **dom** $containers$ $\beta.2$, subset

$\beta.8$ $containers(c').type = $ PACKAGE $\Rightarrow$

           $containers(c').material \neq$ nil $\wedge$-E, $\forall$-E inv-*ContainerMap*, $\beta.7$

$\beta.9$ $containers(c').material \neq$ nil $\Rightarrow$ -E-left, $\beta.8$, $\beta.6$

$\beta.10$ $gather(containers, c') = \{containers(c').material\}$ defn of *gather*

$\beta.11$ $containers(c').material \neq$ LIQUOR

                          $\forall$-E, *pre-COMPACTION*, $\beta.h1$

    infer LIQUOR $\notin gather(containers, c')$ Lemma1, $\beta.10$, $\beta.11$

α $\forall\, c' \in container(cid).contents \cdot$ LIQUOR $\notin gather(containers, c')$

                                        $\forall$-I, β

$\vdots$

infer LIQUOR $\notin gather(containers, cid)$

The remainder of the proof is left as an exercise. The crucial point is the expansion of *gather* from the overall conclusion.

Remarks

The flaw in the compaction operation which admitted compaction of liquor was a consequence of the specification relying on the fact that the container identified by *cid* would be a liner. There was a check in the precondition that *cid* was in the compaction phase, but there is no formal link between the compaction phase and the kind of containers which appear in the input. The link is initially present (the init clause in the state definition sets the expected input type to LINER for the compaction phase), but the compaction operation cannot rely on this still holding at the time it is applied.

When this discussion arose in the inspection of the full specification in the BNFL project, it was argued that there were no operations capable of modifying the expected input types of phases. This relies on an argument that, starting from the initial state, there are no reachable states in which anything other than a liner can be accepted into compaction. Thus, the argument relied on the initial state and the operations to maintain the property, rather than having the property stated explicitly in the invariant: the property was emergent, rather than being an integral part of the model. The risk associated with using this approach is that future modifications to the model may fail to respect the emergent property because it is not documented anywhere in the model. Recording the property in the invariant ensures that future modifications respect it because they must meet their satisfiability proof obligations.

1.5 Issues Raised by the Study

This section brings together evidence from the small study just presented and the full tracking manager project on which it was based, to raise a number of issues which the authors feel are applicable anywhere formal modelling is to be used.

1.5.1 Review Cycle

The full tracking manager project divided the phases of specification and proof completely: first deriving a specification from the informal requirements document and, having reviewed this and confirmed that it was satisfactory, proceeding to the proof stage. Furthermore, the first review of the formal specification was conducted as an *inspection* at the stage where the complete specification was available. In the event it was only found possible to review the state in the first inspection and a second inspection was scheduled which reviewed the operation descriptions.

It is clear that a number of the issues raised during the proof work could have been determined earlier had extra appropriate reviews been scheduled. In particular, it seems that it would be constructive from all points of view to have a formal inspection at the stage where the system state has been defined and to ensure that this inspection is attended by people who are expert in proof matters. (It should also be anticipated that this inspection will uncover enough alternative suggestions that at least one revision cycle with re-inspection should be allowed for in the schedule.) It is important to realise that simplifications of the state at an early stage can economise not only on the effort in specifying individual operations but can, more importantly, have a major impact on the effort required to complete satisfiability proofs etc. Although not undertaken in this project, other experiences suggest that similar observations could be made about implementation proofs.

The inclusion of safety-related properties in invariants means that their proof is part of the satisfiability obligation. A change to the specification (state space, operation definitions or invariant) would necessitate re-discharging the obligations on affected operations, thus ensuring that safety is re-assessed on each change and reissue of the specification. To take advantage of this, it is worth setting up an inspection process which concentrates on discharging satisfiability proof obligations at a suitable level of rigour. Further experience is needed to measure how cost-effective such an approach would be. The specification of this system, possibly in a revised and more general form, could form a useful basis for such an experiment.

1.5.2 Scope of System

There is a class of computer systems which can be regarded as "closed world" systems. Such systems compute a neat mathematical function and their specification can easily be documented in terms of pre/post conditions which say all that is required for safe execution. There is another class of systems where the overall requirements should actually be stated in terms of the connection between what goes on in the computer and what goes on in the physical world: *controlling* the movement of nuclear material would clearly fall into this category. The tracking manager systems which we were asked to specify somehow or another tried to avoid the overall linking with reality by saying that it is an advisory system which would be employed to check functions determined in other ways. In spite of this, one of the conjectures which was to be considered was informally termed "*LIQUOR* cannot be compacted". It is clear that there is some danger of misunderstanding here about what can actually be proved. The tracking manager which was specified cannot compact anything –*LIQUOR* or otherwise– nor can it prevent such compaction taking place. It is important to emphasize that the result of proof exercises conducted on a formal model of a controlling system does not by itself establish safe function of the overall factory site.

1.5.3 Tools

In the tracking manager project, the full formal specification was created with the aid of Adelard SpecBox VDM tools and later checked with the aid of the IFAD VDM-SL Toolbox[2]. Both of these tools offered considerable help to the specifier

---

[2]The reduced specification in this chapter was developed with the aid of the IFAD VDM-SL Toolbox only.

and in particular the latter was successful in removing a number of type errors in the specification. It is clear that it would be a waste of effort to begin undertaking proofs –at whatever level of rigour– before such type errors are eradicated by use of appropriate tools.

However, for the purposes of the proof exercise the available tools offered very little support. It was not felt that any particular proof tool was appropriate for the range of proof styles which have been employed in the study. The proofs in this chapter have therefore been constructed with no other support than a text editor and the LaTeX formatting system. This clearly makes them vulnerable to sources of inconsistency. It is, for example, possible that the statement of a lemma above has been erroneously copied and, however formal the proof is, the lemma will not match its alleged applications.

It is difficult to see how a theorem proving system can offer a significant degree of extra security except for the very formal proofs but this is clearly a topic which justifies further research.

1.5.4   Genericity and Proofs

The present specification describes a specific demonstrator architecture. This is witnessed by the use of operations specific to particular phases, and the use of the initialisation clause to set up a phase structure. Yet some parts of the specification are clearly generic: the container packing and unpacking operations for example. The complex and large-scale task of proving properties about each tracking manager application (which could well be different in each plant) would be eased if more general properties of the generic tracking architecture were proved separately. This implies a modular specification, with a parametric module giving the model of the generic architecture, and its instantiation in the demonstrator. This approach is further discussed in Chapter 2. The authors feel that the safety case for each tracking manager application could be easier to construct if based on such a generic model and would suggest this as a next step in research.

One area in which the tracking manager system has been made generic is that the phase structure is not fixed by the state itself but is determined by initialization of *System*. One could question whether the genericity so produced is in fact the area where change is most likely: one could, for instance, envisage the sorts of containers as being more likely to change than the phases through which containers are processed. Leaving aside the specification issue of whether the application of genericity is even across the system, it is more interesting here to investigate the impact on the proof work of such genericity as has been included. As indicated in the proofs, the way in which the generic system has been instantiated to a particular phase pattern by means of initialisation made it unnecessarily difficult to prove a number of desirable results. Earlier work of the authors [7, 5, 6] has, however, suggested that there is little point in generality in specifications unless the level is so chosen that proofs about the general system particularize to subsequent instantiations. In the case in hand, one would wish to be convinced that there were useful general theorems about the generic phase system which lent themselves to easy understanding in any particular instantiation in that generic system. Indeed, the authors feel that the proof work reported here would have uncovered fewer errors if the specification had been more biased to the specific demonstrator. The work on the demonstrator architecture has not sought to identify such general results, but there would appear to be scope for considerable research into the area of proofs about generic systems.

1.5.5 Testing as a Way of Detecting Problems

A number of problems have been detected in the specification during the attempt to construct the proofs contained in this document. The authors suggest that many of these problems would not have been detected by animation of the specification based on testing. This in no way questions the overall value of tools which can perform simple execution style checks on a specification: such checks can frequently detect errors before one starts the laborious effort of proof. Indeed, where a property appears not to hold, it may be less costly to come up with a test case which serves as a counter-example than to initiate the process of proof, as in the phase entry case above. However, testing often exercises those parts of a specification which one expects to function rather than detecting the unexpected gaps in the specification by conducting proofs about universal properties. An obvious example of this in the work above is the proof about non-compaction of *LIQUOR*. It would have been easy for somebody familiar with the intent of the system to set up tests showing the attempt to compact a *LINER* which contained or did not contain *LIQUOR* but the observation which is detected in the proof attempt is precisely that it is the derivation of the assumption that the *Container* is or is not a *LINER* which is not clearly established by the mechanism of instantiating the generic specification. In the longer term, one can envisage automated test case generation tools which make some contribution to the identification of pathological test cases.

1.6 Conclusions

- This chapter has illustrated, though a compact version of a larger specification, the use made of proof at various levels of rigour in the analysis of the larger formal model of an industrial system.

- Fully formal proof has its place, but we have stressed the use of less detailed proofs as guides to structuring the arguments which should take place during validation and review of a system model.

- In the commercial application of formal modelling, it may well be desirable to minimise the size of the skill base required for successful application of formal techniques, but the experience gained on this study leads the authors to the view that a knowledge of the structure and process of formal proof is desirable in teams undertaking this kind of analysis in future.

- Proof should play a role in the early stages of formal modelling, as part of a process of incremental specification development. This would allow the outcome of a proof study to influence the overall design of a specification, affecting issues such as specification structure, genericity and other "tradeoffs" between alternative formal models.

Acknowledgements

The tracking manager study took place as part of the *Research Study into the use of Computer-based Tracking Systems as valuable support to Safety Cases in Nuclear Power Technology*, a collaboration of Manchester informatics Limited, BNFL (Engineering) and Adelard under the UK Health and Safety Executive's Nuclear Safety Research Programme. The authors are especially grateful to Martyn Spink for composing the original tracking manager model, Bill Neary and Paul Vlissidis, then of BNFL Engineering, for their valuable domain expertise and to Ian Cottam for work in managing the project. JSF gladly acknowledges the support of the Engineering and Physical Science Research Council. CBJ acknowledges the support to his research by grants from the EPSRC and the Royal Society. Finally, both authors thank Juan Bicarregui and Peter Gorm Larsen for their helpful comments on earlier drafts of this chapter.

1.7   Bibliography

[1] P. G. Larsen, B. S. Hansen, H. Brunn, N. Plat, H. Toetenel, D. J. Andrews, J. Dawes, G. Parkin and others, Information technology - Programming languages, their environments and system software interfaces - Vienna Development Method - Specification Language - Part 1: Base language, International Standard, ISO/IEC 13817-1, December 1996.

[2] J. C. Bicarregui, J. S. Fitzgerald, P. A. Lindsay, R. Moore, and B. Ritchie. *Proof in VDM: A Practitioner's Guide*. FACIT. Springer-Verlag, 1994. ISBN 3-540-19813-X.

[3] Robin Bloomfield, Peter Froome, and Brian Monahan. SpecBox: A toolkit for BSI-VDM. *SafetyNet*, (5):4–7, 1989.

[4] René Elmstrøm, Peter Gorm Larsen, and Poul Bøgh Lassen. The IFAD VDM-SL Toolbox: A Practical Approach to Formal Specifications. *ACM Sigplan Notices*, September 1994.

[5] J. S. Fitzgerald. *Modularity in Model-Oriented Formal Specifications and its Interaction with Formal Reasoning*. PhD thesis, Dept. of Computer Science, University of Manchester, UK, 1991. Available as Technical Report UMCS 91-11-2 from Dept. of Computer Science, University of Manchester, UK.

[6] J. S. Fitzgerald. Reasoning about a modular model-oriented formal specification. In David J. Harper and Moira C. Norrie, editors, *Proc. Intl. Workshop on Specifications of Database Systems, University of Glasgow 1991*, Workshops in Computer Science. Springer-Verlag, 1992.

[7] J.S. Fitzgerald and C.B. Jones. Modularizing the Formal Description of a Database System. In D. Bjørner, C.A.R. Hoare, and H. Langmaack, editors, *VDM '90: VDM and Z – Formal Methods in Software Development*, volume 428 of *Lecture Notes in Computer Science*. Springer-Verlag, 1990.

[8] C. B. Jones. *Systematic Software Development Using VDM*. Prentice Hall International(UK), second edition, 1990. ISBN 0-13-880733-7. Out of print. Available by ftp from `ftp.cs.man.ac.uk` in directory `pub/cbj` in file `ssdvdm.ps.gz`

Chapter 2

The Ammunition Control System

Paul Mukherjee and John Fitzgerald

Summary

Proving properties of a specification can deepen our knowledge of the specification, leading to clearer specifications, and more elegant and efficient designs. In this chapter we use an existing specification (Mukherjee and Stavridou's model of UN regulations for safe storage of explosives) to illustrate this idea. In particular we demonstrate how to discharge a satisfiability proof obligation, and how to prove the correctness of a specification modification. We see that both proofs further our understanding of the specification and the system itself.

2.1 Introduction

In this chapter we describe the use of proof on the specification of the Ammunition Control System [8] (ACS). The ACS is a system used throughout the UK for controlling the safe storage of explosives. This specification has previously been analysed using a number of different techniques such as animation in the algebraic language OBJ3 [5] and syntax and type analysis using the IFAD VDM-SL Toolbox [3]. It has also had a validation conjecture discharged. However satisfiability of the specification has never been proved.

Here we prove two quite different properties of the ACS specification: we prove the satisfiability of a particular operation, and we prove the equivalence of the specification with a modified version of it (i.e. we prove the correctness of the modification), using the IFAD modular scheme. Our objectives are to demonstrate the use of proof, and to demonstrate typical domains in which proof might be used.

This chapter is organized as follows: in Section 2.2 we give a description of the ACS specification, sufficient for the purposes of the following sections. Then in Section 2.3

we describe the proof of satisfiability of an operation from the ACS specification. This is followed by a modification to the specification, and a proof of the correctness of this modification in Section 2.4. Finally in Section 2.5 we review the proofs, and discuss the outcomes of the exercise.

2.2 The Specification

The Ammunition Control System (ACS) described in [8] is a computer-based system used by the UK Ministry of Defence (MOD) for monitoring and controlling the safe storage of explosives at storage sites. The system is a transaction processing system; when a site takes delivery of a particular explosive object, the ACS system chooses the most appropriate building in the site for the object's storage. The choice is based on the danger of the object, and its compatibility with other explosive objects. The precise rules used by the MOD are not publically available, but are known to be consistent with the UN regulations for the Transport of Dangerous Goods [2].

The specification presented describes a model for a storage site, and the safety requirements which must be observed when a new explosive object is stored at a given storage site. A full description of the study may be found in [8]. Here we restrict ourselves to those portions of the specification relevant to the proofs we will perform.

2.2.1 Explosives Regulations

Explosives are classified in two complementary ways: the *hazard division*, which indicates how dangerous an explosive is; and the compatibility group, which describes what other goods this explosive may be mixed with in storage. There are four hazard divisions, 1 – 4, where 1 is the most dangerous, 4 the least dangerous. Compatibility groups are assigned letters, A–L, excluding I, and S. In VDM-SL we have:

$$Cg = A \mid B \mid C \mid D \mid E \mid F \mid G \mid H \mid J \mid K \mid L \mid S$$

$$Hzd = \mathbb{N}$$

$$\text{inv } h \triangleq h \geq 1 \wedge h \leq 4$$

2.2.2 The Model

The model for a storage site is a hierarchical one. We describe it in a bottom-up fashion.

The fundamental building block is an *Object*. This consists of a description of the explosive item itself, together with an (x, y) co-ordinate representing the position of the object within the magazine in which it is stored. We first consider the description of the explosive item, denoted by the type *Object-desc*. Nett explosive quantity is measured in Kilograms:

$Kg = \mathbb{R}$

inv $k \triangleq k \geq 0$

Thus we can now define what an object-description is:

$Object\text{-}desc :: neq : Kg$
$\qquad\qquad\quad hzd : Hzd$
$\qquad\qquad\quad cg : Cg$
$\qquad\qquad\quad xlen : Metre$
$\qquad\qquad\quad ylen : Metre$
$\qquad\qquad\quad zlen : Metre$

Here, *neq* stands for the nett explosive quantity of an object, *hzd* stands for the hazard division of an object, *cg* the compatibility group of an object and *xlen*, *ylen* and *zlen* the *x*, *y* and *z* lengths of the object respectively, measured in *Metres* (positive reals).

Now that we have defined the physical properties of objects, we are free to define objects themselves:

$Object :: desc : Object\text{-}desc$
$\qquad\qquad pos : Point$

$Point :: x : Metre$
$\qquad\quad\; y : Metre$

Note that there is no *z* component for objects as they are not stacked, and therefore are always stored at ground level.

A magazine stores a collection of objects. Objects may only be stored in a given magazine provided all the objects are mutually compatible. A magazine is only allowed to store a certain amount of explosive, this amount being known as the *Maximum nett explosive quantity* for the magazine.

For any particular magazine, we will need to know what type of magazine it is (classified according to physical properties), the maximum nett explosive quantity for that magazine, the most dangerous hazard division that the magazine is capable of storing, the physical dimensions of the magazine, and the collection of objects stored in the magazine. In addition, we require that each object in the collection of objects be uniquely labelled to avoid any ambiguity when adding or removing objects to or from the magazine. Finally, we wish to specify that each object in the magazine lies within the bounds of the magazine, and no two objects in the magazine overlap. Thus we get the following definition:

$Magazine :: type : Pes\text{-}types$
$\qquad max\text{-}neq : Kg \mid \text{INFINITY}$
$\qquad hzd : Hzd$
$\qquad length : Metre$
$\qquad breadth : Metre$
$\qquad height : Metre$
$\qquad objects : Object\text{-}label \xleftrightarrow{m} Object$

inv $m \triangleq$
$\quad \forall o \in$ rng $m.objects \cdot$
$\qquad within\text{-}bounds(o, m.length, m.breadth, m.height) \wedge$
$\quad \forall o1, o2 \in$ rng $m.objects \cdot o1 \neq o2 \Rightarrow \neg overlap(o1, o2)$

Here *Object-label* is a synonym for the type of tokens. Note that for relatively inert hazard divisions, the only limitation on the quantity that may be stored in such a magazine is limited by the physical dimensions of the magazine. In such cases the maximum net explosive quantity for the magazine is said to be INFINITY. The functions *suff-space-at, within-bounds* and *overlap* will be defined in section 2.2.3.

Finally, we describe a *Store* to be a map from magazine labels to magazines, where the label uniquely defines the magazine. Again *Magazine-label* is a synonym for tokens.

state *Store* of
$\qquad mags : Magazine\text{-}label \xrightarrow{m} Magazine$
end

This is a slight simplification of the specification given in [8], but is sufficient for our purposes.

2.2.3 Storing Objects

Safe storage of explosive objects depends on their hazard division and compatibility group. The UN regulations give a list of rules describing which compatibility groups may safely be mixed in storage. Details of these rules, and the errors found in them during the formalization process, may be found in [8]. In addition, an explosive object may never be stored in a magazine whose hazard division is less hazardous than the explosive object's.

When we come to specifying the compatibility rules in VDM, we give a set of pairs of compatibility groups. A pair lies in this set only if the two groups are compatible under these rules. As the relation is symmetric, it is not necessary to include a pair (m, n) if the pair (n, m) already lies in the set. (For brevity we do not give the full definition here.)

$\qquad Compatible\text{-}pairs : Cg \times Cg\text{-set} = \ldots$

Note that this relation is not reflexive; for instance, articles of compatibility group

L are specifically required to be stored separate to other articles of the same compatibility group.

If we wish to store a particular object at a particular place in a magazine, we must satisfy four conditions: there is sufficient space for the object at that point in the magazine; the item is not more hazardous than the hazard the magazine was designed to store; the object is compatible with all other objects within the magazine; and the addition of this object does not cause the maximum nett explosive quantity of the magazine to be exceeded. We specify four functions which govern when each of these conditions is met and then combine these to form an overall safety predicate.

Our first function decides when there is sufficient space at a given point in a magazine to house the given object. An object o, may be placed at position (x, y) in a magazine provided that (x, y) lies within the given magazine, and such a placement does not cause the object to overlap with an object already in the magazine.

$suff\text{-}space\text{-}at : Object\text{-}desc \times Magazine \times Point \to \mathbb{B}$

$suff\text{-}space\text{-}at\,(od, m, op) \triangleq$
    let $new\text{-}o = mk\text{-}Object(od, op)$ in
    $within\text{-}bounds(new\text{-}o, m.length, m.breadth, m.height) \wedge$
    $\forall\, o1, o2 \in \text{rng } m.objects \cup \{new\text{-}o\} \cdot$
        $o1 \neq o2 \;\Rightarrow\; \neg\, overlap(o1, o2)$

$within\text{-}bounds : Object \times Metre \times Metre \times Metre \to \mathbb{B}$

$within\text{-}bounds\,(o, l, b, h) \triangleq$
    $0 < o.pos.x + o.desc.xlen \wedge o.pos.x + o.desc.xlen \leq l \wedge$
    $0 < o.pos.y + o.desc.ylen \wedge o.pos.y + o.desc.ylen \leq b \wedge$
    $0 < o.desc.zlen \wedge o.desc.zlen \leq h$

$overlap : Object \times Object \to \mathbb{B}$

$overlap\,(o1, o2) \triangleq$
    $\textbf{abs}\,(o1.pos.x - o2.pos.x) < o1.desc.xlen \wedge$
    $\textbf{abs}\,(o1.pos.y - o2.pos.y) < o1.desc.ylen$

The above function assumes that a candidate point (x, y) has been found so we need to specify a function which does just that; that is, if there exists a point in a magazine at which there is sufficient space to store an object, then the function returns the co-ordinates of that point. This function is called *find-point*.

Due to the design of our model, it is quite straightforward to specify when an object's hazard division allows it to be stored in a given magazine. An object may only be stored in a magazine provided that the hazard division of the object is no less than the hazard division of the magazine. Thus our second function is:

$within\text{-}hazard : Object\text{-}desc \times Magazine \to \mathbb{B}$

$within\text{-}hazard\,(o, m) \triangleq$
$\quad o.hzd \geq m.hzd$

We say that two objects are compatible if under the storage rules they are allowed to be mixed in storage. The compatibility function is defined as:

$compatible : Cg \times Cg \to \mathbb{B}$

$compatible\,(m, n) \triangleq$
$\quad mk\text{-}(m, n) \in Compatible\text{-}pairs \lor mk\text{-}(n, m) \in Compatible\text{-}pairs$

We can then formalize our compatibility requirement for the addition of the object to a magazine. An object may be stored in a magazine only if it is compatible with all other objects in the magazine under the rules governing storage.

$all\text{-}compatible : Object\text{-}desc \times Magazine \to \mathbb{B}$

$all\text{-}compatible\,(o, m) \triangleq$
$\quad \forall\, object \in \mathsf{rng}\ m.objects \cdot compatible(o.cg, object.desc.cg)$

As mentioned before, each magazine has a maximum nett explosive quantity; that is, a capacity of explosive which must not be exceeded. Thus we get the following safety requirement: An object may only be stored in a magazine provided that the addition of this object does not cause the aggregate nett explosive quantity of all the objects in the magazine to exceed the maximum nett explosive quantity of the magazine. So our final function is:

$suff\text{-}capacity : Object\text{-}desc \times Magazine \to \mathbb{B}$

$suff\text{-}capacity\,(o, m) \triangleq$
$\quad$ **if** $m.max\text{-}neq \neq \text{INFINITY}$
$\quad$ **then** $total\text{-}neq(\{object.desc \mid object \in \mathsf{rng}\ m.objects\}) +$
$\qquad\qquad o.neq \leq m.max\text{-}neq$
$\quad$ **else** true

where the function $total\text{-}neq$ computes the sum of the net explosive capacities of a collection of objects. Note that $suff\text{-}space\text{-}at$ is included in the invariant for magazines, whereas the other three predicates relating magazines and objects are not. This is because magazines for which $suff\text{-}space\text{-}at$ is not satisfied can not physically exist (junk elements). However magazines in which the other three predicates are not satisfied can exist, but would be unsafe.

We can now formally describe when the overall safety requirement for storing objects in magazines. An object may be stored at a point (x, y) in a magazine only if the point is currently unoccupied and the four predicates listed above are satisfied.

safe-addition : *Object-desc* × *Magazine* × *Point* → $\mathbb{B}$

safe-addition (*o*, *m*, *p*) $\triangleq$
    (∀ *ob* ∈ rng *m.objects* · *ob.pos* ∉ *p*) ∧
    suff-space-at(*o*, *m*, *p*) ∧ *within-hazard*(*o*, *m*) ∧
    all-compatible(*o*, *m*) ∧ *suff-capacity*(*o*, *m*)

The function *find-point* is used to locate a position within the magazine at which it is safe to store the given explosive object; it implicitly requires that *safe-addition* is satisfied at the chosen point:

find-point (*o* : *Object-desc*, *m* : *Magazine*) *pt* : *Point*
pre ∃ *pt* : *Point* · *safe-addition*(*o*, *m*, *pt*)
post *safe-addition*(*o*, *m*, *pt*)

Finally we look at the operation for the addition of objects to magazines. Using the above predicate we have:

ADD-OBJECT (*o* : *Object-desc*, *obj* : *Object-label*, *ml* : *Magazine-label*)
ext wr *mags* : *Magazine-label* $\xrightarrow{m}$ *Magazine*
pre *ml* ∈ dom *mags* ∧
    obj ∉ dom *mags*(*ml*).*objects* ∧
    ∃ *pt* : *Point* · *safe-addition*(*o*, *mags*(*ml*), *pt*)
post let *p* = *find-point*(*o*, *mags*(*ml*)) in
    let *new-objs* =
        mags(*ml*).*objects* † {*obj* ↦ *mk-Object*(*o*, *p*)} in
    let *new-mag* = μ (*mags*(*ml*), *objects* ↦ *new-objs*) in
    mags = $\overleftarrow{mags}$ † {*ml* ↦ *new-mag*}

In the above precondition, the three conjuncts respectively formalize the following requirements: that the magazine is known in the store; that the label which we wish to give to the object is not already being used in the given magazine and that it is possible to add an object while satisfying the safety requirements of the previous section. In the postcondition we merely update the state to reflect the addition of the new object.

2.3 Satisfiability of *ADD-OBJECT*

An operation specification is said to be *satisfiable* if, for every input and "before" state satisfying the precondition, there exists some result and "after" state satisfying the postcondition. Showing satisfiability is a common proof task in the context of VDM. In this section, we show how the satisfiability of the *ADD-OBJECT* operation can be tackled using the framework presented in the "practitioner's guide" [1]. We will use the proof rules and notation defined in the guide, except for some small deviations.

The proof of *ADD-OBJECT* is typical of many satisfiability proofs, so the lessons from this example can be applied in many other contexts. This section illustrates a systematic approach to the construction of the satisfiability proof. We begin by attempting the main satisfiability proof. This suggests a splitting of the proof task into subtasks based on showing separate lemmas. We construct proofs of the lemmas, breaking these tasks down further as necessary, until we reach a stage where the lemmas relate to properties of the basic types and operators of VDM-SL rather than to the types and functions in the ACS specification.

It is worth reviewing the relevant parts of the specification before launching into the main proof itself. Sometimes it is very tempting to modify the specification to allow the proof task to proceed smoothly. In this case, the operation *ADD-OBJECT* appears normal, but two points are worth special note: the use of the record modification (μ) operator in the third line of the postcondition and the use of nested let expressions in the postcondition. Although μ is used as though it is a general operator on records, there is in fact a different operator for every possible modification of every possible record type ([1], pages 262-263). We make this explicit by defining an auxiliary function *f-new-mag* which achieves the same effect as the μ expression, but for which the proof theory is more straightforward. The treatment of the nested let expressions is discussed at the final stage in the completion of the satisfiability proof in Section 2.3.3 below.

This modification yields the following version of the operation:

$ADD\text{-}OBJECT\,(o:Object\text{-}desc, obj:Object\text{-}label, ml:Magazine\text{-}label)$
ext wr $mags:Magazine\text{-}label \xrightarrow{m} Magazine$
pre $ml \in$ dom $mags \wedge$
    $obj \notin$ dom $mags(ml).objects \wedge$
    $\exists\,pt:Point \cdot safe\text{-}addition(o, mags(ml), pt)$
post let $p = find\text{-}point(o, mags(ml))$ in
    let $new\text{-}objs = mags(ml).objects \dagger \{obj \mapsto mk\text{-}Object(o, p)\}$ in
    let $new\text{-}mag = f\text{-}new\text{-}mag(\overleftarrow{mags}(ml), new\text{-}objs)$ in
    $mags = \overleftarrow{mags} \dagger \{ml \mapsto new\text{-}mag\}$

The auxiliary function is defined as follows:

$f\text{-}new\text{-}mag:Magazine \times (Object\text{-}label \xleftarrow{m} Object) \to Magazine$

$f\text{-}new\text{-}mag\,(m, om) \triangleq$
    $mk\text{-}Magazine\,(m.type, m.max\text{-}neq, m.hzd,$
                  $m.length, m.breadth, m.height,$
                  $om)$

In this study, which concentrates on the production of proofs, rather than on the proof theory, we depart slightly from the notation used in [1] for inference rules. Instead of the "horizontal line" notation separating hypotheses from the conclusion, we will list the hypotheses in a "from" line and give the conclusion in an "infer" line.

The satisfiability proof obligation, called '*ADD-OBJECT*-sat', is stated as follows:

from o : *Object-desc*; obj : *Object-label*; ml : *Magazine-label*;
$\quad \overleftarrow{mags}$: *Magazine-label* $\xrightarrow{m}$ *Magazine*;
$\quad$ pre-*ADD-OBJECT*($o, obj, ml, \overleftarrow{mags}$)
infer $\exists$ *mags* : *Magazine-label* $\xrightarrow{m}$ *Magazine*·
$\qquad$ post-*ADD-OBJECT*($o, obj, ml, \overleftarrow{mags}, mags$)

Notice that this is a slightly simplified version of the obligation given in [1]. The bound variable in the conclusion is not a whole *Store*, but a single *mags* component. As the state consists only of this one component, and has no invariant on it, this simplification is valid.

The remainder of this section describes the proof of '*ADD-OBJECT*-sat'. Rather than provide fully formal proofs in minute detail, the general structure of the proof is presented. More detailed discussion of the proofs can be found in [4].

2.3.1 Main Satisfiability Proof

The proof of '*ADD-OBJECT*-sat' follows the usual pattern for satisfiability proofs. Since the conclusion is an existential quantification, the proof will normally proceed by '$\exists$-I' in which a witness value ([1], page 42) is proposed for the new *mags*. Typically, there are two parts to a proof applying the '$\exists$-I' rule to show satisfiability: showing that the witness value is of the correct type and showing that it satisfies the postcondition. In the case of *ADD-OBJECT*, this yields the following proof structure, where the witness value is shown as '$\mathcal{W}$':

from o : *Object-desc*; obj : *Object-label*; ml : *Magazine-label*;
$\quad \overleftarrow{mags}$: *Magazine-label* $\xrightarrow{m}$ *Magazine*;
$\quad$ pre-*ADD-OBJECT*($o, obj, ml, \overleftarrow{mags}$)
$\quad \vdots$

a$\quad \mathcal{W}$: *Magazine-label* $\xrightarrow{m}$ *Magazine*
$\quad \vdots$

b$\quad$ post-*ADD-OBJECT*($o, obj, ml, \overleftarrow{mags}, \mathcal{W}$)
$\quad \vdots$

infer $\exists$ *mags* : *Magazine-label* $\xrightarrow{m}$ *Magazine* ·
$\qquad$ post-*ADD-OBJECT*($o, obj, ml, \overleftarrow{mags}, mags$) $\qquad\qquad$ $\exists$-I(**a,b**)

Normally, showing type correctness (justifying line **a** in the proof above) takes up most of the effort in a proof of correctness. This is because showing the correct type of the witness value entails showing that the witness respects its type's invariant as well as showing that it has the correct basic structure.

We begin by proposing a witness value to stand for '$\mathcal{W}$' in the proof. The postcondition of *ADD-OBJECT* is not very implicit.In fact, it practically gives a "recipe" for the construction of the witness value. Operation specifications with postconditions of the form "*result = expression*" are quite common in practice and, in such cases, the construction of a witness value for the satisfiability proof is straightforward. The postcondition of *ADD-OBJECT* follows this pattern, although it is slightly disguised by the nested let expressions.

The usual approach to the construction of a witness value is to explicitly define an auxiliary function which, given the operation's inputs and "before" state component, constructs the witness value. Here, the function is called f-*mags*:

$$f\text{-}mags : Object\text{-}desc \times Object\text{-}label \times Magazine\text{-}label \times$$
$$(Magazine\text{-}label \xrightarrow{m} Magazine) \to Magazine\text{-}label \xrightarrow{m} Magazine$$

$$f\text{-}mags\,(o, ol, ml, old) \triangleq$$
$$old \dagger \{ml \mapsto f\text{-}new\text{-}mag(old(ml), f\text{-}new\text{-}objs(old(ml), o))\}$$

The body of the function is inspired by the result expression in the postcondition of *ADD-OBJECT*, with auxiliary functions corresponding to the values defined in the let expressions.

The auxiliary function f-*new-mag* has already been introduced and the function f-*new-objs* builds the new objects mapping for inclusion in the new magazine. The definition of f-*new-objs* is as follows:

$$f\text{-}new\text{-}objs : Magazine \times Object\text{-}label \times Object\text{-}desc \to$$
$$(Object\text{-}label \xleftrightarrow{m} Object)$$

$$f\text{-}new\text{-}objs\,(om, ol, od) \triangleq$$
$$om.objects \dagger \{ol \mapsto mk\text{-}Object(od, find\text{-}point(od, om))\}$$

Using the auxiliary functions defined so far, the proof of satisfiability is as follows:

from $o : Object\text{-}desc$; $obj : Object\text{-}label$; $ml : Magazine\text{-}label$;
$\overleftarrow{mags} : Magazine\text{-}label \xrightarrow{m} Magazine$;
$pre\text{-}ADD\text{-}OBJECT(o, obj, ml, \overleftarrow{mags})$

$\vdots$

a $f\text{-}mags(o, obj, ml, \overleftarrow{mags}) : Magazine\text{-}label \xrightarrow{m} Magazine$

$\vdots$

b $post\text{-}ADD\text{-}OBJECT(o, obj, ml, \overleftarrow{mags}, f\text{-}mags(o, obj, ml, \overleftarrow{mags}))$

$\vdots$

infer $\exists\, mags : Magazine\text{-}label \xrightarrow{m} Magazine \,\cdot$
$post\text{-}ADD\text{-}OBJECT(o, obj, ml, \overleftarrow{mags}, mags)$ $\exists\text{-}I(\mathbf{a}, \mathbf{b})$

Now that the witness value has been proposed, we can be more precise about the work required to complete the proof: justifying lines **a** and **b**. These are substantial tasks, so rather than attempting them *in situ*, we define them as two lemmas to be proved separately, allowing us to complete the satisfiability proof itself, so that, when the lemmas are proved, the whole satisfiability obligation will have been discharged.

The first lemma, called '*f-mags*-form-1', is constructed by taking the hypotheses available in the satisfiability proof and showing that line **a** follows from them:

from o : *Object-desc*; *obj* : *Object-label*; *ml* : *Magazine-label*;
    $\overleftarrow{mags}$: *Magazine-label* $\xrightarrow{m}$ *Magazine*;
    pre-ADD-OBJECT$(o, obj, ml, \overleftarrow{mags})$
infer *f-mags*$(o, obj, ml, \overleftarrow{mags})$: *Magazine-label* $\xrightarrow{m}$ *Magazine*

This lemma asserts that *f-mags*, when used in the context of the satisfiability proof, will return a mapping from Magazine labels to magazines. The second lemma, called 'p-ADD-OBJECT' is derived from line **b** in the same way. It asserts that the witness value satisfies the postcondition:

from o : *Object-desc*; *obj* : *Object-label*; *ml* : *Magazine-label*;
    $\overleftarrow{mags}$: *Magazine-label* $\xrightarrow{m}$ *Magazine*;
    pre-ADD-OBJECT$(o, obj, ml, \overleftarrow{mags})$
infer *post-ADD-OBJECT*$(o, obj, ml, \overleftarrow{mags}, f\text{-}mags(o, obj, ml, \overleftarrow{mags}))$

Using these lemmas, the main satisfiability proof is completed as follows. The proofs of the lemmas are addressed in Sections 2.3.2 and 2.3.3 respectively.

from o : *Object-desc*; *obj* : *Object-label*; *ml* : *Magazine-label*;
    $\overleftarrow{mags}$: *Magazine-label* $\xrightarrow{m}$ *Magazine*;
    pre-ADD-OBJECT$(o, obj, ml, \overleftarrow{mags})$
1   *f-mags*$(o, obj, ml, \overleftarrow{mags})$: *Magazine-label* $\xrightarrow{m}$ *Magazine*
                                                f-mags-form-1 (h1,h2,h3,h4,h5)
2   *post-ADD-OBJECT*$(o, obj, ml, \overleftarrow{mags}, f\text{-}mags(o, obj, ml, \overleftarrow{mags}))$
                                                p-ADD-OBJECT (h1,h2,h3,h4,h5)
infer $\exists$ *mags* : *Magazine-label* $\xrightarrow{m}$ *Magazine* ·
    post-ADD-OBJECT$(o, obj, ml, \overleftarrow{mags}, mags)$ $\exists$-I (1,2)

2.3.2 Formation of the Witness Value

The first lemma on which the satisfiability of *ADD-OBJECT* rests asserts that the witness value is of the correct type. We can expect in advance that its proof will rely on properties of *f-new-mag* and *f-new-objs*, and so we should be ready to deal with these as separate lemmas if required.

The lemma '*f-mags*-form-1' is a *formation* property. Given the hypotheses, the function *f-mags* must return a well-formed mapping as a result. The first stage in constructing the proof of a formation property is typically to reason backwards from the conclusion, expanding the definition of the function under analysis and justifying the conclusion by folding:

from $o : Object\text{-}desc$; $obj : Object\text{-}label$; $ml : Magazine\text{-}label$;
$\quad \overleftarrow{mags} : Magazine\text{-}label \xrightarrow{m} Magazine$;
$\quad pre\text{-}ADD\text{-}OBJECT(o, obj, ml, \overleftarrow{mags})$

$\quad \vdots$

a $\quad \overleftarrow{mags} \dagger \{ml \mapsto f\text{-}new\text{-}mag(\overleftarrow{mags}(ml), f\text{-}new\text{-}objs(\overleftarrow{mags}(ml), obj, o))\}$
$\qquad : Magazine\text{-}label \xrightarrow{m} Magazine$
infer $f\text{-}mags(o, obj, ml, \overleftarrow{mags}) : Magazine\text{-}label \xrightarrow{m} Magazine$ $\qquad\qquad$ folding (a)

Now it can be seen that the body of the function is a mapping overwrite expression. The mapping $\overleftarrow{mags}$ is of the correct type, and *ml* is a *Magazine-label*, so, provided

$$f\text{-}new\text{-}mag(\overleftarrow{mags}(ml), f\text{-}new\text{-}objs(\overleftarrow{mags}(ml), obj, o)) : Magazine$$

we should be able to complete the proof. This last proviso is treated as a lemma, '*f-new-mag*-OK', which is defined as follows:

from $o : Object\text{-}desc$; $obj : Object\text{-}label$; $ml : Magazine\text{-}label$;
$\quad \overleftarrow{mags} : Magazine\text{-}label \xrightarrow{m} Magazine$;
$\quad pre\text{-}ADD\text{-}OBJECT(o, obj, ml, \overleftarrow{mags})$
infer $f\text{-}new\text{-}mag(\overleftarrow{mags}(ml), f\text{-}new\text{-}objs(\overleftarrow{mags}(ml), obj, o)) : Magazine$

Given this lemma, the proof of '*f-mags*-form-1' is completed as follows:

from o : *Object-desc*; *obj* : *Object-label*; *ml* : *Magazine-label*;
 $\overleftarrow{mags}$: *Magazine-label* $\xrightarrow{m}$ *Magazine*;
 pre-ADD-OBJECT$(o, obj, ml, \overleftarrow{mags})$

1 $f\text{-}new\text{-}mag(\overleftarrow{mags}(ml), f\text{-}new\text{-}objs(\overleftarrow{mags}(ml), obj, o))$: *Magazine*
            $f\text{-}new\text{-}mag$-OK (h1,h2,h3,h4,h5)

2 $\{ml \mapsto f\text{-}new\text{-}mag(\overleftarrow{mags}(ml), f\text{-}new\text{-}objs(\overleftarrow{mags}(ml), obj, o))\}$
  :*Magazine-label* $\xrightarrow{m}$ *Magazine* $\{a \mapsto b\}$-form (h3,1)

3 $\overleftarrow{mags} \dagger \{ml \mapsto f\text{-}new\text{-}mag(\overleftarrow{mags}(ml), f\text{-}new\text{-}objs(\overleftarrow{mags}(ml), obj, o))\}$
  :*Magazine-label* $\xrightarrow{m}$ *Magazine* $\dagger$-form (h4,2)

infer $f\text{-}mags(o, obj, ml, \overleftarrow{mags})$: *Magazine-label* $\xrightarrow{m}$ *Magazine*   folding (3)

Now it remains to prove the new lemma. Again, this is a formation rule, and so we begin by expanding the function definition, working backwards from the conclusion, yielding the proof shown in Figure 2.1. The completed proof uses and three lemmas (at lines 10-12) which relate to the use of the function $f\text{-}new\text{-}objs$. We need to show that the function returns a bijective mapping and that the returned mapping respects the two conjuncts in the *Magazine* invariant. The first lemma is '$f\text{-}new\text{-}objs$-form-1':

from o : *Object-desc*; *obj* : *Object-label*; *ml* : *Magazine-label*;
 $\overleftarrow{mags}$: *Magazine-label* $\xrightarrow{m}$ *Magazine*;
 pre-ADD-OBJECT$(o, obj, ml, \overleftarrow{mags})$
infer $f\text{-}new\text{-}objs(\overleftarrow{mags}(ml), obj, o)$: *Object-label* $\xleftrightarrow{m}$ *Object*

The second lemma is '$new\text{-}objs$-bounds'. It asserts that the new object in the witness value is within the physical bounds of the magazine:

from o : *Object-desc*; *obj* : *Object-label*; *ml* : *Magazine-label*;
 $\overleftarrow{mags}$: *Magazine-label* $\xrightarrow{m}$ *Magazine*;
 pre-ADD-OBJECT$(o, obj, ml, \overleftarrow{mags})$
infer $\forall o' \in$ rng $f\text{-}new\text{-}objs(\overleftarrow{mags}(ml), obj, o) \cdot$
  $within\text{-}bounds(o', \overleftarrow{mags}(ml).length, \overleftarrow{mags}(ml).breadth, \overleftarrow{mags}(ml).height)$

The third lemma is '$new\text{-}objs$-olap', which asserts that the new object does not overlap with existing objects.

from o : *Object-desc*; obj : *Object-label*; ml : *Magazine-label*;
$\overleftarrow{mags}$: *Magazine-label* $\xrightarrow{m}$ *Magazine*;
$pre\text{-}ADD\text{-}OBJECT(o, obj, ml, \overleftarrow{mags})$

1    $ml \in$ dom $\overleftarrow{mags} \wedge$
     $obj \notin$ dom $\overleftarrow{mags}(ml).objects \wedge$
     $\exists\, pt : Point \cdot safe\text{-}addition(o, \overleftarrow{mags}(ml), pt)$ unfold (h5)

2    $ml \in$ dom $\overleftarrow{mags}$ $\wedge$-E-right (1)

3    $\overleftarrow{mags}(ml) : Magazine$ at-form (h3,h4,2)

4    $\overleftarrow{mags}(ml).type : Pes\text{-}types$ *type*-form (3)

5    $\overleftarrow{mags}(ml).max\text{-}neq : Kg \mid INFINITY$ *max-neq*-form (3)

6    $\overleftarrow{mags}(ml).hzd : Hzd$ *hzd*-form (3)

7    $\overleftarrow{mags}(ml).length : Metre$ *length*-form (3)

8    $\overleftarrow{mags}(ml).breadth : Metre$ *breadth*-form (3)

9    $\overleftarrow{mags}(ml).height : Metre$ *height*-form (3)

10   $f\text{-}new\text{-}objs(\overleftarrow{mags}(ml), obj, o) : Object\text{-}label \xleftrightarrow{m} Object$
       f-new-objs-form-1 (h1,h2,h3,h4,h5)

11   $\forall\, o' \in$ rng $f\text{-}new\text{-}objs(\overleftarrow{mags}(ml), obj, o) \cdot$
     $within\text{-}bounds(o', \overleftarrow{mags}(ml).length, \overleftarrow{mags}(ml).breadth, \overleftarrow{mags}(ml).height)$
       new-objs-bounds (h1,h2,h3,h4,h5)

12   $\forall\, o1, o2 \in$ rng $f\text{-}new\text{-}objs(\overleftarrow{mags}(ml), obj, o) \cdot$
     $o1 \neq o2 \Rightarrow \neg\, overlap(o1, o2)$ *new-objs*-olap (h1,h2,h3,h4,h5)

13   $inv\text{-}Magazine(\overleftarrow{mags}.type, \overleftarrow{mags}.max\text{-}neq, \overleftarrow{mags}.hzd,$
       $\overleftarrow{mags}.length, \overleftarrow{mags}.breadth, \overleftarrow{mags}.height,$
       $f\text{-}new\text{-}objs(\overleftarrow{mags}, obj, o))$ folding ($\wedge$-I(11,12))

14   $mk\text{-}Magazine(\overleftarrow{mags}.type, \overleftarrow{mags}.max\text{-}neq, \overleftarrow{mags}.hzd,$
       $\overleftarrow{mags}.length, \overleftarrow{mags}.breadth, \overleftarrow{mags}.height,$
       $f\text{-}new\text{-}objs(\overleftarrow{mags}, obj, o)) : Magazine$
       mk-Magazine-form (3,4,5,6,7,8,9,10,13)

infer $f\text{-}new\text{-}mag(\overleftarrow{mags}(ml), f\text{-}new\text{-}objs(\overleftarrow{mags}(ml), obj, o)) : Magazine$
       folding (14)

Figure 2.1: Proof of '*f-new-mag*-OK'

from $o : Object\text{-}desc$; $obj : Object\text{-}label$; $ml : Magazine\text{-}label$;
    $\overleftarrow{mags} : Magazine\text{-}label \xrightarrow{m} Magazine$;
    $pre\text{-}ADD\text{-}OBJECT(o, obj, ml, \overleftarrow{mags})$
infer $\forall\, o1, o2 \in$ rng $f\text{-}new\text{-}objs(\overleftarrow{mags}(ml), obj, o)\cdot$
    $o1 \neq o2 \;\Rightarrow\; \neg\, overlap(o1, o2)$

We will deal with each of these lemmas in order. First, the formation lemma which requires us to show that the addition of the new object does not compromise the bijective nature of the objects mapping in the magazine. The additions to the mapping are the label obj and the object

$$mk\text{-}Object(find\text{-}point(o, \overleftarrow{mags}(ml).objects))$$

In order to ensure that the *objects* mapping remains bijective, we should check that the new object is not already in the range of the mapping. This gives the following outline proof:

from $o : Object\text{-}desc$; $obj : Object\text{-}label$; $ml : Magazine\text{-}label$;
    $\overleftarrow{mags} : Magazine\text{-}label \xrightarrow{m} Magazine$;
    $pre\text{-}ADD\text{-}OBJECT(o, obj, ml, \overleftarrow{mags})$
a $\overleftarrow{mags}(ml).objects : Object\text{-}label \xleftrightarrow{m} Object$
b $mk\text{-}Object(o, find\text{-}point(o, \overleftarrow{mags}(ml))) : Object$
c $mk\text{-}Object(o, find\text{-}point(o, \overleftarrow{mags}(ml))) \notin$ rng $\overleftarrow{mags}(ml).objects$
d $\overleftarrow{mags}(ml).objects \dagger \{obj \mapsto mk\text{-}Object(o, find\text{-}point(o, \overleftarrow{mags}(ml)))\}$
                                                                    bimap-pres(a,h2,b,c)
infer $f\text{-}new\text{-}objs(\overleftarrow{mags}(ml), obj, o) : object\text{-}label \xleftrightarrow{m} Object$ folding (d)

The 'bimap-pres' lemma used in line **d** asserts that adding a maplet to a bijective mapping does not compromise the bijection, provided the range element of the maplet is not already present in the mapping. Formally:

from $m : A \xleftrightarrow{m} B$; $a : A$; $b : B$; $b \notin$ rng m
infer $m \dagger \{a \mapsto b\} : A \xleftrightarrow{m} B$

The lemma is not proved here. A more detailed discussion of the proofs of lemmas used in this section can be found in [4].

To complete the proof of '$f\text{-}new\text{-}objs$-form-1', consider each of the five labelled lines in turn. Line **a** follows directly from the structure of the *Magazine* composite type. Line **b** follows from $mk\text{-}Object$ formation, for o is an object description and *find-point* must return a point (we treat this as a lemma on *find-point*). Line **c**

from $o : Object\text{-}desc$; $obj : Object\text{-}label$; $ml : Magazine\text{-}label$;
    $\overleftarrow{mags} : Magazine\text{-}label \xrightarrow{m} Magazine$;
    $pre\text{-}ADD\text{-}OBJECT(o, obj, ml, \overleftarrow{mags})$

1	$ml \in$ dom $\overleftarrow{mags}$	$\wedge$-E-right(unfold (h5))
2	$\overleftarrow{mags}(ml) : Magazine$	at-form (h3,h4,1)
3	$\overleftarrow{mags}(ml).objects : Object\text{-}label \xleftrightarrow{m} Object$	$Objects$-form (2)
4	$\exists\, pt : Point \cdot safe\text{-}addition(o, \overleftarrow{mags}(ml), pt)$	$\wedge$-E, unfolding (h5)
5	$pre\text{-}find\text{-}point(o, \overleftarrow{mags}(ml))$	folding (4)
6	$find\text{-}point(o, \overleftarrow{mags}(ml)) : point$	$find\text{-}point$-form (h1,2,5)
7	$mk\text{-}Object(o, find\text{-}point(o, \overleftarrow{mags}(ml))) : Object$	$mk\text{-}Object$-form (h1,6)
8	$post\text{-}find\text{-}point(o, \overleftarrow{mags}(ml), find\text{-}point(o, \overleftarrow{mags}(ml)))$	
		$find\text{-}point$-defn (h1,2,5)
9	$safe\text{-}addition(o, \overleftarrow{mags}(ml), find\text{-}point(o, \overleftarrow{mags}(ml)))$	unfolding (8)
10	$\forall\, o \in$ rng $\overleftarrow{mags}(ml).objects \cdot o.pos \neq find\text{-}point(o, \overleftarrow{mags}(ml))$	
		$\wedge$-E, unfolding (9)
11	rng $\overleftarrow{mags}(ml) : Object$-set	rng-form-bimap (3)
12	$mk\text{-}Object(o, find\text{-}point(o, \overleftarrow{mags}(ml))) \notin$ rng $\overleftarrow{mags}(ml).objects$	
		point-excl(6,h1,11,10)
13	$\overleftarrow{mags}(ml).objects \dagger \{obj \mapsto mk\text{-}Object(o, find\text{-}point(o, \overleftarrow{mags}(ml)))\}$	
		bimap-pres(3,h2,7,12)

infer $f\text{-}new\text{-}objs(\overleftarrow{mags}(ml), obj, o) : object\text{-}label \xleftrightarrow{m} Object$ folding (13)

Figure 2.2: Completed proof of '$f\text{-}new\text{-}objs$-form-1'

follows because *safe-addition* (part of *pre-ADD-OBJECT*) ensures that no objects already exist at the same point. This gives the completed version of the proof shown in Figure 2.2. The completed proof of '$f\text{-}new\text{-}objs$-form-1' uses one further lemma. Called 'point-excl', this states that the object constructed at a new point cannot be in the set of existing objects:

from $pt : Point$; $od : Object\text{-}desc$; $s : Object$-set;
    $\forall\, o \in s \cdot o.pos \neq pt$
infer $mk\text{-}Object(od, pt) \notin s$

The proof of this lemma is not discussed here, but is covered in [4].

The proof of '$f\text{-}new\text{-}objs$-form-1', for brevity, uses the "working versions" of the formation rules for the implicitly defined function *find-point*, as defined in [1], pgs. 324-325. The use of these working versions is contingent on the satisfiability of *find-point* having been shown, and again we assume this has been done.

from $o : Object\text{-}desc$; $obj : Object\text{-}label$; $ml : Magazine\text{-}label$;
$\overleftarrow{mags} : Magazine\text{-}label \xrightarrow{m} Magazine$;
$pre\text{-}ADD\text{-}OBJECT(o, obj, ml, \overleftarrow{mags})$

1	$ml \in \text{dom } \overleftarrow{mags}$	$\wedge$-E-right (unfolding (h5))
2	$\overleftarrow{mags}(ml) : Magazine$	at-form (h3,h4,1)
3	$\exists\, pt : Point \cdot safe\text{-}addition(o, \overleftarrow{mags}(ml), pt)$	$\wedge$-E, unfolding (h5)
4	$\cdot pre\text{-}find\text{-}point(o, \overleftarrow{mags}(ml))$	folding (3)
5	$post\text{-}find\text{-}point(o, \overleftarrow{mags}(ml), find\text{-}point(o, \overleftarrow{mags}(ml)))$	
		$find\text{-}point$-defn (h1,2,4)
6	$safe\text{-}addition(o, \overleftarrow{mags}(ml), find\text{-}point(o, \overleftarrow{mags}(ml)))$	unfolding (5)
7	$suff\text{-}space\text{-}at(o, \overleftarrow{mags}(ml), find\text{-}point(o, \overleftarrow{mags}(ml)))$	unfolding (6)
8	$within\text{-}bounds(mk\text{-}Object(o, find\text{-}point(o, \overleftarrow{mags}(ml))),$	
	$\qquad \overleftarrow{mags}(ml).length, \overleftarrow{mags}(ml).breadth, \overleftarrow{mags}(ml).height)$	
		$\wedge$-E, unfolding (7)
9	$inv\text{-}Magazine(\overleftarrow{mags}(ml))$	$inv\text{-}Magazine$-I (2)
10	$\forall\, o' \in \text{rng } \overleftarrow{mags}()\,ml.objects\cdot$	
	$within\text{-}bounds(o', \overleftarrow{mags}(ml).length, \overleftarrow{mags}(ml).breadth, \overleftarrow{mags}(ml).height)$	
		$\wedge$-E, unfolding (9)
11	$\overleftarrow{mags}(ml).objects : Object\text{-}label \xleftrightarrow{m} Object$	$objects$-form (2)
12	$find\text{-}point(o, \overleftarrow{mags}(ml)) : Point$	$find\text{-}point$-form (h1,12)
13	$mk\text{-}Object(o, find\text{-}point(o, \overleftarrow{mags}(ml))) : Object$	$mk\text{-}Object$-form (h1, 12)
14	$\text{rng } \overleftarrow{mags}(ml).objects \dagger \{obj \mapsto mk\text{-}Object(o, find\text{-}point(o, \overleftarrow{mags}(ml)))\}$	
	$= \text{rng } \overleftarrow{mags}(ml).objects \cup \{mk\text{-}Object(o, find\text{-}point(o, \overleftarrow{mags}(ml)))\}$	
		rng-$\dagger$-bimap(11,h2,13,$\wedge$-E(unfold h5))
15	$\text{rng } \overleftarrow{mags}(ml).objects : Object\text{-}\text{set}$	rng-form-bimap (11)

infer $\forall\, o' \in \text{rng } f\text{-}new\text{-}objs(\overleftarrow{mags}(ml), obj, o)\cdot$
$\qquad within\text{-}bounds(o', \overleftarrow{mags}(ml).length, \overleftarrow{mags}(ml).breadth, \overleftarrow{mags}(ml).height)$
$\qquad\qquad\qquad\qquad\qquad\qquad\qquad\qquad \forall\text{-}\cup\text{-inh } (15,11,14,10,8)$

Figure 2.3: Proof of '$new\text{-}objs$-bounds'

We have established the basic type-correctness of the new objects mapping and hence of the magazine added to the state by the *ADD-POINT* operation. It remains to show that the new mapping respects the invariant on *Magazine* by proving the lemmas '$new\text{-}objs$-bounds' and '$new\text{-}objs$-olap'. The proof of '$new\text{-}objs$-bounds' is shown in Figure 2.3. The proof utilises two lemmas. The first, 'rng-$\dagger$-bimap' is a property of bijective mappings:

from $m : A \xleftrightarrow{m} B; a : A; b : B; a \notin \text{dom } m$
infer rng $m \dagger \{a \mapsto b\} = \text{rng } m \cup \{b\}$

This lemma is not further discussed here. The second lemma used, '$\forall$-$\cup$-inh', is a property of sets:

from $s1 : A\text{-set}; a : A; s = s1 \cup \{a\};$
  $\forall x \in s1 \cdot P(x); P(a)$
infer $\forall x \in s \cdot P(x)$

This lemma's proof is also omitted here. For this proof, we again expect *find-point* to have been proved satisfiable, so that the working versions of the function's formation and definition rules can be used.

By this stage in the proof, the lemmas generated from proofs are now no longer lemmas about the particular formal specification under analysis, but relate almost exclusively to the underlying data types and operators in VDM-SL. They represent results which should be provable from the theories given in [1].

The one remaining lemma is the proof of '*new-objs*-olap'. Its proof follows similar lines to that of its companion lemma '*new-objs*-bounds' and the proof is not presented here.

All the lemmas required for the proof of '*f-new-mag*-OK', and thus for '*f-mags*-form-1' have been proved. We have shown that the witness value is a well-formed *Magazine*. It remains to show that this magazine respects the postcondition on *ADD-OBJECT*.

2.3.3   Satisfaction of Postcondition

Recall that satisfaction of *post-ADD-OBJECT* is described in the lemma 'p-ADD-OBJECT' as follows:

from $o : Object\text{-}desc; obj : Object\text{-}label; ml : Magazine\text{-}label;$
  $\overleftarrow{mags} : Magazine\text{-}label \xrightarrow{m} Magazine;$
  $pre\text{-}ADD\text{-}OBJECT(o, obj, ml, \overleftarrow{mags})$
infer $post\text{-}ADD\text{-}OBJECT(o, obj, ml, \overleftarrow{mags}, f\text{-}mags(o, obj, ml, \overleftarrow{mags}))$

Such satisfaction proofs are usually straightforward in cases where the operation specification is quite explicit and the postcondition is of the form "*result = expression*". The witness value has usually been chosen so that it is identical to *expression*,

from o : *Object-desc*; obj : *Object-label*; ml : *Magazine-label*;
  $\overleftarrow{mags}$: *Magazine-label* $\xrightarrow{m}$ *Magazine*;
  pre-*ADD-OBJECT*$(o, obj, ml, \overleftarrow{mags})$

1 f-*mags*$(o, obj, ml, \overleftarrow{mags})$: *Magazine-label* $\xrightarrow{m}$ *Magazine*
$\qquad\qquad\qquad\qquad\qquad\qquad$ f-*mags-form*-1 (h1,h2,h3,h4,h5)

2 f-*mags*$(o, obj, ml, \overleftarrow{mags}) = f$-*mags*$(o, obj, ml, \overleftarrow{mags})$
$\qquad\qquad\qquad\qquad\qquad\qquad\qquad\qquad$ =-self-I (1)

3 f-*mags*$(o, obj, ml, \overleftarrow{mags}) =$
  $\overleftarrow{mags} \dagger \{ml \mapsto f$-*new-mag*$(\overleftarrow{mags}(ml), f$-*new-objs*$(\overleftarrow{mags}(ml), obj, o))\}$
$\qquad\qquad\qquad\qquad\qquad\qquad\qquad\qquad$ unfold (2)

4 f-*mags*$(o, obj, ml, \overleftarrow{mags}) =$
  $\overleftarrow{mags} \dagger \{ml \mapsto f$-*new-mag*$(\overleftarrow{mags}(ml),$
  $\overleftarrow{mags}(ml).objects \dagger \{obj \mapsto mk\text{-}Object(o, find\text{-}point(o, \overleftarrow{mags}(ml)))\})\}$
$\qquad\qquad\qquad\qquad\qquad\qquad\qquad\qquad$ unfold (3)

5 let $p = find\text{-}point(o, \overleftarrow{mags}(ml))$ in
  let $new\text{-}objs = \overleftarrow{mags}(ml).objects \dagger \{obj \mapsto mk\text{-}Object(o, p)\}$ in
  let $new\text{-}mag = f$-*new-mag*$(\overleftarrow{mags}(ml), new\text{-}objs)$ in
  f-*mags*$(o, obj, ml, \overleftarrow{mags}) = \overleftarrow{mags} \dagger \{ml \mapsto new\text{-}mag\}$ $\qquad\qquad$ let, 4
infer post-*ADD-OBJECT*$(o, obj, ml, \overleftarrow{mags}, f$-*mags*$(o, obj, ml, \overleftarrow{mags}))$
$\qquad\qquad\qquad\qquad\qquad\qquad\qquad\qquad$ folding (5)

Figure 2.4: Rigorous proof of satisfaction of *post-ADD-OBJECT*

so the satisfaction proof amounts to showing this identity. The witness value has
already been shown to denote a value of the correct type, so we can easily conclude
the expression

  witness-value = *witness-value*

because equality is reflexive for defined values. We then proceed to expand one side
of the equality until we get the expression in the postcondition, giving "*witness* =
expression*". The same approach is applied to the *ADD-OBJECT* operation.

The only complication here is the use of nested let expressions in the postcondition.
In the rigorous proof presented here, we treat the let expressions in the obvious
way, omitting the details of how this can be justified by appealing to proof rules.
This is discussed in more detail in [4]. The resulting proof of satisfaction of the
postcondition is given in Figure 2.4.

2.3.4 Summary

We have shown how a typical satisfiability proof can be tackled in VDM-SL by breaking the task down into subtasks by means of lemmas. It is worth taking stock of the proof process before considering a less typical proof in the context of the ACS.

The proof of satisfiability often highlights errors in the specification of the operation and related auxiliary functions. The construction of the satisfiability proof for *ADD-OBJECT* raised issues which had not been addressed in any of the previous validations performed on the specification. For example, it became apparent that the original version of *ADD-OBJECT* had too weak a precondition, allowing a magazine label outside the domain of *mags* to be used. In a more subtle example, the specification failed to exclude the possible sharing of positions by objects in certain cases. This is not an argument in favour of formal proof as a validation mechanism, but it is an argument in favour of allowing proof structures to guide the attention of reviewers. For example, it is conceivable that very good tool support could have generated test cases testing which would have made at least the first of these errors apparent. The development of such tool support is an area of ongoing research.

2.4 Modifying the Specification

Our specification of the ammunition control system is static in the sense that modifications to the UN regulations would require wholesale modifications to the specification. However, the specification encompasses both the current safety requirements of the UN regulations, and their *interpretation*. Thus it would be convenient if we were able to separate these two aspects of the specification, so that future modifications to the regulations which do not alter the their interpretation (such as new compatibility groups) could be incorporated with ease. This is a very real requirement, as clearly explosives technology rapidly changes, and therefore new substances with different chemical properties to existing substances will have to be dealt with.

Constructing such a separated specification poses no real problems as such; however we need to demonstrate that the separated specification is equivalent to the original one. In this case, we take equivalence of specifications to mean that each specification captures precisely the same set of models as the other.

In this section we give an example of such a separation, and discharge the proof obligations necessary to establish the equivalence of the original and separated specifications. The separation that we perform concerns the test of whether two objects are compatible. We separate our specification by constructing a parametrised module modules to deal with compatibility groups, then instantiate this in the main specification. We use the modular scheme used in the IFAD VDM-SL Toolbox [3] for this purpose.

2.4.1 Modification to the Specification

We wish to make the treatment of compatibility more flexible. We do this by constructing a new module that deals exclusively with compatibility groups. For each interpretation of the UN regulations, we will instantiate this module with the collection of compatibility groups relevant to the current application, and the rules governing safe combinations of compatibility groups. Thus our module takes a type parameter:modules

> module *Compatibility*
>
> parameters
>
> > types *CG*

We construct a model of a generic compatibility relation, which will be instantiated by each interpretation of the regulations. We say that a compatibility relation is a map from a compatibility group *cg* to a set of compatibility groups *s*, such that each compatibility group in *s* is compatible with *cg*. Thus we have

> types
>
> > $CompatRel = CG \xrightarrow{m} CG\text{-set}$
> >
> > inv $cr \triangleq \forall a \in$ dom $cr \cdot \forall b \in cr(a) \cdot b \in$ dom $cr \wedge a \in cr(b)$

In the invariant we specify the property that compatibility is symmetric.

We can think of the module modules as an abstract data type – users of compatibility groups need not know how the type is specified, they merely need access to operations that manipulate the data type. Thus we have constructor functions for *CompatRel*:

> $emptyCR : () \rightarrow CompatRel$
>
> $emptyCR () \triangleq$
> > $\{\}$

> $addpair : CompatRel \times CG \times CG \rightarrow CompatRel$
>
> $addpair (cr, cg1, cg2) \triangleq$
> > $cr \dagger \{cg1 \mapsto cr(cg1) \cup \{cg2\}, cg2 \mapsto cr(cg2) \cup \{cg1\}\}$
>
> pre $\{cg1, cg2\} \subseteq$ dom cr

Note that a compatibility group cg_2 can only be added to those groups compatible with cg_1 if both cg_1 and cg_2 already lie in the domain of the relation. Thus we need a way of adding compatibility groups to the domain of a relation. The function *addCG* performs this.

$addCG : CG \times CompatRel \rightarrow CompatRel$

$addCG\,(cg, cr) \triangleq$
   if $cg \in$ dom cr
   then cr
   else $cr \dagger \{cg \mapsto \{\}\}$

Then we say that two compatibility groups cg_1 and cg_2 are compatible with respect to compatibility relation cr if $cg_2 \in cr(cg_1)$.

$compatible : CG \times CG \times CompatRel \rightarrow \mathbb{B}$

$compatible\,(cg1, cg2, cr) \triangleq$
   $cg2 \in cr(cg1)$
pre $cg1 \in$ dom cr

In our original specification we represented the compatibility relation as a set of pairs of compatibility groups, with groups cg_1 and cg_2 compatible iff $mk\text{-}(cg_1, cg_2)$ lies in the set, or $mk\text{-}(cg_2, cg_1)$ lies in the set. In order to prove that the new representation is equivalent to the original one, we need some way of relating the two representations. We do this using the function $build\text{-}rel$, which takes a set of pairs of compatibility groups, and returns that element of $CompatRel$ corresponding to this relation. This gives:

$build\text{-}rel : CG \times CG\text{-set} \rightarrow CompatRel$

$build\text{-}rel\,(cgs) \triangleq$
  if $cgs = \{\}$
  then $\{\}$
  else let $mk\text{-}(cg1, cg2) \in cgs$ in
      let $cr = build\text{-}rel(cgs \setminus \{mk\text{-}(cg1, cg2)\})$ in
      let $new\text{-}cr = addCG(cg2, addCG(cg1, cr))$ in
      $new\text{-}cr \dagger \{cg1 \mapsto new\text{-}cr(cg1) \cup \{cg2\}, cg2 \mapsto new\text{-}cr(cg2) \cup \{cg1\}\}$

This completes the module. The only remaining changes we need to make are to the ACS module itself.modules We make two changes to the module. The first alteration is to instantiate the Compatibility module with the type Cg, which we enumerate as previously:

module ACS

  instantiation

    $CgRel$ as $Compatibility\,(CG \rightarrow Cg)$all

  types

    $Cg =$ A | B | C | D | E | F | G | H | J | K | L | S

The second alteration is to the test of compatibility: we use the operation defined in the new Compatibility module.

> *compatible* : $Cg \times Cg \to \mathbb{B}$
>
> *compatible* $(m, n) \triangleq$
>   *CgRel' compatible*$(m, n, CgRel'\,build\text{-}rel(Compatible\text{-}pairs))$

This completes our description of the new specification. A couple of points arise: firstly, it is clear to see that the new specification is much more flexible that the original one, without greatly altering it. Secondly, in this instance we can think of the module mechanism as allowing us to specify information hiding (in this case, we are hiding the details of the compatibility relation). modules

Note that there are many ways that we could have specified the Compatibility module. For instance, we could have had a second parameter, which took a set of pairs of compatibility groups, and then had a state based module using this set of pairs. However, we chose this approach described because it is simple and it provides the desired functionality. Since we are performing two tasks here (delegating some functionality to a new module, modules and using maps rather than sets), we could have explicitly constructed the new specification in two stages (leading to two tiers of proof). However the complexity of the task was not considered sufficient to justify such an approach.

2.4.2 Proving Equivalence

We now turn our attention to proving that the new specification is equivalent to the original one. Here, by "equivalent" we mean that every model of the original specification is also a model of the modified specification, and vice-versa. Alternatively (but equivalently) we can think of it as each specification refining the other.

As the only modification we have made to our specification concerns dealing with compatibility, our equivalence condition will revolve around this part of the specification. In particular, we wish to prove that if two compatibility groups x and y are compatible in the original specification, then they are compatible in the modified specification, and vice-versa. Translating this into a predicate, our overall proof goal is:

$$\forall cp : (CG \times CG)\text{-set}, x, y : CG\cdot$$
$$CgRel'\,compatible(x, y, CgRel'\,build\text{-}rel(cp))$$
$$\Leftrightarrow \quad mk\text{-}(x, y) \in cp \lor mk\text{-}(y, x) \in cp$$

Replacing *CgRel' compatible* with its definition, and relaxing the notation a little, we get the following equivalent proof goal:

$$\forall s : (CG \times CG)\text{-set}, x, y : CG\cdot$$
$$y \in \text{dom } build\text{-}rel(s) \land x \in build\text{-}rel(s)(y) \;\Leftrightarrow\; (mk\text{-}(x, y) \in s \lor mk\text{-}(y, x) \in s)$$

We prove this equivalence in two stages: in stage 1, we prove the sub-goal

$\forall s : (CG \times CG)\text{-set}, x, y : CG \cdot$

$\quad (mk\text{-}(x, y) \in s \lor mk\text{-}(y, x) \in s) \Rightarrow y \in \text{dom } build\text{-}rel(s) \land x \in build\text{-}rel(s)(y).$

Then in stage 2, we prove the converse, namely:

$\forall s : (CG \times CG)\text{-set}, x, y : CG \cdot$

$\quad y \in \text{dom } build\text{-}rel(s) \land x \in build\text{-}rel(s)(y) \Rightarrow (mk\text{-}(x, y) \in s \lor mk\text{-}(y, x) \in s).$

Proof of Stage 1

If we define p as the following predicate:

$\qquad p : CG \times CG\text{-set} \to \mathbb{B}$

$\qquad p\,(s) \triangleq$
$\qquad\quad \forall x, y : CG \cdot mk\text{-}(x, y) \in s \Rightarrow \{x, y\} \subseteq \text{dom } build\text{-}rel(s) \land$
$\qquad\qquad\qquad\qquad\qquad\qquad\qquad\quad x \in build\text{-}rel(s)(y) \land$
$\qquad\qquad\qquad\qquad\qquad\qquad\qquad\quad y \in build\text{-}rel(s)(x)$

Then we prove by induction over s that

$$\forall s : (CG \times CG)\text{-set} \cdot p(s)$$

Separating out the two cases for the induction, we prove the following results:

1. $p(\{\,\})$

2. $\forall a, b : CG; s' : (CG \times CG)\text{-set}; p(s'); mk\text{-}(a, b) \notin s' \vdash p(add(mk\text{-}(a, b), s'))$

The first of these is trivial to prove, so assuming the proof of the second case, we get theorem 2 below:

from $s : CG \times CG\text{-set}$
1	from $x : CG; y : CG$	
1.1	$mk\text{-}(x, y) \notin \{\}$	$\{\,\}$-is-empty(h1)
1.2	$\neg\, mk\text{-}(x, y) \in \{\}$	$\notin$-defn(1.1)
1.3	$\neg\, mk\text{-}(x, y) \in \{\} \lor$	
	$(\{x, y\} \subseteq \text{dom } build\text{-}rel(\{\}) \land x \in build\text{-}rel(\{\})(y) \land$	
	$y \in build\text{-}rel(\{\})(x))$	$\lor$-I-right(1.2)
1.4	$mk\text{-}(x, y) \in \{\} \Rightarrow$	
	$(\{x, y\} \subseteq \text{dom } build\text{-}rel(\{\}) \land x \in build\text{-}rel(\{\})(y) \land$	
	$y \in build\text{-}rel(\{\})(x))$	$\Rightarrow$-defn(1.3)
	infer $p(\{\})$	p-defn(1.4)
2	from $a : CG; b : CG; s' : CG \times CG\text{-set}; p(s'); mk\text{-}(a, b) \notin s'$	
	infer $p(add(mk\text{-}(a, b), s'))$	Theorem 1(h2)
	infer $p(s)$	set-indn(1,2,h)

To prove the inductive step (theorem 1, shown in figure 2.5), we observe that we need to prove an implication. By the implication formation rule ($\Rightarrow$ -I), this means that we need to prove that we can infer the conclusion from the hypothesis, and also that the hypothesis is well-defined. The latter part is a straightforward application of type reasoning (lines 7 – 10). To prove the former, we need to prove

$$\forall x, y, a, b : CG; s' : CG \times CG\text{-set}; p(s'); mk\text{-}(a, b) \notin s' \vdash$$
$$\{x, y\} \subseteq \text{dom } build\text{-}rel(add(mk\text{-}(a, b), s')) \wedge$$
$$x \in build\text{-}rel(add(mk\text{-}(a, b), s'))(y) \wedge$$
$$y \in build\text{-}rel(add(mk\text{-}(a, b), s'))(x)$$

We then distinguish two cases: $mk\text{-}(x, y) = mk\text{-}(a, b)$ (line 4) and $mk\text{-}(x, y) \in s'$ (line 5). We prove the conclusion in each of these cases, then infer that the conclusion must hold when $mk\text{-}(x, y) \in add(mk\text{-}(a, b), s')$ (line 6).

One point worthy of note is the use of lemma 1 on line 5.7: this is an example of what we might think of as a commuting result: having proved $t(x, y)$ we can infer $t(y, x)$. This greatly eases reasoning, and also helps the readability of proofs. The proof of lemma 1 itself is essentially just a re-arrangement of the type invariant:

from $cr : CompatRel; x : CG; y : CG; x \in \text{dom } cr; y \in cr(x)$

1	$\forall a \in \text{dom } cr \cdot \forall b \in cr(a) \cdot b \in \text{dom } cr \wedge a \in cr(b)$	*inv-CompatRel*
2	$\forall b \in cr(x) \cdot b \in \text{dom } cr \wedge x \in cr(b)$	$\forall$-E(1,h)
infer	$y \in \text{dom } cr \wedge x \in cr(y)$	$\forall$-E(2,h)

Proof of Stage 2

We wish to prove

$$\forall s : (CG \times CG)\text{-set}, x, y : CG \cdot \cdot$$
$$(y \in \text{dom } build\text{-}rel(s) \wedge x \in build\text{-}rel(s)(y)) \Rightarrow (mk\text{-}(x, y) \in s \vee mk\text{-}(y, x) \in s).$$

One more, we perform induction over the set s. The base case is theorem 3 (shown in figure 2.6); the induction is performed in theorem 4 (figure 2.7).

This theorem has two parts: line 1 and line 2. Line 1 is the base case (proved above) and line 2 is the inductive case. For the inductive case, we wish to prove an implication of the form $A \Rightarrow B$, so we first prove $A \vdash B$ (line 2.1) then prove $\delta(A)$ (lines 2.2 – 2.8). We then infer $A \Rightarrow B$ by the implication-introduction rule ($\Rightarrow$ -I).

To prove

$$\begin{array}{c}(y \in \text{dom } build\text{-}rel(add(mk\text{-}(a, b), s'))\wedge \\ x \in build\text{-}rel(add(mk\text{-}(a, b), s'))(y))\end{array} \vdash \begin{array}{c}mk\text{-}(x, y) \in add(mk\text{-}(a, b), s') \vee \\ mk\text{-}(y, x) \in add(mk\text{-}(a, b), s')\end{array}$$

from $x : CG; y : CG; a : CG; b : CG; s' : CG \times CG$-set$; p(s'); mk\text{-}(a, b) \notin s'$

1 $\{a, b\} \subseteq$ dom $build\text{-}rel(add(mk\text{-}(a, b), s)) \wedge$
  $a \in build\text{-}rel(add(mk\text{-}(a, b), s))(b) \wedge$
  $b \in build\text{-}rel(add(mk\text{-}(a, b), s))(a)$ Lemma 2(h)

2 $\forall x, y : CG \cdot mk\text{-}(x, y) \in s' \Rightarrow$
  $(\{x, y\} \in$ dom $build\text{-}rel(s') \wedge x \in build\text{-}rel(s')(y) \wedge$
  $y \in build\text{-}rel(s')(x))$ p-defn(h)

3 $mk\text{-}(x, y) \in s' \Rightarrow (\{x, y\} \in$ dom $build\text{-}rel(s') \wedge$
  $x \in build\text{-}rel(s')(y) \wedge y \in build\text{-}rel(s')(x))$ $\forall$-E(h,2)

4 from $mk\text{-}(a, b) = mk\text{-}(x, y)$

4.1 $a = x \wedge b = y$ tuple-defn(h4)

   infer $\{x, y\} \subseteq$ dom $build\text{-}rel(add(mk\text{-}(a, b), s')) \wedge$
   $x \in build\text{-}rel(add(mk\text{-}(a, b), s'))(y) \wedge$
   $y \in build\text{-}rel(add(mk\text{-}(a, b), s'))(x)$ =-subs(1,4.1)

5 from $mk\text{-}(x, y) \in s'$

5.1 $\{x, y\} \in$ dom $build\text{-}rel(s') \wedge$
   $x \in build\text{-}rel(s')(y) \wedge y \in build\text{-}rel(s')(x)$ $\Rightarrow$-E(h5,3)

5.2   dom $build\text{-}rel(add(mk\text{-}(a, b), s')) =$
   $\{a, b\} \cup$ dom $build\text{-}rel(s')$ Lemma 3(h)

5.3 $\{x, y\} \subseteq \{a, b\} \cup$ dom $build\text{-}rel(s')$ $\cup$-I-left-$\subseteq$(5.1)

5.4 $\{x, y\} \subseteq$ dom $build\text{-}rel(add(mk\text{-}(a, b), s'))$ =-subs(5.2,5.3)

5.5 $build\text{-}rel(s')(y) \subseteq build\text{-}rel(add(mk\text{-}(a, b), s'))(y)$

                   Lemma 4(5.1)

5.6 $x \in build\text{-}rel(add(mk\text{-}(a, b), s'))(y)$ $\subseteq$-I(5.1,5.5)

5.7 $y \in build\text{-}rel(add(mk\text{-}(a, b), s'))(x)$ Lemma 1(5.6)

   infer $\{x, y\} \subseteq$ dom $build\text{-}rel(add(mk\text{-}(a, b), s')) \wedge$
   $x \in build\text{-}rel(add(mk\text{-}(a, b), s'))(y) \wedge$
   $y \in build\text{-}rel(add(mk\text{-}(a, b), s'))(x)$ $\wedge$-I(5.4,5.6,5.7)

6 from $mk\text{-}(x, y) \in add(mk\text{-}(a, b), s')$

6.1 $mk\text{-}(x, y) = mk\text{-}(a, b) \vee mk\text{-}(x, y) \in s'$ $\in$-add-E(h6)

   infer $\{x, y\} \subseteq$ dom $build\text{-}rel(add(mk\text{-}(a, b), s')) \wedge$
   $x \in build\text{-}rel(add(mk\text{-}(a, b), s'))(y) \wedge$
   $y \in build\text{-}rel(add(mk\text{-}(a, b), s'))(x)$ $\vee$-E(6.1,4,5)

7 $mk\text{-}(a, b) : CG \times CG$ tuple-form(h)

8 $add(mk\text{-}(a, b), s') : CG \times CG$-set add-form(7,h)

9 $mk\text{-}(x, y) : CG \times CG$ tuple-form(h)

10 $\delta(mk\text{-}(x, y) \in add(mk\text{-}(a, b), s'))$ δ-in-set(9,8)

infer $mk\text{-}(x, y) \in add(mk\text{-}(a, b), s') \Rightarrow$
  $(\{x, y\} \subseteq$ dom $build\text{-}rel(add(mk\text{-}(a, b), s')) \wedge$
  $x \in build\text{-}rel(add(mk\text{-}(a, b), s'))(y) \wedge$
  $y \in build\text{-}rel(add(mk\text{-}(a, b), s'))(x))$ $\Rightarrow$-I(6,10)

Figure 2.5: Proof of Theorem 1

from $x : CG; y : CG$
1     $build\text{-}rel(\{\}) =$
         if $\{\} = \{\}$ then $\{\}$
         else let $cr = build\text{-}rel(\{\})$ in
            let $new\text{-}cr = addCG(b, addCG(a, cr))$ in
              $new\text{-}cr \dagger \{a \mapsto new\text{-}cr(a) \cup \{b\},$
                      $b \mapsto new\text{-}cr(b) \cup \{a\}\}$ $build\text{-}rel\text{-defn}(h)$
2   if $\{\} = \{\}$ then $\{\}$
       else let $cr = build\text{-}rel(\{\})$ in
          let $new\text{-}cr = addCG(b, addCG(a, cr))$ in
           $new\text{-}cr \dagger \{a \mapsto new\text{-}cr(a) \cup \{b\},$
                  $b \mapsto new\text{-}cr(b) \cup \{a\}\} = \{\}$ condition-true(h)
3    $build\text{-}rel(\{\}) = \{\}$ =-trans$(1,2)$
4   dom $\{\} = \{\}$ dom -defn-$\{\mapsto\}$
5   dom $build\text{-}rel(\{\}) = \{\}$ =-subs$(3,4)$
6    $\neg\, y \in \{\}$ $\{\,\}$-is-empty(h)
7    $\neg\, y \in$ dom $build\text{-}rel(\{\})$ =-subs$(5,6)$
8    $\neg\, (y \in$ dom $build\text{-}rel(\{\}) \wedge x \in build\text{-}rel(\{\})(y))$ $\neg$-$\wedge$-I-right(7)
9    $\neg\, (y \in$ dom $build\text{-}rel(\{\}) \wedge x \in build\text{-}rel(\{\})(y)) \vee$
      $(mk\text{-}(x, y) \in \{\} \vee mk\text{-}(y, x) \in \{\})$ $\vee$-I-right(8)
infer $(y \in$ dom $build\text{-}rel(\{\}) \wedge x \in build\text{-}rel(\{\})(y)) \Rightarrow$
      $(mk\text{-}(x, y) \in \{\} \vee mk\text{-}(y, x) \in \{\})$ $\Rightarrow$ -defn(9)

Figure 2.6: Proof of Theorem 3

we distinguish three cases: the two trivial ones in which $\{x, y\} = \{a, b\}$, and the third in which $mk\text{-}(x, y) \neq mk\text{-}(a, b) \wedge mk\text{-}(y, x) \neq mk\text{-}(a, b)$ (line 2.1.3). In the latter case the desired conclusion is yielded by Lemma 5, which we discuss below.

Finally, to prove $\delta(A)$, we explicitly construct A and use our type hypotheses to verify definedness at each stage of the construction. Thus we prove the required inference.

As stated above, the main result used in this induction is Lemma 5, shown in figure 2.8. The proof for this lemma proceeds in two parts. In the former (lines 1–11), x, y, a and b are manipulated until we are able to partition inequalities in the manner shown on line 11. This partition is then used in a case-by-case analysis (lines 12–15) using Lemmas 6–9. These lemmas, listed in appendix 2.7, are all technical results, and all appeal to the definition of *build-rel* for their proof. Details may be found in [7].

from $x : CG; y : CG; s : CG \times CG$-set
1    $y \in$ dom $build\text{-}rel(\{\}) \wedge x \in build\text{-}rel(\{\})(y) \Rightarrow$

    $(mk\text{-}(x, y) \in \{\} \vee mk\text{-}(y, x) \in \{\})$ Theorem 3(h)

2   from $a : CG; b : CG; s' : CG \times CG$-set; $mk\text{-}(a, b) \notin s'$;

        $y \in$ dom $build\text{-}rel(s') \wedge x \in build\text{-}rel(s')(y) \Rightarrow$

        $mk\text{-}(x, y) \in s' \vee mk\text{-}(y, x) \in s'$

2.1   from $y \in$ dom $build\text{-}rel(add(mk\text{-}(a, b), s')) \wedge$

        $x \in build\text{-}rel(add(mk\text{-}(a, b), s'))(y)$

2.1.1   from $mk\text{-}(x, y) = mk\text{-}(a, b)$

2.1.1.1 $mk\text{-}(x, y) \in add(mk\text{-}(a, b), s')$ $\in\text{-}add$-I-elem(h2.1.1)

    infer $mk\text{-}(x, y) \in add(mk\text{-}(a, b), s') \vee$

    $mk\text{-}(y, x) \in add(mk\text{-}(a, b), s')$ $\vee$-I-right(2.1.1.1)

2.1.2   from $mk\text{-}(y, x) = mk\text{-}(a, b)$

2.1.2.1 $mk\text{-}(y, x) \in add(mk\text{-}(a, b), s')$ $\in\text{-}add$-I-elem(h2.1.2)

    infer $mk\text{-}(x, y) \in add(mk\text{-}(a, b), s') \vee$

    $mk\text{-}(y, x) \in add(mk\text{-}(a, b), s')$ $\vee$-I-right(2.1.2.1)

2.1.3   from $mk\text{-}(x, y) \neq mk\text{-}(a, b) \wedge mk\text{-}(y, x) \neq mk\text{-}(a, b)$

2.1.3.1 $y \in$ dom $build\text{-}rel(s') \wedge x \in build\text{-}rel(s')(y)$

        Lemma 5(h,h2.1,h2.1.3)

2.1.3.2 $mk\text{-}(x, y) \in s' \vee mk\text{-}(y, x) \in s'$ $\Rightarrow$ -E(h2,2.1.3.1)

    infer $mk\text{-}(x, y) \in add(mk\text{-}(a, b), s') \vee$

    $mk\text{-}(y, x) \in add(mk\text{-}(a, b), s')$ $\in\text{-}add$-I-set-$\vee$(2.1.3.2)

    infer $mk\text{-}(x, y) \in add(mk\text{-}(a, b), s') \vee$

    $mk\text{-}(y, x) \in add(mk\text{-}(a, b), s')$ $=$-cases(2.1.1,2.1.2,2.1.3)

2.2 $add(mk\text{-}(a, b), s') : CG \times CG$-set add-form(h2)

2.3 $build\text{-}rel(add(mk\text{-}(a, b), s')) : CompatRel$ $build\text{-}rel$-defn(2.2)

2.4   dom $build\text{-}rel(add(mk\text{-}(a, b), s')) : CG$ dom -form(2.3)

2.5 $\delta(y \in$ dom $build\text{-}rel(add(mk\text{-}(a, b), s')))$ δ-in(2.4,h)

2.6 $build\text{-}rel(add(mk\text{-}(a, b), s'))(y) : CG$-set $CompatRel$-defn(2.3)

2.7 $\delta(x \in build\text{-}rel(add(mk\text{-}(a, b), s'))(y))$ δ-in(2.6,h)

2.8 $\delta(y \in$ dom $build\text{-}rel(add(mk\text{-}(a, b), s')) \wedge$

    $x \in build\text{-}rel(add(mk\text{-}(a, b), s'))(y))$ δ-$\wedge$-inherit(2.5,2.7)

    infer $(y \in$ dom $build\text{-}rel(add(mk\text{-}(a, b), s')) \wedge$

    $x \in build\text{-}rel(add(mk\text{-}(a, b), s'))(y)) \Rightarrow$

    $(mk\text{-}(x, y) \in add(mk\text{-}(a, b), s') \vee$

    $mk\text{-}(y, x) \in add(mk\text{-}(a, b), s'))$ $\Rightarrow$ -I(2.1,2.8)

infer $(y \in$ dom $build\text{-}rel(s) \wedge x \in build\text{-}rel(s)(y)) \Rightarrow$

$mk\text{-}(x, y) \in s \vee mk\text{-}(y, x) \in s$ set-indn(1,2)

Figure 2.7: Proof of Theorem 4

from $x : CG; y : CG; a : CG; b : CG; s : CG \times CG$-set;
    $y \in$ dom $build\text{-}rel(add(mk\text{-}(a, b), s))$;
    $x \in build\text{-}rel(add(mk\text{-}(a, b), s))(y)$;
    $mk\text{-}(x, y) \neq mk\text{-}(a, b) \land mk\text{-}(y, x) \neq mk\text{-}(a, b)$

1	from $x = a \land y = b$	
	infer $mk\text{-}(x, y) = mk\text{-}(a, b)$	mk-defn(h,h1)
2	$\neg((x = a \land y = b) \land mk\text{-}(x, y) \neq mk\text{-}(a, b))$	$\neg$-$\land$-i-sqt(1)
3	$\neg(x = a \land y = b)$	$\neg$-$\land$-E-right(h,2)
4	$x \neq a \lor y \neq b$	$\land$-defn(3)
5	from $x = b \land y = a$	
	infer $mk\text{-}(y, x) = mk\text{-}(a, b)$	mk-defn(h,h5)
6	$\neg((x = b \land y = a) \land mk\text{-}(y, x) \neq mk\text{-}(a, b))$	$\neg$-$\land$-i-sqt(5)
7	$\neg(x = b \land y = a)$	$\neg$-$\land$-E-right(h,6)
8	$x \neq b \lor y \neq a$	$\land$-defn(7)
9	$(x \neq a \lor y \neq b) \land (x \neq b \lor y \neq a)$	$\land$-I(4,8)
10	$((x \neq a \lor y \neq b \land x \neq b) \lor$	
	$(x \neq a \lor y \neq b \land y \neq a))$	$\land$-$\lor$-dist-expand(9)
11	$(x \neq a \land x \neq b) \lor (y \neq b \land x \neq b) \lor$	
	$(x \neq a \land y \neq a) \lor (y \neq b \land y \neq a)$	$\land$-$\lor$-dist-expand(10)
12	from $x \neq a \land x \neq b$	
	infer $y \in$ dom $build\text{-}rel(s) \land x \in build\text{-}rel(s)(y)$	Lemma 6(h,h12)
13	from $y \neq b \land x \neq b$	
	infer $y \in$ dom $build\text{-}rel(s) \land x \in build\text{-}rel(s)(y)$	Lemma 7(h,h13)
14	from $x \neq a \land y \neq a$	
	infer $y \in$ dom $build\text{-}rel(s) \land x \in build\text{-}rel(s)(y)$	Lemma 8(h,h14)
15	from $y \neq b \land y \neq a$	
	infer $y \in$ dom $build\text{-}rel(s) \land x \in build\text{-}rel(s)(y)$	Lemma 9(h,h15)
infer $y \in$ dom $build\text{-}rel(s) \land x \in build\text{-}rel(s)(y)$		$\lor$-E(11,12,13,14,15)

Figure 2.8: Proof of Lemma 5

Summary

Having proved the equivalence of the separated specification and the original specification, it is useful to step back and consider what we have achieved. At the outset, we suggested that we wished to modify the specification, then "demonstrate that the [modified] specification is equivalent to the original one." At this stage the notion of equivalence is left relatively vague and is only really detailed in section 2.4.2. Thus while we were modifying the specification, we were relying on some intuitive notion of equivalence, which (as it turned out) was sufficient. However in other cases formalizing our equivalence requirement then attempting to prove equivalence might lead to deficiencies in the specification being highlighted. This is not unexpected, as we can not always expect our intuition to be sufficiently precise to match the degree of rigour demonstrated in the proofs above. Nor is this unwelcome, for as described in [6], undertaking proof, whether successful or otherwise, gives us deeper insight into the underlying domain, in this case our specification.

Turning to the proofs themselves, the complete proofs run to nearly thirty pages, which is surprising given the relatively modest goal, notwithstanding the degree of formality used. However much of this is relatively straightforward symbolic manipulation, which could easily be automated. Somewhat more surprising is the proportion of the proof which was simple case analysis, as exemplified by the proofs presented here. On reflection, this case analysis reflects the structure of the specification, as there we see a number of conditional expressions. In fact it is interesting to see the degree to which the structure of the proofs is dictated by the structure of the specification; conditional expressions give rise to proofs based around case analysis, and recursive functions lead to inductive proofs. This emphasizes the relationship between specifications and proofs, in that when proving a property of the specification, we use the structure of the specification to structure the proof; the success (or otherwise) of the proof can then feed back into the specification.

2.5 Discussion

Our objective in this chapter has been to demonstrate the use of a variety of proof techniques in two scenarios: as a tool for ensuring the well-formedness of a specification; and as a mechanism for performing design in a rigorous manner. Thus we have proved the satisfiability of an operation, and we have proved the correctness of a design decomposition. Although we have used the specific example of the Ammunition Control System, the approach and techniques are not specific to this example, nor even to VDM-SL itself. The underlying theme throughout has been that proof deepens our understanding of specifications. We can draw an analogy with [6], where it is argued that proof deepens our understanding of theorems, and eventually improves them. Here, though our objects of interest differ (specifications rather than theorems) the same conclusion can be drawn.

One question that arose in this (and previous) exercises, is the extent to which we should alter the specification to simplify proofs. That is, some expressions give rise to simpler proof obligations than other expressions, which in a given context are equivalent. In this situation it seems that we can safely replace the original expressions with new ones, simplifying our proof obligations whilst leaving the meaning of the specification unchanged. However it is important to bear in mind that the specification document is meant as a communication medium between the various parties involved in the construction of a system. Such modification whilst preserving the meaning of the specification, need not preserve the clarity nor even the style of the original document. Moreover, as the number of such modifications increases, it becomes more tempting to accept the equivalence of the new specification with the old, with less rigour. Thus we argue that such modifications should be kept to a minimum, and, when used, should always be justified formally.

A problem that arose concerned the size and intricacy of the proofs described in section 2.4, which, as stated there, occupy nearly 30 pages. As the use of lemmas exploiting similar structure in distinct portions of the proof increased, so the relationship between proofs and the overall result weakened. Eventually the issue that two lemmas might be mutually dependent was confronted, as it was not obvious that this was not the case. Verifying that such mutual dependencies do not exist is both non-trivial and prone to errors when performed by hand. Therefore a simple tool was constructed to analyse proofs: for a given collection of proofs, it parses each proof then forms a list of the results (theorems and lemmas) on which this proof depends. A directed graph is then constructed in which nodes are results and arcs denote dependence of the proof of a result. This graph can be tested for cycles using standard algorithms. In this case no such cycles were found, so we can be confident that there is no circular reasoning in our proofs. However in the first instance a number of results were discovered upon which no other results depended! Thus this tool undoubtedly improved the quality of the proofs themselves, and therefore increased our confidence in the proofs.

Is there any place for hand proofs today, given the availability of powerful theorem provers such as PVS and Isabelle? (See Chapters 6 and 7. In an ideal world, no! As hinted above, a large proportion of the tasks associated with proof are better performed mechanically. However in practice this is not always possible, for a number of reasons. For instance, we might be using domain-specific extensions to the formal notation that are not supported by the proof tool. In such situations knowledge of how to perform hand proof is vital. Moreover at present, theorem provers are only able to prove non-trivial results when directed by a human user, so even using such tools, knowledge and understanding of the craft of proof is invaluable.

2.6 Bibliography

[1] J.C. Bicarregui, J.S. Fitzgerald, P.A. Lindsay, R. Moore, and B. Ritchie. *Proof in VDM: A Practitioner's Guide.* Springer-Verlag, 1994.

[2] Committee of Experts on the Transport of Dangerous Goods, New York. *Recommendations on the Transport of Dangerous Goods*, 5th revised edition,

1988.

[3] R. Elmstrøm, P.G. Larsen, and P.B. Lassen. The IFAD VDM-SL Toolbox: A Practical Approach to Formal Specifications. *ACM Sigplan Notices*, 29(9), 1994.

[4] J. S. Fitzgerald. A proof of Satisfiability in Mukherjee and Stavridou's Ammunition Control System. Technical Report 616, Dept. of Computing Science, University of Newcastle upon Tyne, Newcastle upon Tyne, NE1 7RU, UK, 1997.

[5] J. Goguen and T. Winkler. Introducing OBJ3. Technical Report SRI-CSL-88-9, SRI International, August 1988.

[6] I. Lakatos. *Proofs and Refutations*. Cambridge University Press, 1976.

[7] P. Mukherjee. Proof of Equivalence in the ACS specification. Technical Report SCS 97.34, University of Leeds, 1997.

[8] P. Mukherjee and V. Stavridou. The Formal Specification of Safety Requirements for Storing Explosives. *Formal Aspects of Computing*, 5(4):299–336, 1993.

2.7   Auxiliary Results

This section gives the statements of the results used in the equivalence proof in Section 2.4. The proofs of these results may be found in [7].

Lemma 2

from $a : CG; b : CG; s : CG \times CG$-set
infer $\{a, b\} \subseteq$ dom $build\text{-}rel(add(mk\text{-}(a, b), s)) \wedge$
$a \in build\text{-}rel(add(mk\text{-}(a, b), s))(b) \wedge$
$b \in build\text{-}rel(add(mk\text{-}(a, b), s))(a)$

Lemma 3

from $a : CG; b : CG; s : CG \times CG$-set
infer dom $build\text{-}rel(add(mk\text{-}(a, b), s)) = \{a, b\} \cup$ dom $build\text{-}rel(s)$

Lemma 4

from $a : CG; b : CG; y : CG; s : CG \times CG$-set; $y \in$ dom $build\text{-}rel(s)$
infer $build\text{-}rel(s)(y) \subseteq build\text{-}rel(add(mk\text{-}(a, b), s))(y)$

Lemma 5

from $a : CG; b : CG; c : CG; d : CG; s : CG \times CG$-set;
    $b \in$ dom $build\text{-}rel(add(mk\text{-}(c, d), s))$;
    $a \in build\text{-}rel(add(mk\text{-}(c, d), s))(b)$;
    $mk\text{-}(a, b) \neq mk\text{-}(c, d) \wedge mk\text{-}(b, a) \neq mk\text{-}(c, d)$
infer $b \in$ dom $build\text{-}rel(s) \wedge a \in build\text{-}rel(s)(b)$

Lemma 6

from $a : CG; b : CG; c : CG; d : CG; s : CG \times CG$-set;
    $b \in$ dom $build\text{-}rel(add(mk\text{-}(c, d), s))$;
    $a \in build\text{-}rel(add(mk\text{-}(c, d), s))(b); a \neq c; a \neq d$
infer $b \in$ dom $build\text{-}rel(s) \wedge a \in build\text{-}rel(s)(b)$

Lemma 7

from $a : CG; b : CG; c : CG; d : CG; s : CG \times CG$-set;
    $b \in$ dom $build\text{-}rel(add(mk\text{-}(c, d), s))$;
    $a \in build\text{-}rel(add(mk\text{-}(c, d), s))(b); b \neq d; a \neq d$
infer $b \in$ dom $build\text{-}rel(s) \wedge a \in build\text{-}rel(s)(b)$

Lemma 8

from $a : CG; b : CG; c : CG; d : CG; s : CG \times CG$-set;
    $b \in$ dom $build\text{-}rel(add(mk\text{-}(c, d), s))$;
    $a \in build\text{-}rel(add(mk\text{-}(c, d), s))(b); a \neq c; b \neq c$
infer $b \in$ dom $build\text{-}rel(s) \wedge a \in build\text{-}rel(s)(b)$

Lemma 9

from $a : CG; b : CG; c : CG; d : CG; s : CG \times CG$-set;
   $b \in$ dom $build\text{-}rel(add(mk\text{-}(c, d), s))$;
   $a \in build\text{-}rel(add(mk\text{-}(c, d), s))(b); b \neq d; b \neq c$
infer $b \in$ dom $build\text{-}rel(s) \wedge a \in build\text{-}rel(s)(b)$

Chapter 3

Specification and Validation of a Network Security Policy Model

Peter Lindsay

Summary

This case study concerns the specification and validation of a Security Policy Model (SPM) for an electronic network. The network is intended to provide processing and transmission services for electronic messages, including sensitive and classified material, over distributed sites and supporting multiple levels of security classification. The SPM is formally specified in VDM-SL and validated by showing that the model is mathematically consistent and satisfies certain security properties. Rigorous proofs are provided. In addition, the case study illustrates some new techniques concerning proof obligations for exception conditions in VDM-SL.

3.1 Introduction

3.1.1 Background and Context

This chapter describes the specification and validation of a formal Security Policy Model (SPM) for an electronic-message processing and transmission service. The SPM is a distillation of the important security requirements of the software system that provides the service. The SPM described here is based on a security model originally proposed for an Australian Government agency's secure distributed network; the model has been changed in certain ways, however, to protect sensitive details.

A high degree of assurance in the correctness of the model and the system's security was required – roughly equivalent to the requirements for level E5 in the ITSEC computer security standard [1]. A particular accreditation requirement was that the SPM be described in a formal language and that formal proofs of correctness be performed. This chapter describes a formal specification of the SPM in VDM-SL [4], but rather than present formal proofs, the proofs are given rigorously here, for clarity and ease of understanding.

By way of context for the specification and validation of the SPM, the overall computer system security objectives will be outlined in the rest of this section. The process by which the security objectives were attained will not be discussed here, however, nor how particular aspects of the model were determined to be the appropriate ones for study. The interested reader is referred to Landwehr's excellent survey article [6] for explanation of computer security terminology and for further background on the use and need for security models.

3.1.2   Software System Requirements

The system's primary function is to provide a secure message processing and transmission service for a government agency whose offices are distributed across many locations. Messages generated and processed on the system range in sensitivity from unclassified to classified material with different levels of security classification. The system is also required to provide a message transmission service for other government agencies, which send and receive messages via the network.

An important feature of the agency's message processing procedures is analysis of messages. Each message is subjected to review by one or more analysts, to determine if the content of the message warrants additional dissemination and whether additional relevant information should be appended to the message. Analysis occurs both at the location where the message is generated (by a local expert) and at the organisation's headquarters by a team of experts (called central analysts).

In outline, the processing activities applied to a message from conception to delivery are as follows:

1. The author generates a message together with its classification and a list of proposed recipients.

2. The author sends the message for review by a local analyst, which may result in information being added, the destination list changing, or in the message's classification being modified.

3. The local analyst sends the message for review by central analysts, which may result in similar modifications of the message. Central analysis may involve review by one or more analysts, depending upon the message's content.

4. When central analysis is complete, the message is added to a queue for delivery.

5. The system transmits the message to appropriate locations, where local analysis may take place prior to delivery of the message to its intended recipients.

3.1.3   Security Threats and Security Objectives

The security threats identified for the message processing system include the following:

1. Users may gain access to classified messages which they are not cleared to access.

2. Classified messages may (accidentally or deliberately) be delivered to users or agencies who are not cleared to receive them.

3. During processing, information may (accidentally or deliberately) be added whose classification is higher than that of the message, without subsequent adjustment of the message's classification.

4. Users of external agency facilities may try to subvert the system, for example by sending messages containing malevolent code such as computer viruses.

The agency's overall computer security objectives for the system are as follows:

1. To preserve the *confidentiality* of messages – i.e., to ensure that no message is distributed to an individual who is not sufficiently cleared to receive it, nor sent to an agency with a lower classification (no unauthorised disclosure).

2. To preserve the *integrity* of messages – i.e., to ensure that message contents are not accidentally or deliberately changed in transit (no unauthorised modification).

3. To ensure *accountability* of users for their actions – i.e., to ensure that anyone who authorises transmission of a message is identifiable and a record is kept of their actions. This is an important deterrent against deliberate breaches of security.

3.1.4   Conceptual Model of the Security Policy

The following principles underlie the conceptual model of the electronic security policy for the new system:

1. Users are *partitioned* according to their clearance. This applies both to users who are internal to the agency and those in connected external agencies.

2. Confidentiality of information is preserved by controlling the flow of information between user partitions.

3. *Seals* are applied to parts of messages to enable the integrity of their classification and contents to be checked. Any changes to the classification or contents of a message need authorisation before the message can be transferred between partitions.

4. Accountability is enforced by maintaining a *complete audit trail* of system
   and user actions related to authorisation of messages and attempts to transfer
   messages between partitions.

The mechanisms which achieve these principles are outlined below.

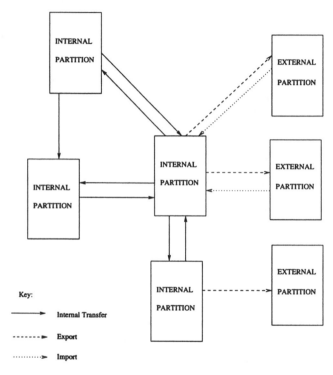

Figure 3.1: Conceptual model of security partitions.

Partitions

Conceptually, the system is divided into a number of *internal partitions* – serving a
community of users within the agency who are cleared to access messages passed to
(or within) that partition – and a set of *external partitions*, serving other agencies
connected to the message processing system (see Fig. 3.1).

A partition can hold messages that are classified up to, and including, the classification of the partition. A user may have access to more than one internal partition,
provided of course they have sufficient clearance. Note also that there is not necessarily a physical relationship between the location of users and an internal partition:
a single internal partition may be spread over many different physical locations that
comprise the distributed system.

Transfers

The operations which move messages from one partition to another are called *transfers*. For precision, transfers between internal partitions will be called *internal transfers*; transfers from internal partitions to external partitions will be called *exports*; and transfers from external partitions to internal partitions will be called *imports*. A non-hierarchical *adjoinment* relation will be used to record how partitions are connected to one another via network gateways. Note that in some cases the flow of information is one-way only (see Fig. 3.1).

Certain constraints will be imposed on the transfer operations by the security policy. In particular, a message will only be transferred from one partition to another if the two partitions adjoin, the receiving partition has sufficient clearance to accept the message, and any changes made to the message have been authorised. Fig. 3.2 illustrates how a message is processed by the system.

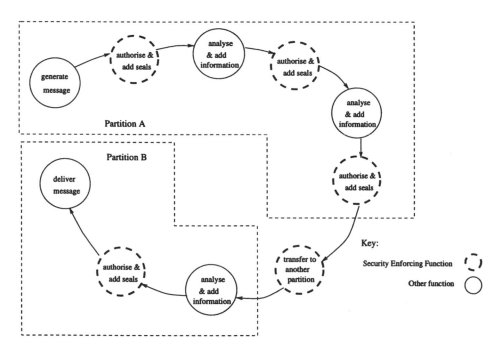

Figure 3.2: Example life-cycle of a message in the message processing system.

Seals

Conceptually, a seal binds the classification of a message part to its contents in a trusted manner. Intuitively, an electronic seal is a kind of encrypted check-sum. The sealing function will be carefully protected from unauthorised use. The essential property of a seal is that authorised users can check the integrity of message parts and their classification by regenerating the seal and checking that it hasn't changed.

Each internal partition has its own protected sealing mechanism. In addition to their use for checking integrity, this SPM uses seals as a mechanisms for maintaining confidentiality, by checking seals before transfer is allowed. This principle is explained in detail in the body of the chapter. In essence, the sealing mechanism provides a *trusted path* between the authoriser and trusted software performing gateway or access control decisions.

Audit trail

Details of each use of a message authorisation operation or transfer operation — successful or unsuccessful — are recorded as part of a security audit trail, including the identity of the authoriser.

3.1.5 The Security Enforcing Functions

The conceptual model of security policy is achieved through four *Security Enforcing Functions*(SEFs), outlined below:

- An *Authorise Message* function, to authorise transfers and apply seals. Authorising requires the user to check the content of the message and to confirm the message is correctly classified. Upon authorisation, seals are added to the message.

- An *Internal Transfer* function, to perform transfers between internal partitions. The function confirms that the message has been sealed and that the destination partition has sufficient clearance to receive the message.

- An *Export* function to perform transfers from internal partitions to external partitions. A confirmation procedure similar to that for Internal Transfer is performed.

- An *Import* function to perform transfers from external partitions to internal partitions. Since in this case the message has been received from an external agency, it is not considered to have been authorised in the required manner. The Import function thus checks that the message contains no viruses, hostile software, etc, before sealing and transferring the message into an internal partition.

The system has many other functions, but the above four are the ones that are concerned with enforcing security.

3.1.6 Specification and Validation of the SPM

In the remainder of this chapter, the Security Policy Model is formally specified in VDM-SL:

- Section 3.2 defines a data model which describes the main system entities at an appropriate level of abstraction.

- Section 3.3 defines the abstract state of the network at any time as consisting of: the conceptual location of messages; the active user sessions; and the complete audit trail of user and system actions. The main security properties are defined as constraints (invariants) on the allowable states.

- In Section 3.4, the four Security Enforcing Functions are modelled as state-changing operations. Exception conditions are used to model abnormal operation, including accidental or deliberate attempts to subvert security.

The SPM is validated in various ways in Section 3.5. In particular, it is shown that the specification is mathematically consistent, the Security Enforcing Functions preserve the desired security properties, and the specification is complete with respect to its input space. Finally Section 3.6 draws some conclusions about the use of specification and proof on this example.

3.2 The Data Model

This section gives mathematical definitions of the main system entities and the relationships between them, including the various static security-enforcing properties of the network. In what follows, *primitive types* are types which will not be defined further here.

3.2.1 Partitions

The primitive type *Partition* will be used to model the set of all possible partitions. The sets of internal and external partitions will be modelled as constants, with declarations:

intpartns: *Partition*-**set**
extpartns: *Partition*-**set**

The adjoinment relation will be modelled as a binary relation on partitions:

adjoins: *Partition* × *Partition* → **B**

Thus, $adjoins(p_1, p_2)$ stands for the assertion that messages are physically able to flow from partition p_1 to partition p_2. Note that the configuration of partitions may change from time to time, but that operations for reconfiguring the network are outside the scope of the SPM described here.

3.2.2   Users and User Sessions

The primitive type *UserId* will be used to model the set of identifiers of users. It is assumed that user identifiers are unique and are sufficient to enable a user to be identified unambiguously. (User authentication mechanisms are outside the scope of the SPM described here.) A binary predicate

hasAccess: *UserId* × *Partition* → **B**

will model the check that a given user has access to a given partition. Note that a user may be able to access multiple partitions (but not simultaneously).

The concept of *sessions* is introduced for periods of use of the system by internal users. Work areas can be shared by a number of users and it is not practical to authenticate users' identities at all times; sessions thus allow an extra level of identification for accountability.

The primitive type *SessionId* will be used to model the set of identifiers of individual user sessions. Conceptually, each session has a unique identifier, together with a record of the partition in which it is being run and the identity of the user who is running it:

$$Session :: \quad sid \; : \; SessionId$$
$$pid \; : \; Partition$$
$$uid \; : \; UserId$$

inv $s, p, u \triangleq p \in intpartns \land hasAccess(u, p)$

The invariant says that sessions run in internal partitions only, and that some kind of access control is in place to ensure that only users who can access the given partition are able to run sessions there.

3.2.3   Classifications

The primitive type *Classif* will be used to model the set of all possible classifications of messages. In practice, classifications are not simply hierarchical in nature, but have multiple dimensions. The binary predicate

hasClearance: *Partition* × *Classif* → **B**

will be used to model the relationship between partitions and the classifications of messages they are cleared to receive. The clearance of an individual will be determined implicitly by the partitions they are able to access.

3.2.4   Messages

The central concept of the model is a *message*, which consists of a destination list, a classification, and a set of *message parts*:

Message :: *destins* : *Destination*-**set**
         classif : *Classif*
          body : *MessagePart**

A *destination* consists of a user identifier for the intended recipient, together with the partition in which they will receive the message:

Destination :: *uid* : *UserId*
          pid : *Partition*

The system does not actively check that the intended recipient has access to the destination partition. (Access control is applied at the partition itself.)

The primitive type *Content* is used to model the set of all possible contents of messages. A message part consists of some content, an optional user identifier to note the person who has authorised the content, and an optional seal (explained below):

MessagePart ::   *content* : *Content*
          authoriser : [*UserId*]
              seal : [*Seal*]

Creation and processing of the message parts are outside the scope of the SPM. Seals and user identifiers would not be edited under normal circumstances, but the model covers the possibility of malicious editing.

3.2.5   Seals

Seals are applied to individual message parts to enable integrity of their classification, contents and authoriser to be checked. Each of the internal partitions has its own sealing mechanism, which is assumed to be protected in such a way that only authorised users of that partition can access the mechanism, and then only via the Security Enforcing Functions. Intuitively, a seal is a kind of encrypted checksum which binds the classification, content and authoriser to the message part; any attempt to modify these will be detected by regenerating and checking the seal.

The primitive type *Seal* will be used to model the set of all possible seals. The function

generateSeal: *Partition* × *Classif* × *Content* × *UserId* → *Seal*

will be used to model the generation of seals in internal partitions.

The following function checks the integrity of a message part with respect to a given partition and classification:

hasValidSeal : *MessagePart* × *Partition* × *Classif* → **B**

hasValidSeal(*mp*, *p*, *c*) $\triangleq$ *mp.authoriser* ≠ **nil** ∧
    mp.seal = *generateSeal*(*p*, *c*, *mp.content*, *mp.authoriser*)

Note that the seal may be valid in one partition but not in another. (There will be functions for changing the seals on message parts when messages are transferred from one partition to another.)

The following lemma is a logical consequence of the above definition:

ValidSeal Lemma If a message part's seal is valid, then it is non-nil and an authoriser is identifier for the message part:

$\forall mp$: *MessagePart*, p: *Partition*, c: *Classif* ·
$\quad hasValidSeal(mp, p, c) \Rightarrow mp.seal \neq$ **nil** $\land mp.authoriser \neq$ **nil**

3.2.6   Sealing

The following function models sealing of an individual message part:

$sealMsgPart$: *Partition* × *Classif* × *MessagePart* × *UserId* → *MessagePart*

$sealMsgPart(p, c, mp, u) \quad \triangle \quad$ **if** $hasValidSeal(mp, p, c)$ **then** mp
$\quad$ **else** $mk\text{-}MessagePart(mp.content, u, generateSeal(p, c, mp.content, u))$

Note that if message part already has a valid seal then neither it nor the authoriser identifier are changed.

The following function models the sealing of an entire message:

$sealMessage$: *Partition* × *Message* × *UserId* → *Message*

$sealMessage(p, m, u) \quad \triangle$
$\quad \mu(m, body \mapsto [sealMsgPart(p, m.classif, m.body(i), u) \mid i \in \textbf{inds } m.body])$

The following lemma is a logical consequence of the above definition:

Main Sealing Lemma Sealing a message does not change its destination list, its classification or the content of its parts, and the authoriser field is changed only for message parts without valid seals:

$\forall p$: *Partition*, m: *Message*, u: *UserId* ·
$\quad$ **let** $m' = sealMessage(p, m, u)$ **in**
$\qquad m'.destins = m.destins \land$
$\qquad m'.classif = m.classif \land$
$\qquad$ **len** $m'.body =$ **len** $m.body \land$
$\qquad \forall i \in \textbf{inds } m.body ·$ **let** $mp = m.body(i), mp' = m'.body(i)$ **in**
$\qquad\quad mp'.content = mp.content \land$
$\qquad\quad$ **if** $hasValidSeal(mp, p, m.classif)$
$\qquad\quad$ **then** $mp'.authoriser = mp.authoriser$
$\qquad\quad$ **else** $mp'.authoriser = u$

Note that sealed message parts can be inspected without breaking the seal, but any changes to the message part will be detectable. If a message is resealed after message parts have been changed, then the person who authorises the resealing will be identified as the authoriser of the new and changed parts (only).

3.2.7 Changing Seals

The following functions change the seals on a transferred message so that they are valid in its new partition. The functions will be assumed to be protected in such a way that they can be invoked only by the system, and then only at network gateways.

$changeSeal : Partition \times Classif \times MessagePart \rightarrow MessagePart$

$changeSeal(p, c, mp) \quad \triangleq$
   $\mu(mp, seal \mapsto generateSeal(p, c, mp.content, mp.authoriser))$

pre $mp.authoriser \neq$ **nil**

$changeSeals : Partition \times Message \rightarrow Message$

$changeSeals(p, m) \quad \triangleq$
   $\mu(m, body \mapsto [changeSeal(p, m.classif, m.body(i)) \mid i \in$ **inds** $m.body])$

pre $\forall mp \in$ **elems** $m.body \cdot mp.authoriser \neq$ **nil**

The following lemma is a logical consequence of the above definition:

Resealing Lemma Resealing a message does not change its destination list, its classification, nor the content or authoriser fields of its parts:

$\forall p: Partition, m: Message \cdot$
   $(\forall mp \in$ **elems** $m.body \cdot mp.authoriser \neq$ **nil**$) \Rightarrow$
   let $m' = changeSeals(p, m)$ **in**
      $m'.destins = m.destins \wedge$
      $m'.classif = m.classif \wedge$
      len $m'.body =$ **len** $m.body \wedge$
      $\forall i \in$ **inds** $m.body \cdot$ **let** $mp = m.body(i), mp' = m'.body(i)$ **in**
         $mp'.content = mp.content \wedge$
         $mp'.authoriser = mp.authoriser$

3.2.8 Other Integrity Checks

The following predicate checks whether all message parts of a given message have valid seals:

$allSealsAreValid : Message \times Partition \rightarrow$ **B**

$allSealsAreValid(m, p) \quad \triangleq \quad \forall mp \in$ **elems** $m.body \cdot hasValidSeal(mp, p, m.classif)$

The following predicate checks that a message has no seals (valid or otherwise):

$hasNoSeals : Message \rightarrow \mathbf{B}$

$hasNoSeals(m) \quad \underline{\triangle} \quad \forall mp \in \mathbf{elems}\ m.body \cdot mp.seal = \mathbf{nil}$

The following function strips all seals off the message parts in a given message:

$stripSeals : Message \rightarrow Message$

$stripSeals(m) \quad \underline{\triangle} \quad \mu(m, body \mapsto [\mu(m.body(i), seal \mapsto \mathbf{nil}) \mid i \in \mathbf{inds}\ m.body])$

The following lemma is a logical consequence of the above definition:

StripSeals Lemma After applying *stripSeals*, the message has no seals:

$\forall m: Message \cdot hasNoSeals(stripSeals(m))$

3.2.9   Content Checks

A primitive predicate

$contentUserChecked: Content \times UserId \rightarrow \mathbf{B}$

will model the assertion that the content of a message part has been authorised by the given user. Through the use of seals it will follow that, if this predicate is true, then the message part's content has not subsequently changed in any way.

Similarly, a primitive predicate

$contentAutoChecked: Content \rightarrow \mathbf{B}$

will model the assertion that an automated check (e.g. for malicious code) has been applied successfully. This check will be applied to all messages imported from an external partitions. A primitive function

$filterContent: Content \rightarrow Content$

will model a function which removes potentially dangerous content (program code, etc) from a message part.

The following functions are used to rebuild a message after its contents have been filtered:

$rebuildMsgPart : MessagePart \rightarrow MessagePart$

$rebuildMsgPart(mp) \quad \underline{\triangle} \quad mk\text{-}MessagePart(filterContent(mp.content), \mathbf{nil}, \mathbf{nil})$

$rebuildMessage : Message \rightarrow Message$

$rebuildMessage(m) \quad \underline{\triangle}$
$\quad \mu(m, body \mapsto [rebuildMsgPart(mp.body(i)) \mid i \in \mathbf{inds}\ mp.body])$

The following lemma is a logical consequence of the above definitions:

RebuildMessage Lemma Rebuilt messages have no seals:

$$\forall m: Message \cdot hasNoSeals(rebuildMessage(m))$$

3.2.10 Accountability Records

The primitive type *AccRecord* will be used to model the set of all possible *accountability records* which may be stored as part of the system's audit trail.

3.2.11 The Message Pool

The final concept in the data model is that of a *message pool*, which represents the complete collection of messages that are undergoing processing within the network. Message identifiers will be introduced, to simplify modelling of the processing and delivery of messages within the network. Intuitively, a message's attributes may change during processing, but the *identity* of the message will be preserved by each of the Security Enforcing Functions, to allow trace-back.

The primitive type *MsgId* will be used to model the set of all possible message identifiers. The following type will be used to model pools of messages, indexed by the partition in which they reside and their message identifier:

$$MessagePool = Partition \xrightarrow{m} (MsgId \xrightarrow{m} Message)$$

Note that, a message may be transferred to more than one partition, but during processing there is (conceptually) at most one copy of the message in each partition.

The following function updates message d, with name n, in partition p in the message pool – or adds it, if it didn't already exist:

$$updateMsgPool : MessagePool \times Partition \times MsgId \times Message \rightarrow MessagePool$$

$$updateMsgPool(pool, p, n, d) \quad \triangleq \quad pool \dagger \{p \mapsto (pool(p) \dagger \{n \mapsto d\})\}$$

The following lemma is a logical consequence of the definition:

UpdateMessagePool Lemma Apart from the new message *new*, all messages in the updated message pool were already present before the update took place:

let $pool' = updateMsgPool(pool, to, n, new)$ **in**
$\forall p \in \textbf{dom}\, pool' \cdot \forall d \in \textbf{rng}\, pool'(p) \cdot$
$\quad (p = to \wedge d = new) \vee (p \in \textbf{dom}\, pool \wedge d \in \textbf{rng}\, pool(p))$

3.3 The System State

The system state consists of three state variables: a message pool, representing the conceptual location of messages; a set of currently active sessions; and a sequence of

$$
\begin{array}{l}
\textbf{state } SecureNetwork \textbf{ of} \\
\qquad pool \;:\; MessagePool \\
\quad sessions \;:\; Session\text{-set} \\
\quad audittrail \;:\; AccRecord^* \\
\textbf{inv } pool, sessions, audittrail \;\triangle \\
\quad \textbf{dom } pool \subseteq intpartns \cup extpartns \;\wedge \\
\quad (\forall p \in \textbf{dom } pool \cap extpartns \cdot \forall m \in \textbf{rng } pool(p) \cdot hasNoSeals(m)) \;\wedge \\
\quad \forall p \in \textbf{dom } pool \cap intpartns \cdot \forall m \in \textbf{rng } pool(p) \cdot \forall mp \in \textbf{elems } m.body \cdot \\
\qquad hasValidSeal(mp, p, m.classif) \;\Rightarrow \\
\qquad\qquad hasClearance(p, m.classif) \;\wedge \\
\qquad\qquad contentUserChecked(mp.content, mp.authoriser) \\
\textbf{end}
\end{array}
$$

Figure 3.3: The state of the secure network, with its important security properties.

accountability records, representing the complete audit trail. The following *security properties* are required to hold at all times:

1. Messages reside only in recognised internal and external partitions.

2. Messages in external partitions have no seals. (Seals should be stripped off messages before they are exported.)

3. If any part of a message in an internal partition has a valid seal, then

   - the partition has clearance to store the message, and
   - the content of that part has been checked by the authorising person and has not subsequently changed.

   This clause formalises the trusted-path property which the sealing mechanism is intended to provide (Section 3.1.4).

The security properties are expressed as an invariant of the state in Figure 3.3.

3.4   Operations Modelling the SEFs

This section gives a formal specification of the four Security Enforcing Functions (SEFs) described in Section 3.1.5 above. Each SEF is modelled as a VDM operation which may change the values of the state variables.

In what follows, and in the subsequent validation, preconditions of operations will have two parts:

1. An *environmental precondition*, which models the important security characteristics of the operation's interface and the conditions under which the operation can be performed. (Certain implementation-level restrictions will not

be modelled here, such as checking that the audit trail recording mechanism is working.)

2. A *precondition for success*, which models the additional conditions which determine whether an attempt has been made to subvert security, for example by attempting to transfer a message to a partition which does not have clearance to receive it.

VDM exception conditions (see p.214 [4]) will be used here to model accidental or deliberate attempts to breach security. An exception is raised whenever the environmental precondition is satisfied but the precondition for success is not. The general form of the specification of the SEFs is thus:

Operation (*inputs*)
ext ...
pre $P \wedge S$
post A_0
errs $FAILURETYPE_1: P \wedge E_1 \rightarrow A_1$

$\qquad \vdots$

$\qquad FAILURETYPE_n: P \wedge E_n \rightarrow A_n$

where P represents the environmental precondition, S represents the precondition for success, A_0 represents the action upon success, and $A_1, \ldots, A_n$ represent the individual actions upon failure.

3.4.1 The Authorise Message Operation

Description: The *AuthoriseMessage* operation is invoked by a user from a session within an internal partition. By authorising a message, the user is taking responsibility for checking the contents of all message parts which did not have a valid seal.

Environmental precondition: The message should reside in the partition in which authorisation takes place, in a currently active session.

Preconditions for success:

1. The partition should have sufficient clearance to store the message. (This check will for example prevent someone who is used to working in multiple partitions from accidentally creating a message in a partition which does not have appropriate clearance.)

2. All addresses in the destination list should refer to the current partition or to an immediately adjoining partition, and the latter should have clearance to receive the message.

$AuthoriseMessage$ (s: $Session$, p: $Partition$, n: $MsgId$)

ext wr $pool$, $audittrail$
　　rd $sessions$

pre $s \in sessions \land s.pid = p \land hasAccess(s.uid, p) \land$
　　$p \in \textbf{dom}\ pool \land n \in \textbf{dom}\ pool(p) \land$
　　$sealingAllowed(p, pool(p)(n))$

post let $old = \overleftarrow{pool}(p)(n)$, $c = old.classif$, $new = sealMessage(p, old, s.uid)$ **in**
　　$(\forall mp \in \textbf{elems}\ old.body \cdot \neg hasValidSeal(mp, p, c) \Rightarrow$
　　　$contentUserChecked(mp.content, mp.authoriser)) \land$
　　$pool = updateMsgPool(\overleftarrow{pool}, p, n, new) \land$
　　$audittrail = \overleftarrow{audittrail} \frown [authoriseSuccess(s, p, new)]$

errs $AUTHORISEMESSAGEFAIL$:
　　　$s \in sessions \land s.pid = p \land hasAccess(s.uid, p) \land$
　　　$p \in \textbf{dom}\ pool \land n \in \textbf{dom}\ pool(p) \land$
　　　$\neg sealingAllowed(p, pool(p)(n))$
　　　　　$\rightarrow\ pool = \overleftarrow{pool} \land$
　　　　　　$audittrail = \overleftarrow{audittrail} \frown [authoriseFailure(s, p, pool(p)(n))]$

Figure 3.4: The operation for authorising a message and adding seals.

Action upon success: Fresh seals are added to all message parts and the audit trail is updated.

Action upon failure: A record of the invalid attempt to authorise a message is added to the audit trail but the message is not changed in any way.

The formal specification of the $AuthoriseMessage$ operation is given in Figure 3.4, where

$sealingAllowed$: $Partition \times Message \rightarrow \textbf{B}$

$sealingAllowed(p, m)\ \triangleq\ hasClearance(p, m.classif) \land$
　　$\forall a \in m.destins \cdot a.pid \neq p$
　　$\Rightarrow\ adjoins(p, a.pid) \land hasClearance(a.pid, m.classif)$

3.4.2　The Internal Transfer Operation

Description: The $InternalTransfer$ operation is invoked automatically when a message n arrives at an internal network gateway, from partition $from$ to partition to.

Environmental precondition: Partitions *from* and *to* should be internal partitions which adjoin, and the message should currently reside in the *from* partition.

Preconditions for success:

1. All seals in the message should be valid with respect to the *from* partition.

2. The *to* partition should appear among the addresses in the message's destination list.

3. To *to* partition should have sufficient clearance to receive the message.

Action upon success: The message is copied across to the new partition, with fresh seals, and the audit trail is updated accordingly.

Action upon failure: A record of the invalid attempt to transfer a message is added to the audit trail.

The formal specification of the *InternalTransfer* operation is given in Figure 3.5, where

$transferAllowed : Partition \times Partition \times Message \rightarrow \mathbf{B}$

$transferAllowed(from, to, m) \quad \triangleq \quad allSealsAreValid(m, from) \wedge$
$(\exists a \in m.destins \cdot a.pid = to) \wedge hasClearance(to, m.classif)$

3.4.3 The Export Operation

Description: The *Export* operation is invoked automatically when a message *n* arrives at a network gateway from an internal partition *from* to an external partition *to*.

Environmental precondition: Partitions *from* and *to* should be adjoining partitions – *from* internal and *to* external. The message should currently reside in the *from* partition.

Preconditions for success: As for *InternalTransfer*.

Action upon success: The message is copied across to the new partition, with seals removed, and the audit trail is updated.

Action upon failure: A record of the invalid attempt to export a message is added to the audit trail.

The formal specification of the *Export* operation is given in Figure 3.6.

$InternalTransfer$ $(from: Partition, to: Partition, n: MsgId)$
ext wr $pool, audittrail$
pre $from \in \mathbf{dom}\, pool \cap intpartns \wedge$
$\quad to \in intpartns \wedge adjoins(from, to) \wedge$
$\quad n \in \mathbf{dom}\, pool(from) \wedge$
$\quad transferAllowed(from, to, pool(from)(n))$
post let $new = changeSeals(to, \overleftarrow{pool}(from)(n))$ **in**
$\quad pool = updateMsgPool(\overleftarrow{pool}, to, n, new) \wedge$
$\quad audittrail = \overleftarrow{audittrail} \frown [transferSuccess(from, to, n)]$
errs $TRANSFERFAIL:$
$\quad\quad from \in \mathbf{dom}\, pool \cap intpartns \wedge$
$\quad\quad to \in intpartns \wedge adjoins(from, to) \wedge$
$\quad\quad n \in \mathbf{dom}\, pool(from) \wedge$
$\quad\quad \neg\, transferAllowed(from, to, pool(from)(n))$
$\quad\quad\quad \rightarrow\; pool = \overleftarrow{pool} \wedge$
$\quad\quad\quad\quad audittrail = \overleftarrow{audittrail} \frown [transferFailure(from, to, n)]$

Figure 3.5: The operation for copying a message from one internal partition to another.

3.4.4 The Import Operation

Description: The *Import* operation is invoked automatically when a message n arrives at a network gateway from an external partition *from* to an internal partition *to*.

Environmental precondition: Partitions *from* and *to* should be adjoining partitions — *from* external and *to* internal. The message should currently reside in the *from* partition.

Preconditions for success:

1. The *to* partition should appear among the addresses in the message's destination list.

2. To *to* partition should have sufficient clearance to receive the message.

3. The automated check should have been applied successfully to the contents of all message parts.

Action upon success: The message is copied across to the new partition, with its contents filtered to remove any potentially dangerous content and with fresh seals added; the audit trail is updated accordingly.

Export (*from*: *Partition*, *to*: *Partition*, *n*: *MsgId*)

ext wr *pool*, *audittrail*

pre *from* ∈ **dom** *pool* ∩ *intpartns* ∧
    to ∈ *extparts* ∧ *adjoins*(*from*, *to*) ∧
    n ∈ **dom** *pool*(*from*) ∧
    transferAllowed(*from*, *to*, *pool*(*from*)(*n*))

post let *new* = *stripSeals*($\overleftarrow{pool}$(*from*)(*n*)) **in**

    pool = *updateMsgPool*($\overleftarrow{pool}$, *to*, *n*, *new*) ∧
    audittrail = $\overleftarrow{audittrail}$ ⌢ [*exportSuccess*(*from*, *to*, *n*)]

errs *EXPORTFAIL*:
        from ∈ **dom** *pool* ∩ *intpartns*∧
        to ∈ *extparts* ∧ *adjoins*(*from*, *to*)∧
        n ∈ **dom** *pool*(*from*)∧
        ¬ *transferAllowed*(*from*, *to*, *pool*(*from*)(*n*))
            → *pool* = $\overleftarrow{pool}$∧
                audittrail = $\overleftarrow{audittrail}$ ⌢ [*exportFailure*(*from*, *to*, *n*)]

Figure 3.6: The operation for copying a message from an internal partition to an external partition.

Action upon failure:

1. If the *to* partition does not have sufficient clearance to receive the message, a record of the invalid attempt to import a message is added to the audit trail.

2. If the import check fails, a record of the attempt to import a potentially dangerous message is added to the audit trial.

The formal specification of the *Import* operation is given in Figure 3.7, where

importAllowed : *Partition* × *Partition* × *Message* → **B**

importAllowed(*from*, *to*, *m*) ≜
    (∃*a* ∈ *m*.*destins* · *a*.*pid* = *to*) ∧ *hasClearance*(*to*, *m*.*classif*) ∧
    ∀*mp* ∈ **elems** *m*.*body* · *contentAutoChecked*(*mp*.*content*)

3.5 The Proofs

This section validates the Security Policy Model by showing that the specification is mathematically consistent, the Security Enforcing Functions preserve the security

Import (*from*: *Partition*, *to*: *Partition*, *n*: *MsgId*)

ext wr *pool*, *audittrail*

pre *from* ∈ **dom** *pool* ∩ *extpartns* ∧
  to ∈ *intparts* ∧ *adjoins*(*from*, *to*) ∧
  n ∈ **dom** *pool*(*from*) ∧
  importAllowed(*to*, *pool*(*from*)(*n*))

post let *new* = *rebuildMessage*($\overleftarrow{pool}$(*from*)(*n*)) **in**
  pool = *updateMsgPool*($\overleftarrow{pool}$, *to*, *n*, *new*) ∧
  audittrail = $\overleftarrow{audittrail}$ ⁀ [*importSuccess*(*from*, *to*, *new*)]

errs *IMPORTTRANSFERFAIL*:
  from ∈ **dom** *pool* ∩ *extpartns* ∧
  to ∈ *intparts* ∧ *adjoins*(*from*, *to*) ∧
  n ∈ **dom** *pool*(*from*) ∧
  ¬ *hasClearance*(*to*, *pool*(*from*)(*n*).*classif*)
    → *pool* = $\overleftarrow{pool}$ ∧
      audittrail = $\overleftarrow{audittrail}$ ⁀ [*importTransferFailure*(*from*, *to*, *n*)]

  IMPORTFAIL:
  from ∈ **dom** *pool* ∩ *extpartns* ∧
  to ∈ *intparts* ∧ *adjoins*(*from*, *to*) ∧
  n ∈ **dom** *pool*(*from*) ∧
  hasClearance(*to*, *pool*(*from*)(*n*).*classif*) ∧
  ¬ *importAllowed*(*to*, *pool*(*from*)(*n*))
    → *pool* = $\overleftarrow{pool}$ ∧
      audittrail = $\overleftarrow{audittrail}$ ⁀ [*importFailure*(*from*, *to*, *n*)]

Figure 3.7: The operation for copying a message from an external partition to an internal partition.

properties defined as part of the state invariant, and the specification is complete with respect to its input space.

3.5.1 Consistency Proofs

There are five parts to the proof of mathematical consistency of the model [2]:

1. The specification is syntax and type correct.

2. All function definitions are well formed and agree with the given signatures.

3. All uses of partial functions are well formed, in the sense that the function's arguments are in its domain.

4. All data type invariants are satisfiable (and hence all data types are non-empty).

5. The success or failure of each operation is uniquely determined: i.e., the precondition for success and the exception conditions do not overlap. To the best of our knowledge, this condition has not been made explicit in the literature before now. (Strictly, it is a consistency property of the application domain, in which exception conditions have a particular interpretation: it is thus closer to a "proof opportunity" than a proof obligation in the strictest sense of the word.)

The first two parts are straightforward.

For the third part, note that all uses of partial functions in this specification have one of the following forms:

i. $m.body(i)$ where m: *Message*

ii. $pool(p)$ or $pool(p)(n)$ where *pool*: *MessagePool*

iii. *changeSeal*(p, c, mp)

iv. *changeSeals*(p, m)

For (i), it is easy to check that $i \in$ **inds** m in each case. For (ii), it is easy to check that $p \in$ **dom** *pool* and $n \in$ **dom** *pool*(p) in each case. For (iii), the only use of *changeSeal* in the specification is in the definition of *changeSeals*, whose precondition guarantees the preconditions of *changeSeal* are satisfied. For (iv), the only use is *changeSeals*$(to, \overline{pool}(from)(n))$ in the postcondition of *InternalTransfer*. The precondition of *InternalTransfer* guarantees that, for the message in question, all message parts have valid seals, and hence (by the ValidSeal Lemma in Section 3.2.5) that they all identify an authoriser, as required.

Turning now to data type invariants, the only occurrences in the specification are for *Session* and the state of the system. Both are easily seen to be satisfiable: e.g. the state invariant is satisfied when the message pool is empty.

Given an operation with precondition for success S and given exception conditions $E_1, \ldots, E_n$, proving non-overlap amounts to showing $\neg(S \wedge E_i)$ and $\neg(E_i \wedge E_j)$ for $i \neq j$. For the *AuthoriseMessage*, *InternalTransfer* and *Export* operations, there is a single exception condition and it is of the form $\neg S$, so non-overlap is obvious. For the *Import* operation, there are two exception conditions, of the form $\neg Q$ and $Q \wedge \neg S$ respectively, where $S \Rightarrow Q$. The proofs of the required properties are straightforward.

3.5.2 Preservation of the Security Properties

For each operation, there is a VDM proof obligation to show that, for any state and inputs which satisfy the operation's precondition, there is a corresponding state which satisfies the operation's postcondition. (This is usually called the *satisfiability* proof obligation for operations [2].) For each of the four operations considered here, the values of the post-state are defined explicitly in terms of the pre-state and the inputs, so the proof obligation reduces to showing that the new values preserve the system's state invariant.

Since the message pool is the only state variable mentioned in the state invariant, and since the exception cases of the operations do not actually change the message pool in any way, it suffices to consider only the successful cases of the four operations. Each of the properties defined in Section 3.3 shall be considered in turn below.

Property 1: message location

Property 1 says that all messages reside in internal and external partitions only:

dom *pool* $\subseteq$ *intpartns* $\cup$ *extpartns*

For each operation, preservation of this property follows easily from the fact that

$$pool = updateMsgPool(\overleftarrow{pool}, p, n, new) \;\Rightarrow\; \textbf{dom}\, pool \subseteq \textbf{dom}\, \overleftarrow{pool} \cup \{p\}$$

and the fact that $p \in$ *intpartns* $\cup$ *extpartns*; the latter is a consequence of the environmental precondition in each case.

Property 2: messages in external partitions

Property 2 says that messages in the external partitions have no seals:

$\forall p \in \textbf{dom}\, pool \cap extpartns \cdot \forall m \in \textbf{rng}\, pool(p) \cdot hasNoSeals(m)$

To show that this property is preserved, it suffices to consider the *Export* operation only, since the other operations do not affect the messages in the external partitions. Let *to* be the destination partition and let *new* be the exported message. It follows from the UpdateMessagePool lemma that *new* is the only new message in the pool. Since, by the induction hypothesis, all other messages in external partitions have no seals, it suffices to show that *new* has no seals. From the postcondition of *Export* we know that *new* is of the form *stripSeals*(*m*) for some message *m*, so the desired result follows from the StripSeals lemma. The proof is given in detail in Fig. 3.8.

Property 3: messages in internal partitions

Paraphrased, Property 3 says that, for those parts of messages in internal partitions which have a valid seal, then the partition has clearance to store the message and the content has been user-checked:

$\forall p \in \textbf{dom}\, pool \cap intpartns \cdot \forall m \in \textbf{rng}\, pool(p) \cdot \forall mp \in \textbf{elems}\, m.body \cdot$
$\quad hasValidSeal(mp, p, m.classif) \;\Rightarrow$
$\quad\quad hasClearance(p, m.classif) \wedge$
$\quad\quad contentUserChecked(mp.content, mp.authoriser)$

```
from ∀p ∈ dom pool⃪ ∩ extpartns · ∀m ∈ rng pool⃪(p) · hasNoSeals(m)
1        new = stripSeals(old)                                    post-Export
2        pool = updateMsgPool(pool⃪, to, n, new)                   post-Export
3        from p ∈ dom pool ∩ extpartns,  m ∈ rng pool(p)
3.1          p ∈ dom pool                                         sets, 3.h1
3.2          (p = to ∧ m = new) ∨ (p ∈ dom pool⃪ ∧ m ∈ rng pool⃪(p))
                                    UpdateMessagePool lemma, 2, 3.1, 3.h2
3.3              from p = to,  m = new
3.3.1                hasNoSeals(stripSeals(old))                  StripSeals lemma
3.3.2                hasNoSeals(new)                              subs, 1, 3.3.1
                 infer hasNoSeals(m)                              subs, 3.3.h2, 3.3.2
3.4              from p ∈ dom pool⃪,  m ∈ rng pool⃪(p)
3.4.1                p ∈ extpartns                                sets, 3.h1
3.4.2                p ∈ dom pool⃪ ∩ extpartns                     sets, 3.4.h1, 3.4.1
                 infer hasNoSeals(m)        Induction Hypothesis h1, 3.4.2, 3.4.h2
         infer hasNoSeals(m)                        cases, 3.2, 3.3, 3.4
infer ∀p ∈ dom pool ∩ extpartns · ∀m ∈ rng pool(p) · hasNoSeals(m)
                                                                 ∀-intro,3
```

Figure 3.8: Proof of preservation of Property 2 by *Export*.

To show that this property is preserved, it suffices to consider only the operations which affect the messages in the internal partitions: *AuthoriseMessage, Internal-Transfer* and *Import*. As for the proof of Property 2 above, it suffices to show that the desired property holds for the *new* message. Specifically, it suffices to show that: the destination partition *to* has sufficient clearance to receive *new*; and that each message part of *new* with a valid seal has had its contents checked by the given authoriser. These properties are proved below for each of the three operations in turn.

AuthoriseMessage:

For the *AuthoriseMessage*(s, p, n) operation, *new* is the result of adding fresh seals for partition p to the message *old* identified by n. Since sealing does not affect the message's classification, it follows that *old* and *new* have the same classification. Also, the *AuthoriseMessage* operation can be performed only if the *sealingAllowed* test is passed, from which it follows that p must have sufficient clearance to store *old* and hence must have sufficient clearance to store *new*, as desired.

Since, as a result of sealing, all parts of *new* have valid seals, it is necessary to show that all parts have had their content checked by the given autoriser (and have not

from $new = sealMessage(p, old, s.uid)$
1      $new.classif = old.classif$ Main Sealing Lemma, h1
2      $sealingAllowed(p, old)$ pre-$AuthoriseMessage$
3      $hasClearance(p, old.classif)$ defn of $sealingAllowed$, 2
4      $hasClearance(p, new.classif)$ subs, 1, 3
5   **from** $i \in$ **inds** $new.body$, $mp' = new.body(i)$,
           $hasValidSeal(mp', p, new.classif)$
         let $mp = old.body(i)$ **in**
5.1 $mp'.content = mp.content$ Main Sealing Lemma, h1, 5.h2
5.2 $\neg\, hasValidSeal(mp, p, old.classif) \Rightarrow$
         $contentUserChecked(mp.content, s.uid)$
             post-$AuthoriseMessage$
5.3   **from** $hasValidSeal(mp, p, old.classif)$
5.3.1 $hasClearance(p, old.classif) \wedge$
         $contentUserChecked(mp.content, mp.authoriser)$
             Induction Hypothesis, 5.3.h1
5.3.2 $contentUserChecked(mp.content, mp.authoriser)$
             $\wedge$-elim, 5.3.1
5.3.3 $mp'.authoriser = mp.authoriser$
             Main Sealing Lemma, h1, 5.h2, 5.3.h1
     infer $contentUserChecked(mp.content, mp'.authoriser)$
             subs, 5.3.2, 5.3.3
5.4   **from** $\neg\, hasValidSeal(mp, p, old.classif)$
5.4.1 $contentUserChecked(mp.content, s.uid)$
             modus ponens, 5.4.h1, 5.2
5.4.2 $mp'.authoriser = s.uid$
             Main Sealing Lemma, h1, 5.h2, 5.4.h1
     infer $contentUserChecked(mp.content, mp'.authoriser)$
             subs, 5.4.1, 5.4.2
5.5 $contentUserChecked(mp.content, mp'.authoriser)$ cases, 5.3, 5.4
5.6 $contentUserChecked(mp'.content, mp'.authoriser)$ subs, 5.1, 5.5
5.7 $hasClearance(p, new.classif) \wedge$
         $contentUserChecked(mp'.content, mp'.authoriser)$
              $\wedge$-intro, 4, 5.6
     infer $hasValidSeal(mp', to, new.classif) \Rightarrow$
         $hasClearance(to, new.classif) \wedge$
         $contentUserChecked(mp'.content, mp'.authoriser)$
             $\Rightarrow$-intro, 5.7
infer $\forall mp' \in$ **elems** $new.body \cdot hasValidSeal(mp', p, new.classif) \Rightarrow$
     $hasClearance(p, new.classif) \wedge$
     $contentUserChecked(mp'.content, mp'.authoriser)$ $\forall$-intro', 5

Figure 3.9: Proof of preservation of Property 3 by *AuthoriseMessage*.

changed since then). Let mp' be one of the parts of the message *new* and let mp be the corresponding part of message *old*. Since sealing does not affect message contents, it follows that mp and mp' have the same content, hence it suffices to show that mp has been checked. By invoking the *AuthoriseMessage* operation, the operator is taking responsibility for having checked all message parts which did not have a valid seal, so it only remains to consider the parts which have valid seals. But sealing does not change the value of the *content* or *authoriser* fields for such parts, so this case follows directly from the induction hypothesis. This completes the proof for this operation. The proof for the *new* message case is given in detail in Fig. 3.9.

Internal Transfer:

The *InternalTransfer* proof is similar to the *AuthoriseMessage* proof above. Let *new* be the message created by changing the seals on the message *old* from those for the originating partition *from* to those of the destination partition *to*. As before, *old* and *new* must have the same classification. Thus, from *transferAllowed(from, to, old)*, it follows that *to* has sufficient clearance to store *new*.

It also follows from *transferAllowed(from, to, old)* that all message parts in *old* have valid seals, and hence from Property 3 applied inductively to *old* that all message parts have had their contents checked. Since resealing does not change the contents or authorisers of message parts, it follows that all message parts in *new* have had their contents checked, which completes the proof for this operation. The proof is given in detail in Fig. 3.10.

Import:

The *Import* proof is quite straightforward, since all seals are stripped off the imported message, and so there is essentially nothing to check. The proof is given in detail in Fig. 3.11.

This completes the proof that all operations preserve Property 3.

3.5.3 Completeness Proofs

This section is concerned with the proof that the specification is complete with respect to its input space. Because the modelling is relatively straightforward in this case, there is little to prove. For each SEF, the environmental precondition describes the constraints which are to be imposed on inputs to the SEFs by their interface to the system environment; it thus suffices to show that, for each SEF, the environmental precondition P implies the precondition for success S or one of the exception conditions E_i: i.e.,

$$P \Rightarrow S \vee E_1 \vee \ldots \vee E_n$$

from $new = changeSeals(to, old)$
1      $new.classif = old.classif$ Resealing Lemma, h1
2      $transferAllowed(from, to, old)$ pre-$InternalTransfer$
3      $hasClearance(to, old.classif)$ defn of $transferAllowed$, 2
4      $hasClearance(to, new.classif)$ subs, 1, 3
5   **from** $i \in \mathbf{inds}\ new.body,\ mp' = new.body(i),$
              $hasValidSeal(mp', to, new.classif)$
              let $mp = old.body(i)$ **in**
5.1 $mp'.content = mp.content$ Resealing Lemma, h1, 5.h2
5.2 $allSealsAreValid(old, from)$ defn of $transferAllowed$, 2
5.3 $hasValidSeal(mp, from, old.classif)$
                                                   defn of $allSealsAreValid$, 5.2
5.4 $hasClearance(from, old.classif) \wedge$
              $contentUserChecked(mp.content, mp.authoriser)$
                                                      Induction Hypothesis, 5.3
5.5 $contentUserChecked(mp.content, mp.authoriser)$ $\wedge$-elim, 5.4
5.6 $mp'.authoriser = mp.authoriser$ Resealing Lemma, h1, 5.h2
5.7 $contentUserChecked(mp'.content, mp'.authoriser)$
                                                            subs, 5.1, 5.5, 5.6
5.8 $hasClearance(to, new.classif) \wedge$
              $contentUserChecked(mp'.content, mp'.authoriser)$
                                                          $\wedge$-intro, 4, 5.7
        infer $hasValidSeal(mp', to, new.classif) \Rightarrow$
              $hasClearance(to, new.classif) \wedge$
              $contentUserChecked(mp'.content, mp'.authoriser)$ $\Rightarrow$-intro, 5.8
infer $\forall mp' \in \mathbf{elems}\ new.body \cdot hasValidSeal(mp', to, new.classif) \Rightarrow$
        $hasClearance(to, new.classif) \wedge$
        $contentUserChecked(mp'.content, mp'.authoriser)$ $\forall$-intro', 5

Figure 3.10: Proof of preservation of Property 3 by *InternalTransfer*.

---

from $new = rebuildMessage(old)$
1    $hasNoSeals(new)$ RebuildMessage Lemma, h1
2    $\forall mp \in$ **elems** $new.body \cdot mp.seal =$ **nil**   defn of $hasNoSeals$, 1
3   **from** $mp \in$ **elems** $new.body$
3.1 $mp.seal =$ **nil** $\forall$-elim, 2, 3.h1
3.2 $\neg\, hasValidSeal(mp, to, new.classif)$ ValidSeal Lemma, 3.1
    infer $hasValidSeal(mp', to, new.classif) \Rightarrow$
        $hasClearance(to, new.classif)\wedge$
        $contentUserChecked(mp'.content, mp'.authoriser)$
                                          $\Rightarrow$-intro', 3.2
infer $\forall mp' \in$ **elems** $new.body \cdot hasValidSeal(mp', to, new.classif) \Rightarrow$
    $hasClearance(to, new.classif)\wedge$
    $contentUserChecked(mp'.content, mp'.authoriser)$ $\forall$-intro', 3

Figure 3.11: Proof of preservation of Property 3 by *Import*.

For each of the operations *AuthoriseMessage*, *InternalTransfer* and *Export*, there is a single exception condition, which is of the form $\neg S$, where S is the precondition for success. In each of these cases, the result thus follows easily from the following propositional tautology

$$P \Rightarrow S \vee \neg S$$

upon showing that S is well formed, which is straightforward.

For the *Import* operation, there are two exception conditions, of the form $\neg Q$ and $Q \wedge \neg S$ respectively, where S is the precondition for success. The result follows easily from the following propositional tautology:

$$P \Rightarrow S \vee \neg Q \vee (Q \wedge \neg S)$$

This completes the proof of completeness.

3.6   Conclusions

In conclusion, this chapter has presented a formal Security Policy Model for an electronic message processing and transmission network with multi-level security classification requirements. The VDM-SL specification language was used to define the model. The model was validated by proving that it is mathematically consistent and that it satisfies its required security properties.

A key feature of the Security Policy Model is the use of a sealing mechanism to preserve integrity of messages. The formal specification states precise requirements for how the sealing mechanism should operate. It also explains how the sealing mechanism provides a trusted path between the authoriser and trusted software performing gateway or access control decisions. The proofs confirm in principle that the mechanism achieves its purpose. This in turn conveys a certain degree of assurance that the model is sound.

The main value of the formal model is that it makes the security policy clear and precise. (See Boswell's paper [3] on use of Z for specification and validation of a security policy model for the NATO Air Command and Control System for more discussion.) For the application in question, most of the benefit of the formalisation process was felt to come from being required to make the security policy explicit, and in particular from trying to express exactly what can be inferred from the fact that a seal is valid (Property 3 above).

However, the formalisation did reveal an oversight in an earlier version of the model, which may have had important security implications. The problem was that the earlier model did not explicitly require that messages in external partitions have all seals removed before being imported; as a result, the proof that *Import* preserves Property 3 could not be completed. Upon reflection, it became apparent that the original model was open to "spoofing", whereby an external user with access to a copy of the sealing function could introduce unauthorised messages into the system. Being required to formalise the desired property and perform the proofs thus resulted in the oversight being revealed and the model being improved.

Note in passing that fully formal proofs were constructed and mechanically checked for an earlier version of the specification, using the Mural formal development support environment [4]. To save work, the formal specification was modified so that the four operations shared a common structure, and lemmas were derived which could be proved once and then applied to all four operations. Formal proofs are needed for high degrees of assurance, but rigorous proofs were more appropriate for this chapter, for clarity and ease of understanding. Note however that the amount of additional effort required to construct fully formal proofs is small [2].

Finally, note that the consistency and completeness proof obligations for exception conditions were developed by the first author in the course of this work, and do not appear to have been published before now.

Acknowledgements

The author gratefully acknowledges the substantial contribution to the work reported here by Peter James of Admiral Computing Australia, especially in relation to guidance on requirements for the case study. The idea of using integrity seals as a mechanism for providing a trusted path is due to Les Cook. Thanks are also due to Tom Allen for his earlier input.

3.7 Bibliography

[1] Information Technology Security Evaluation Criteria (ITSEC). Commission of the European Communities, June 1991. Provisional Harmonised Criteria.

[2] J.C. Bicarregui, J.S. Fitzgerald, P.A. Lindsay, R. Moore, and B. Ritchie. *Proof in VDM: A Practitioner's Guide*. FACIT Series. Springer-Verlag, 1994. ISBN no. 3-540-19813-X.

[3] T. Boswell. Specification and validation of a security policy model. In *Proc. 1st Int. Symp. of Formal Methods Europe (FME'93)*, LNCS 670, pages 42–51. Springer Verlag, 1993.

[4] C.B. Jones. *Systematic Software Development Using VDM*. Prentice-Hall International, second edition, 1990.

[5] C.B. Jones, K.D. Jones, P.A. Lindsay, and R. Moore. *Mural: A Formal Development Support System*. Springer-Verlag, 1991.

[6] C.E. Landwehr. Formal models for computer security. *ACM Computing Surveys*, 13(3):243–278, Sept 1981.

Chapter 4

The Specification and Proof of an EXPRESS to SQL "Compiler"

Juan Bicarregui and Brian Matthews

Summary

EXPRESS and SQL are two ISO standard languages for modelling data. However, EXPRESS is abstract in the sense that it is intended to be used to define application-oriented data types, whereas SQL is concrete in that all data must be modelled using relation tables. In this chapter, we specify and prove some properties of an EXPRESS to SQL "compiler" which implements the ISO standard STEP Data Access Interface (SDAI) for the storage and retreval of EXPRESS instance data.

The "compiler" is formalised as a refinement: an abstract model of the EXPRESS database is given which defines operations for the storage and retreval based on a model of the EXPRESS data types on VDM; then a specification of a relational database is given as a basis for a refinement of the EXPRESS database; and then concrete versions of the operations are defined on top of the relational model. These operations are, in effect, the semantic functions of the compiler. The equivalence of the abstract and concrete specifications is the justification of the correctness of the compiler.

We outline the specifications and prove an obligation concerning the refinement. A number of issues concerning modelling style arise in comparing the EXPRESS data types with those of VDM and concerning the structuring of the development to facilitate proofs. The specification was developed using the IFAD VDM-SL Toolbox and the proofs constructed by hand.

4.1   STEP and EXPRESS

EXPRESS is an "information modelling" language developed within the ISO *Standard for the Exchange of Product model data* (STEP) [1]. By defining standard languages for the representation of data models and data compliant with those models, and by standardising particular data models for specific application areas, STEP provides a vendor-neutral mechanism for the representation of product data and hence facilitates the open exchange of data between applications.

The STEP standard is divided into a number of parts. Some parts define "generic technologies" for the definition of models and data, others give particular data models (*Application Protocols*) for representation of data in specific application areas. For example the application protocol for geometric and topological representation, defines that a circle should be represented by its centre and radius, rather than say by a diameter or by three points on the circumference.

The generic technologies include EXPRESS (Part 11) which is a language for the definition of data models and EXPRESS-I (Part 12) for representation of data. Part 21 gives a syntax for a condensed form of EXPRESS-I and Parts 22-26 give a standard API for accessing an EXPRESS-based database, the SDAI (STEP Data Access Interface). An abstract definition of the SDAI is given based on a partial model of EXPRESS in EXPRESS and an informal definition of the operations to manipulate this model. Concrete versions of the SDAI are defined in a number of "language bindings" giving the data structures for implementations in particular languages.

4.1.1   The Context

The work described in the chapter was undertaken in the context of the Process-Base project[1] which concerns the development of an Application Protocol for Process Plants (AP221 and AP227) and is also developing software supporting translation between the APs and some native CAD formats (AutoCAD and PID) for 2D schematics, 3D models and functional data.

The translation between native and STEP data formats is achieved by some application specific conversion software. Because data is structured radically differently in the standard and native models this software requires intensive access to all parts of the data and data models.

The implementation is achieved by interrogation of an SDAI database built on top of relational technology. Effectively two separate repositories are created, one loaded with each data model. Translation takes place by selecting from the source database the components required to construct each data item in the target database. The EXPRESS "shell" built on top of the relational database is the EXPRESS to SQL "compiler" referred to in the title of this chapter.

---

[1]ESPRIT Project 6212, ProcessBase

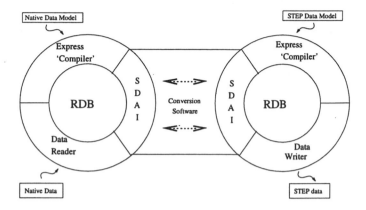

Figure 4.1: The conversion takes place between 2 virtual SDAIs.

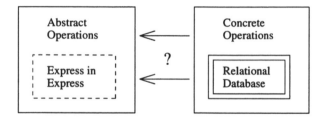

Figure 4.2: The compiler is formalised as a refinement

4.1.2   The Specifications

The abstract specification is conceptually a single module. Its major datatypes are an abstract syntax for the EXPRESS language itself. These are based on the definition of EXPRESS in EXPRESS given in the SDAI but are remodelled to account for some differences between the VDM and EXPRESS. The concrete specification is conceptually two modules. modules The first follows the definition of SQL in VDM given in [5]. This should be simple enough to be implemented on top of any relational database. The second builds on this to give an implementation of the SDAI. (In fact, some datatypes common to abstract and concrete specifications are given as a separate module.) The refinement relation between specifications is the justification of the correctness of the compiler (Figure 4.2).

4.1.3   Related Work

EXPRESS is independent of any particular database technology, however, several implementations of EXPRESS tools founded on relation database technology exist, for example, [15, 16, 18, 13, 17]. These were compared in a preliminary study to this work [9]. One implementation of EXPRESS in SQL was reverse engineered to define the translation and the compiler formalised as a refinement between specifications based upon an existing VDM definition of the semantics of SQL and the definition of EXPRESS in EXPRESS given in ISO 10303 Part 22.

Formal definitions exist for several aspects of this development including a VDM formalisation of the semantic of SQL [5], two EXPRESS models of EXPRESS itself [3, 7], and a VDM definition of part of the SDAI [8]. An interesting development which is trying to define a unifying semantic model for several languages is [4].

VDM is a mature notation for the definition of formal languages. (e.g. [20, 21, 22, 23, 24, 25]). It is undergoing standardisation by BSI and ISO[11]. Several support tools for VDM are available, the present work was undertaken using the IFAD VDM-SL Toolbox [19]

4.1.4   Overview

Section 2 gives an outline of some key concepts of the EXPRESS language and Section 3 the abstract specification of the EXPRESS database. Section 4 gives a simplified relational database and Section 5 defines the EXPRESS database operations on top of this. Section 6 discusses the approach taken.

4.2   An Outline of EXPRESS

EXPRESS is a language for defining data models. It has three levels of granularity. The coarsest level components are Schema which are akin to modules; modules the second and third are Entities and Attributes which loosely correspond to datatypes (or object classes) and fields (or instance variables) respectively.

We present some of the most important features of the EXPRESS language through a simple example based on one given in [6].

4.2.1   Entities

The EXPRESS entity *car* describes the components of a car. As in a VDM record type, each component is given a name and a type.

```
ENTITY car                      ;
      model_type : car_model    ;
        made_by : manufacturer ;
        mnfg_no : STRING        ;
  registration_no : STRING      ;
 production_year : INTEGER      ;
       owned_by : owner         ;
END-ENTITY
ENTITY car_model                ;
        name : STRING           ;
     made_by : manufacturer ;
  consumption : REAL            ;
END-ENTITY
```

Where Rules.

It is clear that the *made_by* attribute should be the same for a car and for the model of that car. This can be formalised as a "where rule" given in the definition of car, for example

WHERE made_by :=: model_type.made_by

This constraint is akin to an invariant in VDM. Note that *:=:* is object identity (see later).

Derived Attributes.

An alternative way to model this constraint would be to give the *made_by* attribute as a *derived attribute* of car.i.e.

DERIVE made_by := model_type.made_by

This indicates that the maker of a car can be derived (in this case trivially) from the maker of the model of the car.

In VDM, the same information could be extracted by use of an auxiliary function.

Object Identifiers.

A fundamental difference between an EXPRESS entities and record types in say VDM, is that an EXPRESS entity declaration indicates an implicit indirection in the data. Following the object-oriented style, each instance of an entity corresponds to a identified object and an environment is assumed which dereferences object identifiers. For example, an instance of a car might be

#1 = car(#2,#3, "VW233445", "N123PQR", 1995, #4)

#2 = car_model("GOLF", #3, 2.6)

#3 = manufacturer(...)

...

where the *#i* represent the object identifiers. Note that the same manufacturer appear in both the *car* and *car_model* instances.

Uniqueness Constraints.

A number of constraints can be given which restrict the universe of instances. Uniqueness of attributes or combinations of attributes can be specified across all instances of an entity. For example, the rule *single* states that the registration number should be globally unique over all cars and *joint* states that, together, the *made_by* and *mnfg_no* fields are also globally unique.

UNIQUE   single : registration_no   ;
*   joint : made_by, mnfg_no ;*

Existence Constraints.

It is also possible to give constraints which describe the necessity of the existence of some instance. For example, if *owner* is defined by

ENTITY *owner*   ;
  owns : *SET OF car* ;
END-ENTITY

then, in the entity definition for cars, one can state that every car must have an owner by giving *owned_by* as an "inverse attribute" as follows:

INVERSE owned_by : owner FOR owns

This stipulates that every car must appear uniquely in the set of cars owned by some owner. This is equivalent to a clause in the invariant

inv-car(c) $\triangleq$ *c* $\in$ *c.owned_by.owns*

By defining specific pieces of syntax for many common modelling situations, EXPRESS entities give a means to specify certain types of relational constraints concisely. This approach can be more "engineer friendly" than the explicit formalisation of such constraints in the general logic of invariant predicates. However the interpretation of these constructs can be somewhat confusing to the newcomer.

4.2.2   Other Type Constructors

EXPRESS also includes a number of other type constructors which can be used without the overhead of object indirection. Type expressions using these constructors are named in defined types. For example there are arrays, lists, sets, bags, enumerated types and select types (unions). However, there are no map or function types and tuples can only be constructed through the use of entities.

4.2.3 Subtypes

The object-flavoured nature of EXPRESS is reinforced by its use of subtypes. A subtype inherits and extends the set of attributes of its supertype. There are three ways in which inheritance can be employed.

Simple inheritance is declared in both supertype and subtype, for example by the combination

ENTITY C SUPERTYPE OF ONEOF (A,B) ....

and

ENTITY A SUBTYPE of C ....
ENTITY B SUBTYPE of C ....

Here A inherits from C and so does B.

A form of multiple inheritance is declared by

ENTITY C SUPERTYPE OF AND (A,B) ....

which allows instances with the fields of A *and* B and C

The third form *ANDOR(A,B)* is equivalent to *ONEOF(A, B, AND(A,B))*.

A supertype can be declared as *abstract* in which case it can only be instantiated through its subtypes.

The *SUPERTYPE* clause can be omitted and inferred from the subtypes declarations. However, the use of *ANDOR* as the default combinator for the subtypes when no supertype clause is given makes its omission highly non-compositional. explicitly.

Subtyping provides a way to condense a data model definition by avoiding repetition of combinations of attributes which are common to several entity definitions. However, it is possible to expand out the subtype hierarchy to give a model with an equivalent set of valid instances. For present purposes, we assume that all subtyping has been expanded out.

Thus EXPRESS provides many (though not all) of the forms of type construction available in VDM and includes a form of subtyping and object identity not available there.

4.3   The Abstract EXPRESS Database

The SDAI standard defines three components in the abstract definition of the interface. Firstly, the "data dictionary" defines the types used. This is the abstract syntax for the data models written in EXPRESS (the meta-data) the instance data written in EXPRESS-I (the actual data). The second component is the "session" which represents the components manipulated during execution (the state). These two components are given as formal models in EXPRESS. Thirdly, there are the operations which, although described in terms of the formal models are given informally in the standard.

The abstract VDM specification is built from two modules. modules One module defines the types used as parameters to the operations, the other defines the abstract state and operations.

Rather than give a VDM model which is as close as possible to the EXPRESS model in the standard (the approach which is followed in [8]), we make certain modelling decisions in "translating" from EXPRESS to VDM. The new model makes use of the facilities available in VDM to replace some of the features of the EXPRESS model which could not be modelled directly.

In an informal translation such as this, there remains a danger that the model we construct does not correspond to that in the standard. However, this approach was adopted after early attempts to follow the EXPRESS style in VDM encountered difficulties with handling object identifiers and the environment to dereference them. This confirmed previous experience [10] that trying to translate directly from one language to an apparently similar one can lead to problems.

4.3.1   The EXPRESS and EXPRESS-I Abstract Syntax

The first module modules defines the abstract syntax for the EXPRESS Types, that is, the meta-data and instance data stored by the database. This follows the structure of the data dictionary in the SDAI. It will be shared by both abstract and concrete specifications.

module *ET*

     exports all

The following sections do not attempt to be comprehensive in their coverage of the EXPRESS language, but rather describe those aspects which lead to interesting modelling issues.

Schema Definitions.

We begin by giving a model for schemas. A schema definition has a set of entities which it declares, a set of types it declares, and some global rules.

$$schema\text{-}def :: exp\text{-}types : type\text{-}name \xrightarrow{m} type\text{-}def$$
$$entities : entity\text{-}name \xrightarrow{m} entity\text{-}def$$
$$global\text{-}rules : global\text{-}rule\text{-}\mathsf{set};$$

In keeping with VDM style, we exploit the fact that the *type-names* and *entity-names* are unique and use these as the indices in map types.

In the EXPRESS model, these names are given as components of the entity and type definitions, sets of which are components of schema definitions. Constraints are then given which state that the names are unique within the parent object. For example, the model of entity definition ensures that the entity names are unique within the parent schema by the following combination of an inverse attribute and a uniqueness rule:

INVERSE parent-schema : schema-definition FOR entities

UNIQUE UR1: entity-name, parent-schema

This construction is rather common in EXPRESS.

Type Definitions.

Entity names and a number of other type constructors can be used in type definitions. For brevity we do not go into this further here.

$$type\text{-}def = entity\text{-}name \mid \dots ;$$

Entity Definitions.

Freed from its name, an entity definition is simply a map from attribute names to attribute definitions.

$$entity\text{-}def = attribute\text{-}name \xrightarrow{m} attribute\text{-}def ;$$

Attribute Definitions.

Attribute definitions can be of one of three forms, defined in EXPRESS using a subtype/supertype relationship:

ENTITY attribute ABSTRACT SUPERTYPE OF (

   ONEOF(derived_attribute, explicit_attribute, inverse_attribute))

For brevity, we only model explicit attributes here[2].

---

[2]One way in which it is possible to model the subtype/supertypes relationship in VDM is to expand out the supertype's attributes into each subtype. Another is to define the supertype's attributes as a composit type and explicitly include this an attribute in the subtypes. Note that this latter approach can be taken without the cost in complexity that the extra level of indirection would have introduced if using EXPRESS entities.

$$attribute\text{-}def = entity\text{-}name \mid$$
$$type\text{-}name \mid$$
$$aggregate\text{-}def \mid$$
$$\ldots;$$

An attribute definition is the type of the attribute. It can either be an entity type, indicated by the entity name, or any named type, or some particular forms of type expressions, such as aggregate types which generalise sets, bags, lists and arrays. It is unclear why not all forms of type expression are permitted as the types of attributes.

Models.

A *model* is the set of instances of the entities of a schema. For consistency with the use of "schema definition" above, here we call it a "data definition"

$$data\text{-}def = instance\text{-}ref \xrightarrow{m} instance\text{-}def;$$

The SDAI states that "the *underlying-schema* of the model must be the schema that defines the structure of the data that appears in the model", but does not formalise this. Formalising this requirement includes ensuring that each instance in the model is an instance of an entity in the underlying schema. This constraint emerges here as part of the invariant when instance data and meta data are brought together.

Instances.

The SDAI defines a hierarchy of kinds of instance: an *application-instance* is an instance of an entity defined in an application schema and an *sdai-instance* is an instance of an entity defined in one of the schemas of the SDAI definition itself. The latter are divided into *dictionary-instances* and *session_instances*. The different classes are then used to distinguish types of instances when required. However, all of these instances have the same attributes so here we do not need to model them separately but rather can define functions that distinguish them if necessary.

$$instance\text{-}def :: entity : entity\text{-}name$$
$$attributes : attribute\text{-}name \xrightarrow{m} attribute\text{-}value;$$

$$attribute\text{-}value = instance\text{-}ref \mid$$
$$expression \mid$$
$$aggregate\text{-}value \mid$$
$$\ldots;$$

The *entity* field of an instance definition is the entity-definition of which this is an instance. This "cross-linking" is required because this schema-centered model does not tie instances to entities in any other way. (Some alternative approaches are discussed in 4.3.3.) In general, this form of duplication is undesirable as it leads to many consistency checks in invariants and operations. belongs"

4.3.2 The State and Operations

The second module modules of the abstract specification defines the state and operations. It imports the EXPRESS types from the last module.

module *AEDB*

> imports
>
>> from *ET* all

In an SDAI "session"[3]. a database has a number of *dbs* indexed by schema names Also, if there are several models for the same schema, these appear as separate *dbs*, each with its own copy of the schema definition. (The alternative of composing each schema definition with a set of models is also discussed in Section 4.3.3.)

However, for simplicity, we specify a database described by a single schema. The state brings together the schema and data in a database segment (a real database may incorporate a number of these). The database is initially empty[4].

> state *db* of
> *schema : schema-def*
> *model : data-def*
>
> inv mk-*db* (s, im) $\triangleq$
>> $\forall\, ir \in$ dom *im* ·
>>> $\exists\, en \in$ dom *s.entities* ·
>>>> *isa-instance-of* $(ir, en, \text{mk-}db\,(s, im))$;
>
>> init *db* $\triangleq$ *db* = mk-*db* (mk-*schema-def* $(\{\mapsto\}, \{\mapsto\}, \{\,\}), \{\mapsto\})$
> end

The instance and meta data are tied together via the *entity* field in the instance definitions. The invariant states that all the instances must be instances of some entity definition in the schema by using the function *isa-instance-of*. This function takes as arguments the instance reference, the entity name, and the whole database. The last is required in order that the first two can be dereferenced.

---

[3]In the SDAI, a session supports a number of repositories, here (like most of the implementations) we assume the EXPRESS database contains a single repository.

[4]The syntax *ET'* is used for referring to constructs from the imported module.

$isa\text{-}instance\text{-}of : instance\text{-}ref \times entity\text{-}name \times db \rightarrow \mathbb{B}$

$isa\text{-}instance\text{-}of\,(ir, en, d) \;\triangleq$
   let $id = d.instance\text{-}map\,(ir),$
       $em = d.schema.entities$ in
   $names\text{-}match\,(id.entity, en) \;\wedge$
   $doms\text{-}equal\,(id.attributes, em\,(en)) \;\wedge$
   $\forall\,an \in$ dom $id.attributes \cdot$
       $isa\,(id.attributes\,(an), em\,(en)\,(an), d);$

Three conditions are required to be satisfied for an instance to be a valid instance of an entity. Firstly, the names of the instance and the entity must match, secondly, the attributes must have the same names in instance and entity definition, and lastly each attribute value must be of type of the corresponding attribute definition. This last condition is formalised by the function *isa* which is a general type checking function which can be applied to any value/type pair and recursively recursively calls *isa-instance-of* in the case that the pair is an instance/entity.

$names\text{-}match : entity\text{-}name \times entity\text{-}name \rightarrow \mathbb{B}$

$names\text{-}match\,(en1, en2) \;\triangleq$
   $en1 = en2;$

$doms\text{-}equal : (@A \xrightarrow{m} @B) \times (@A \xrightarrow{m} @C) \rightarrow \mathbb{B}$

$doms\text{-}equal\,(m1, m2) \;\triangleq$
   dom $m1 =$ dom $m2;$

$isa : attribute\text{-}value \times attribute\text{-}def \times db \rightarrow \mathbb{B}$

$isa\,(av, ad, d) \;\triangleq$
   cases mk- (av, ad) :
     mk- (mk-*instance-ref* (-), mk-*entity-name* (-)) $\rightarrow$
       $isa\text{-}instance\text{-}of\,(av, ad, d),$
     mk- (mk-*expression* (-), mk-*type-name* (-)) $\rightarrow$
       $\ldots\ldots$
   end;

A number of auxiliary function are also provided for convenience in the operation definitions that follow. For example:

$delete\text{-}instance : db \times instance\text{-}ref \rightarrow db$

$delete\text{-}instance\,(d, ir) \;\triangleq$
   $\mu\,(d, instance\text{-}map \mapsto \{ir\} \lhd d.instance\text{-}map)$
   pre $ir \in$ dom $d.instance\text{-}map$;

$add\text{-}instance : instance\text{-}def \times db \rightarrow db \times instance\text{-}ref$

$add\text{-}instance\,(i, d) \;\triangleq$
  let $nir = new\text{-}ir\,(d),$
      $ndb = \mu\,(d, instance\text{-}map \mapsto d.instance\text{-}map \uplus \{nir \mapsto i\})$ in
  mk- (ndb, nir)
pre $i.entity \in$ dom $d.schema.entities \wedge$
    dom $i.attributes =$ dom $d.schema.entities\,(i.entity) \wedge$
    $\forall\,an \in$ dom $i.attributes \cdot$
        $isof\text{-}type\,(i.attributes\,(an), d.schema.entities\,(i.entity)\,(an), d);$

$new\text{-}ir : db \rightarrow instance\text{-}ref$

$new\text{-}ir\,(d) \;\triangleq$
  let $ir : instance\text{-}ref$ be st $ir \notin$ dom $d.instance\text{-}map$ in
  ir

The Operations.

The SDAI defines some 50 operations, not all of which were formalised in VDM. There are also some operations required to complete the description of the EX-PRESS database which are not defined in the SDAI. These concern instantiating the database by reading EXPRESS data models and instances from file.

Here we give a few example a pair of operations which add and delete entities within the database and a pair which add and delete instances.

$add\text{-}entity\,(en : ET\text{`}entity\text{-}name, ed : ET\text{`}entity\text{-}def)$
ext wr $schema : ET\text{`}schema\text{-}def$
pre $en \notin$ dom $schema.entities$
post $schema.entities = \overleftarrow{schema.entities} \dagger \{en \mapsto ed\} \wedge$
    $schema.exp\text{-}types = \overleftarrow{schema.exp\text{-}types} \wedge$
    $schema.global\text{-}rules = \overleftarrow{schema.global\text{-}rules}$

$delete\text{-}entity\,(en : ET\text{`}entity\text{-}name)$
ext rd $model : ET\text{`}data\text{-}def$
    wr $schema : ET\text{`}schema\text{-}def$
pre $en \in$ dom $schema.entities \wedge$
    $\forall\,i \in$ rng $model \cdot i.entity \neq en$
post $schema.entities = \{en\} \lhd \overleftarrow{schema.entities} \wedge$
    $schema.exp\text{-}types = \overleftarrow{schema.exp\text{-}types} \wedge$
    $schema.global\text{-}rules = \overleftarrow{schema.global\text{-}rules}$

$add\text{-}instance\,(i : ET`instance\text{-}def, en : ET`entity\text{-}name)\; ir : ET`instance\text{-}ref$
ext rd $schema : ET`schema\text{-}def$
     wr $model : ET`data_d ef$
pre $en \in$ **dom** $schema.entities\;\wedge$
     $ET`names\text{-}match\,(i.entity, en)\;\wedge$
     dom $i.attributes =$ **dom** $schema.entities\,(en)\;\wedge$
     $\forall\, an \in$ **dom** $i.attributes\;\cdot$
         $ET`isa\,(i.attributes\,(an),$
                 $schema.entities\,(en)\,(an),$
                 mk-*db\,(schema, model))$
post let mk- $(ndb, nir) = ET`add\text{-}instance\,(i,$ **mk-***db\,(\overleftarrow{schema}, \overleftarrow{model}))$ **in**
     mk-*db\,(schema, model) = ndb \wedge ir = nir$;

$delete\text{-}instance\,(ir : ET`instance\text{-}ref)$
ext rd $schema : ET`schema\text{-}def$
     wr $model : ET`data_d ef$
pre $ir \in$ **dom** $data\text{-}def$
post mk-*db\,(schema, model) =$
     $ET`delete\text{-}instance\,($**mk-***db\,(\overleftarrow{schema}, \overleftarrow{model}), ir)$

4.3.3   Reflections on the Abstract Specification

The most fundamental difference in style between EXPRESS and VDM arises from the dereferencing implicit in instances of EXPRESS entities. In VDM, when indirection is required it must be made explicit by use fo a map type; in EXPRESS, each entity definition indicates an indirection in the corresponding instance data.

No uniform approach was taken here in determining which EXPRESS entities should be given object identifiers in the VDM model. However, often a strong indication that a map type was required came from the use of the combination of inverse attribute and uniqueness rule described above.

The data model given in [2] is rather concrete and includes a great proliferation of cross-references and repetition of data which makes it difficult to give a sufficiently strong invariant and operation definitions. The ubiquity of object identifiers in EXPRESS models can lead to a blurring of the roles of composit types as tuple constructors and to indicate indirection in the data.

The treatment here has removed many of these cross-references but there is still some "redundancy" remaining. The model given here can be seen as schema-centred in that the meta data and instance data are separated at the level of schema. The overall model of *db* is

$$entity\text{-}name \xrightarrow{m} (attribute\text{-}name \xrightarrow{m} attribute\text{-}def)$$
$$\times$$
$$instance\text{-}ref \xrightarrow{m} entity\text{-}name$$
$$\times$$
$$(attribute\text{-}name \xrightarrow{m} attribute\text{-}val)$$

This makes instance references unique throughout the instances of the schema and requires the three consistency clauses given above.

An alternative, class-centered, model would bring the instance references within the entity definitions to give

$$entity\text{-}name \xrightarrow{m} (attribute\text{-}name \xrightarrow{m} attribute\text{-}def)$$
$$\times$$
$$instance\text{-}ref \xrightarrow{m} (attribute\text{-}name \xrightarrow{m} attribute\text{-}val)$$

Here instance references are only unique within the instances of a class and only the *isa* and *doms-equal* clauses are required.

A third possible model would be instance-centered.

$$instance\text{-}ref \xrightarrow{m} entity\text{-}name$$
$$\times$$
$$(attribute\text{-}name \xrightarrow{m} (attribute\text{-}def$$
$$\times$$
$$attribute\text{-}val))$$

Now, only the *isa* constraint is required in the invariant although a new one is now needed which states that all instances of the same entity have the same structure.

This last model highlights the fact that the entity names could be considered to be redundant, entities with the same structure being equivalent. However, this value-based rather than an instance-based approach does diminish the potential for the classification of instances. It is a matter for debate which of these models is more abstract or more convenient in use. Which model is preferred is a matter of choice but experience shows that it is often convenient to use whichever model has simplest invariant.

4.4 A Relational Database

The basis for the concrete specification of the EXPRESS database is a VDM definition of an idealised relational database given in [5].

4.4.1 Signature

We are careful only to export the types and operations which we want to make available to the implementation. Note that the structure of the types is exported meaning that the default constructors and selectors are also exported. This is considerably more concise than defining and exporting each function explicitly.

module *RDB*

> exports

>> types struct *Relation*,
>>   struct *RelationName*,
>>   struct *Field*,
>>   struct *Fields*,

>>   . . .

There are just seven operations in the idealised database.

$$operations\ Create : RelationName \times Fields \xrightarrow{o} (),$$
$$Expand : RelationName \times Field \xrightarrow{o} (),$$
$$Drop : RelationName \xrightarrow{o} (),$$
$$Insert : Ins \mid InsSel \xrightarrow{o} (),$$
$$Update : Upd \mid UpdCond \xrightarrow{o} (),$$
$$Delete : Del \mid DelCond \xrightarrow{o} (),$$
$$Select : (Sel \mid SelCond) \times Environment \xrightarrow{o} Relation$$

4.4.2 Datatypes

A number of type declarations are required to support the definition of the operations. [5] defines some "syntactic types" which are the types which are used in the parameters and results of the operations, and "semantic types" which are used to model the internal structures of the database. Here we give a top-down presentation of some of the types without distinguishing the two classes.

$$Database = RelationName \xrightarrow{m} Relation;$$

$$Relation :: scheme : Scheme$$
$$tuples : Tuple\text{-}\mathsf{set}$$

inv mk-*Relation* $(s, ts) \triangleq$
$\quad \forall t \in ts \cdot$
$\qquad$ dom $t =$ dom $s \wedge$
$\qquad \forall att \in$ dom $t \cdot Compatible\text{-}type\,(t\,(att), s\,(att));$

$$Scheme = AttributeName \xrightarrow{m} Attribute;$$

$$Tuple = AttributeName \xrightarrow{m} Value;$$

$$Attribute = DataType$$

$Fields = Field$-**set**;

$Field :: name : AttributeName$
$\qquad\quad type : DataType$;

$DataType =$ INTEGER $\mid$ STRING $\mid$ $RelationName$

$\cdots$

There are many more syntactic domains for queries in the full specification which are used for selections, conditions, comparisons, boolean operations, arithmetic operations, etc.

4.4.3 The State and Operations

The state of the module is a single database. It is initially empty.

state rdb **of**
$\quad db : Database$
$\quad$ **init** $rdb \triangleq db = $ mk-rdb ($\{\mapsto\}$)
end

Note that this model only supports a single schema.

A number of auxiliary functions are used in the definition of the operations. One which is necessary in the following given here.

$Make\text{-}Scheme : Fields \rightarrow Scheme$

$Make\text{-}Scheme\,(fs) \triangleq$
$\quad \{f.name \mapsto f.type \mid f \in fs\}$;

The seven operation given in the signature are sufficient to implement the abstract operations given above. Just one example is given here.

$Create\,(r : RelationName, fs : Fields)$
ext wr $db : Database$
pre $r \notin$ **dom** $db \wedge$
$\quad \forall fi, fj \in fs \cdot$
$\quad\quad fi \neq fj \Rightarrow fi.name \neq fj.name$
post let $rel = $ mk-$Relation\,(Make\text{-}Scheme\,(fs), \{\})$ **in**
$\quad db = db \dagger \{r \mapsto rel\}$

4.4.4 Reflections on the Relational Database Specification

The full specification of the relational database runs to some 10 pages of VDM. Although this was taken directly from a published specification, some significant effort was required to fully formalise the specification and put it into the support tool. It is reassuring to note that only very minor errors were found during this process. Of course, the effort required to achieve full formality is repaid by the possibilities arising from automatic manipulation of the formal description, for example, proof obligation and test case generation, animation and even code generation.

4.5   A Concrete EXPRESS Database

A refinement of the abstract EXPRESS database was built on top of the relational database.

The concrete EXPRESS database module modules import the abstract syntax of EXPRESS defined in the abstract specification and the relational database.

module *CEDB*

    imports

        from *ET* all ,

        from *RDB* all

The state of the concrete EXPRESS database is exactly a relational database.

We first define some auxiliary functions.

functions

$$make\text{-}entity\text{-}name : RDB`RelationName \rightarrow ET`entity\text{-}name$$
$$make\text{-}entity\text{-}name\,(r) \triangleq$$
$$\quad \dots ;$$

$$make\text{-}RelationName : ET`entity\text{-}name \rightarrow RDB`RelationName$$
$$make\text{-}RelationName\,(e) \triangleq$$
$$\quad \dots ;$$

$$make\text{-}attribute\text{-}name : RDB`AttributeName \rightarrow ET`attribute\text{-}name$$
$$make\text{-}attribute\text{-}name\,(an) \triangleq$$
$$\quad \dots ;$$

$$make\text{-}AttributeName : ET`attribute\text{-}name \rightarrow RDB`AttributeName$$
$$make\text{-}AttributeName\,(an) \triangleq$$
$$\quad \dots ;$$

$$make\text{-}DataType : ET`attribute\text{-}def \rightarrow RDB`DataType$$

$$make\text{-}DataType\,(an) \triangleq$$
cases an :
    mk-$ET`entity\text{-}name\,(n) \rightarrow make\text{-}RelationName\,(n),$
    mk-$ET`type\text{-}name\,("Integer") \rightarrow$ INTEGER,
    mk-$ET`type\text{-}name\,("String") \rightarrow$ STRING
end

These are not specified in any more detail, except that they are all bijections, and have the following inverse properties.

$$\forall\,en \in ET`entity\text{-}name \cdot make\text{-}entity\text{-}name\,(make\text{-}RelationName\,(en)) = en$$
$$\forall\,rn \in RDB`RelationName \cdot make\text{-}RelationName\,(make\text{-}entity\text{-}name\,(rn)) = rn$$
$$\forall\,an \in ET`attribute\text{-}name \cdot make\text{-}attribute\text{-}name\,(make\text{-}AttributeName\,(an)) = an$$
$$\forall\,an \in RDB`AttributeName \cdot make\text{-}AttributeName\,(make\text{-}attribute\text{-}name\,(an)) = an$$

The definitions of operations in this model are generally straightforward, they break down the abstract structures and rebuild the relevant concrete structures. We give just a single example of an explicit version of the abstract operations defined on top of the relational database.
operations

$$add\text{-}entity : ET`entity\text{-}name \times ET`entity\text{-}def \xrightarrow{o} ()$$

$$add\text{-}entity\,(en,\,ed) \triangleq$$
let $fields = \{$mk-$RDB`Field$
                $(make\text{-}AttributeName\,(an),$
                  $make\text{-}DataType\,(ed\,(an)))) \mid an \in$ dom $ed\}$ in
$RDB`Create(make\text{-}RelationName\,(en),\,fields)$

Thus the design has the character of a programming task.

4.6 A Refinement Proof

In this section, we give a proof that the relational database based specification is a refinement of the abstract model. We restrict our interest to just one operation, add_entity. Note that in this section, for clarity, we omit the module prefixes.

4.6.1 The Retrieve Function

The refinement proof is based around the retrieve function, relating the concrete state to the abstract. In this case, the concrete state is the relational database model; the abstract the model of EXPRESS.

The retrieve function on the relational database state is broken down into the composition of retrieve functions on the constituent types in the state. This is only a partial definition; we omit for example, all the details of the *retr_model* function, as this plays no part in this part of the refinement proof.

functions

$$retr : rdb \rightarrow db$$

$$retr\,(r) \triangleq$$
$$\quad \mathsf{mk\text{-}}db\,(retr\text{-}schema\,(r), retr\text{-}model\,(r));$$

$$retr\text{-}schema : rdb \rightarrow schema\text{-}def$$

$$retr\text{-}schema\,(r) \triangleq$$
$$\quad \mathsf{mk\text{-}}schema\,(retr\text{-}exp\text{-}types\,(r), retr\text{-}entities\,(r), retr\text{-}global\text{-}rules\,(r));$$

$$retr\text{-}entities : rdb \rightarrow (entity\text{-}name \xrightarrow{m} entity\text{-}def)$$

$$retr\text{-}entities\,(\mathsf{mk\text{-}rdb}\,(rdb)) \triangleq$$
$$\quad \{make\text{-}entity\text{-}name\,(rn) \mapsto retr\text{-}entity\text{-}def\,(rdb\,(rn)) \mid rn \in \mathsf{dom}\ rdb\};$$

$$retr\text{-}entity\text{-}def : Relation \rightarrow entity\text{-}def$$

$$retr\text{-}entity\text{-}def\,(\mathsf{mk\text{-}}Relation\,(s, \text{-})) \triangleq$$
$$\quad \{make\text{-}attribute\text{-}name\,(an) \mapsto retr\text{-}attribute\text{-}def\,(s\,(an)) \mid an \in \mathsf{dom}\ s\};$$

$$retr\text{-}attribute\text{-}def : Attribute \rightarrow attribute\text{-}def$$

$$retr\text{-}attribute\text{-}def\,(\mathsf{mk\text{-}}Attribute\,(dt)) \triangleq$$
$$\quad \mathsf{cases}\ dt :$$
$$\quad\quad RelationName \rightarrow \mathsf{mk\text{-}}entity\text{-}name\,(dt),$$
$$\quad\quad \text{INTEGER} \rightarrow \mathsf{mk\text{-}}type\text{-}name\,("INTEGER"),$$
$$\quad\quad \text{STRING} \rightarrow \mathsf{mk\text{-}}type\text{-}name\,("STRING")\dots$$
$$\quad \mathsf{end}$$

Note that *retr_attribute_def* and *mk_DataType* are inverses.

Proofs about the retrieve function.   Two obligations need to be proven about the retrieve function: *retr-S-adeq* (the is surjective) and *init-adeq* (the initial concrete state is retrieved to the initial abstract state). In this case these give rise to the following proof obligations.

$$\frac{d : db}{\exists\, r : rdb \cdot retr\,(r) = d}$$

$$\frac{d : db, r : rdb, d = retr\,(r), rinit\text{-}rdb\,(r)}{rinit\text{-}db\,(d)}$$

The second clearly holds: the retrieve function maps the empty map onto the empty map. The first requires the consideration of the invariants on the two states. This is more complicated, and is omitted here.

4.6.2 The Refinement Proof Obligations

Two proof obligations are required for each operation: *OP-dom-obl*, which demonstrates that the abstract precondition implies the concrete precondition, and *OP-res-obl*, which demonstrates that the abstract precondition and concrete postcondition together satisfy the abstract postcondition. Here, we only consider one operation, *add_entity*.

We first consider the obligation *add-entity-dom-obl*. This translates into the following:

$$\frac{\begin{array}{c} en : entity\text{-}name, \\ ed : entity\text{-}def, \\ c : cedb, \\ en \notin \mathsf{dom}\,(retr\,(c).schema.entities) \end{array}}{make\text{-}RelationName\,(en) \notin \mathsf{dom}\,(c.db)}$$

Once definedness is established, the proof can proceed via forward reasoning, generating new hypotheses from the existing ones. The last hypothesis can be simplified by equal substitution using the *f-defn* rules for the retrieve functions:

$$\begin{aligned}
&en \notin \mathsf{dom}\,(retr\,(c).schema.entities) \\
&\quad = en \notin \mathsf{dom}\,(retr\text{-}entities\,(c)) \\
&\quad = en \notin \mathsf{dom}\,\{make\text{-}entity\text{-}name\,(rn) \mapsto retr\text{-}entity\text{-}def\,(c.db\,(rn)) \\
&\qquad\qquad\qquad\qquad | \; rn \in \mathsf{dom}\,(c.db)\} \\
&\quad = en \notin \{make\text{-}entity\text{-}name\,(rn) \; | \; rn \in \mathsf{dom}\,(c.db)\}
\end{aligned}$$

Since *make_RelationName* is an injection, we can apply this function to this last hypothesis, pushing it through the set comprehension giving a new hypotheses, which can be simplified as follows:

$$\begin{aligned}
&make\text{-}RelationName\,(en) \notin \{make\text{-}RelationName\,(make\text{-}entity\text{-}name\,(rn)) \\
&\qquad\qquad\qquad\qquad\qquad | \; rn \in \mathsf{dom}\,(c.db)\} \\
&\quad = make\text{-}RelationName\,(en) \notin \{rn \; | \; rn \in \mathsf{dom}\,(c.db)\} \\
&\quad = make\text{-}RelationName\,(en) \notin \mathsf{dom}\,(c.db)
\end{aligned}$$

and the obligation holds. The second obligation *add-entity-res-obl* is more complicated, and we only give a proof sketch. The form of the obligation is as follows.

$$en{:}\,entity\text{-}name,$$
$$ed{:}\,entity\text{-}def,$$
$$c{:}\,cedb,$$
$$en \notin \mathrm{dom}(retr(c).schema.entities),$$

let $fields = \{$
  $\quad$mk-$Field(make\text{-}AttributeName(an),make\text{-}DataType(ed(an)))$
  $\quad\quad\quad\quad | \; an \in \mathrm{dom} \; ed$
  $\quad\} $ in
post-$Create(make\text{-}RelationName(en),fields)$

$retr\,(c).schema.entities = retr\,(\overleftarrow{c}).schema.entities \dagger \{en \mapsto ed\} \wedge$
$retr\,(c).schema.exp\text{-}types = retr\,(\overleftarrow{c}).schema.exp\text{-}types \wedge$
$retr\,(c).schema.global\text{-}rules = retr\,(\overleftarrow{c}).schema.global\text{-}rules$

The fifth hypothesis of this obligation is complex. It is derived from the post-condition of the concrete *add-entity* operation. As this operation calls the *Create* operation, the post-condition of the latter operation is substituted.

We can split the goal into three, one for each conjunction. It is the first one which we are primarily interested in. Again, we proceed by using a forward proof. Most of the information required to prove this goal is encapsulated within the last hypothesis. This can be simplified as follows. We first expand out the post-condition of Create, leading to the following nested expression.

let $fields = \{$
  $\quad\quad\quad$mk-$Field(make\text{-}AttributeName(an),make\text{-}DataType(ed(an)))$
  $\quad\quad\quad\quad\quad\quad | \; an \in \mathrm{dom} \; ed$
  $\quad\quad\quad\} $ in
let $rel = $ mk-$Relation(Make\text{-}Scheme(fields),\{\})$ in
  $\quad\quad\quad c.db = \overleftarrow{c}.db \dagger \{make\text{-}RelationName\,(en) \mapsto rel\}$

By the equational congruence rule (=-*extend*), we can apply the retrieve function to both sides of this expression (the let clauses are omitted for clarity in the following proof steps):

$$retr\,(c.db) = retr\,(c.db \dagger \{make\text{-}RelationName\,(en) \mapsto rel\})$$

Expanding the definition of *retr* gives:

mk-$db\,(retr\text{-}schema\,(c.db), retr\text{-}model\,(c.db)) =$
  $\quad$mk-$db(retr\text{-}schema\,(\overleftarrow{c}.db \dagger \{make\text{-}RelationName\,(en) \mapsto rel\}),$
  $\quad\quad\quad retr\text{-}model\,(\overleftarrow{c}.db \dagger \{make\text{-}RelationName\,(en) \mapsto rel\}))$

As it is the schema component we are primarily interested, we can use the selector definition rule *schema-defn* to give the equation:

$$retr\,(c.db).schema = retr\text{-}schema\,(\overleftarrow{c}.db \dagger \{make\text{-}RelationName\,(en) \mapsto rel\})$$

Again using the selectors, this can be decomposed into the following three hypotheses:

$$retr\,(c.db).schema.entities =$$
$$retr\text{-}schema\,(\overleftarrow{c}.db \dagger \{make\text{-}RelationName\,(en) \mapsto rel\}).entities$$
$$retr\,(c.db).schema.exp\text{-}types =$$
$$retr\text{-}schema\,(\overleftarrow{c}.db \dagger \{make\text{-}RelationName\,(en) \mapsto rel\}).exp\text{-}types$$
$$retr\,(c.db).schema.global\text{-}rules =$$
$$retr\text{-}schema\,(\overleftarrow{c}.db \dagger \{make\text{-}RelationName\,(en) \mapsto rel\}).global\text{-}rules$$

We are only interested in the first of these which can be rewritten to the following hypothesis.

$$retr\,(c.db).schema.entities =$$
$$retr\text{-}entities\,(\overleftarrow{c}.db \dagger \{make\text{-}RelationName\,(en) \mapsto rel\})$$

Now we can push *retr-entities* through the overriding since we know from the previous proof obligation that $make\text{-}RelationName(en) \notin \mathsf{dom}(old(c).db)$. This gives:

$$retr\,(c.db).schema.entities =$$
$$retr\text{-}entities\,(\overleftarrow{c}.db) \dagger retr\text{-}entities\,(\{make\text{-}RelationName\,(en) \mapsto rel\})$$

Unfolding the definition of *retr-entities* gives:

$$retr\,(c.db).schema.entities =$$
$$retr\,(\overleftarrow{c}.db).schema.entities \dagger$$
$$\{make\text{-}entity\text{-}name\,(make\text{-}RelationName\,(en)) \mapsto retr\text{-}entity\text{-}def\,(rel)\}$$

and unfolding again on both sides:

$$retr\,(c).schema.entities =$$
$$retr\,(\overleftarrow{c}).schema.entities \dagger \{en \mapsto retr\text{-}entity\text{-}def\,(rel)\}$$

Unfolding the *retr-entity-def(rel)*, expanding the definition of *rel* as in the let clause, we can give the following steps:

$$retr\,(c).schema.entities$$
$$= retr\,(\overleftarrow{c}).schema.entities \dagger \{en \mapsto$$
$$retr\text{-}entity\text{-}def\,(make\text{-}Relation\,(Make\text{-}Scheme\,(fields),\{\}))\,\}$$
$$= retr\,(\overleftarrow{c}).schema.entities \dagger \{\,en \mapsto$$
$$retr\text{-}entity\text{-}def\,(\mathsf{mk\text{-}Relation}($$
$$\{f.name \mapsto \mathsf{mk\text{-}}Attribute\,(f.type) \mid f \in fields\}), \{\})\}$$
$$= retr\,(\overleftarrow{c}).schema.entities \dagger \{\,en \mapsto$$
$$\{\,make\text{-}attribute\text{-}name\,(an) \mapsto retr\text{-}attribute\text{-}def\,(att) \mid$$
$$\mathsf{mk\text{-}}(an,att)^5 \in \{f.name \mapsto \mathsf{mk\text{-}}Attribute\,(f.type) \mid f \in fields\}\,\}\}$$

Now, the definition of *fields* states that the first component (i.e. *f.name*) of each pair is *mk-AttributeName(an)* for *an* ∈ dom *ed*, and thus performing this expansion gives:

$retr\,(c).schema.entities$
$\quad = retr\,(\overleftarrow{c}).schema.entities\dagger\,\{\ en \mapsto$
$\qquad\quad \{\ make\text{-}attribute\text{-}name\,(an) \mapsto retr\text{-}attribute\text{-}def\,(att)\ |$
$\qquad\qquad\quad \text{mk-}(an, att) \in \{f.name \mapsto \text{mk-}Attribute\,(f.type)\ |\ f \in$
$\qquad\qquad\qquad \{\ \text{mk-}Field\ (\ make\text{-}AttributeName\,(an),$
$\qquad\qquad\qquad\qquad\qquad make\text{-}DataType\,(ed\,(an))\ )\ |\ an \in \text{dom}\ ed\}\}\}\}$

$\quad = retr\,(\overleftarrow{c}).schema.entities\,\dagger\,\{en \mapsto$
$\qquad\quad \{make\text{-}attribute\text{-}name\,(an) \mapsto retr\text{-}attribute\text{-}def\,(att)\ |$
$\qquad\quad \text{mk-}(an, att) \in \{\text{mk-}(make\text{-}AttributeName\,(an),$
$\qquad\qquad\quad make\text{-}DataType\,(ed\,(an)))|\ an \in \text{dom}\ ed\}\}\}$

$\quad = retr\,(\overleftarrow{c}).schema.entities\,\dagger\,\{en \mapsto$
$\qquad\quad \{\ an \mapsto retr\text{-}attribute\text{-}def\,(att)\ |\ \text{mk-}(an, att) \in$
$\qquad\quad \{\text{mk-}(an, make\text{-}DataType\,(ed\,(an)))\ |\ an \in \text{dom}\ ed\}\ \}\ \}$

$\quad = retr\,(\overleftarrow{c}).schema.entities\dagger\,\{\ en \mapsto$
$\qquad\quad \{\ an \mapsto retr\text{-}attribute\text{-}def\,(make\text{-}DataType\,(ed\,(an)))\ |$
$\qquad\qquad an \in \text{dom}\ ed\}\}$

retr-attribute-def is the inverse of *make-DataType*, and so:

$\quad retr\,(c).schema.entities$
$\qquad = retr\,(\overleftarrow{c}).schema.entities\,\dagger\,\{en \mapsto \{an \mapsto ed\,(an)\ |\ an \in \text{dom}\ ed\}\}$
$\qquad = retr\,(\overleftarrow{c}).schema.entities\,\dagger\,\{en \mapsto ed\}$

and the proof is complete.

4.6.3 Thoughts on the Refinement Proof

This example is of a "medium-complexity" proof, but typical of the style required to discharge such obligations. The proof of the obligations for the *add-instance* operation are more complex, due to the necessity to ensure the integrity of the data.

Much of the complexity of the proofs is contained within the retrieve function. The proof of the surjectivity of the retrieve is more problematic, due to the recursive definitions used.

It is striking that this task could be described as "low-level theorem proving". Most of the proof steps are small and relatively trivial: unfolding of function definitions and let clauses; extensive simple equational reasoning; and the application of retrieve

---

[5]In this proof sketch, mk-$(x, y) \in m$ is being used as a shorthand for $x \in \text{dom}\ m \wedge y = m\,(x)$.

function to generate new equational congruences. However, there are a large number of these steps, even in a modest proof such as this one. The steps are tedious, with substitutions and expansions into large, unwieldy terms, and are thus are highly prone to human error.

This emphasises the need for appropriate machine support. Proofs of this type are needed for each of the operations, with many such low-level reasoning steps, which are prime candidates for automation, and many repeated chains of reasoning, calling for the construction of repositories of reusable lemmas.

4.7 General Experiences and Conclusions

Concurrent engineering of the abstract specification, refinement and implementation worked well. A major task was the understanding of the SDAI standard; by working on specification and implementation together, the abstract model in the standard and the language bindings were both considered which was a help when trying to interpret the standard.

No routine technique was found to develop a VDM model from an EXPRESS one. No uniform approach was appropriate for object identifiers or subtypes, rather it was necessary build the VDM model as dictated by an understanding of the overall specification. Unsurprisingly perhaps, it is not appropriate to try to use EXPRESS style in VDM!

The implicit dereferencing available in EXPRESS has both benefits and drawbacks. In its favour is that many concise forms can be defined for particular situations, on the other hand, it can overly complicate the data to require an indirection every time a tuple is created. It is unfortunate that there is no other way of constructing tuples in EXPRESS.

The IFAD VDM-SL Toolbox was invaluable for writing, typesetting and typecheck- ing the specifications. There is no doubt that the task would have been more time consuming and error prone without it. Many errors were found in the specification whilst it was developed and some minor ones in the previously published module. The animation and testing facilities available in the toolbox were not used.

The Toolbox also provides a facility for generation of C++ code which could be very useful. Code generated from the specification of the "EXPRESS shell" could form the basis of an actual implementation of the software. However, if this were to be used, it would have to be integrated (and maintained) with other software which would interface to the relational database and the EXPRESS application. Although this was not attempted, the documentation for the code generator describes the structure of the resulting code. The present authors were surprised to find that the code generation process builds classes according to the type constructors of VDM rather than the data structures of the application data model. It could make the integration task unnecessarily difficult. Similar problems will of course be present with any automatic code generation tool [12].

Although, the formalisation of the refinement and proofs were not completed in full detail, it was certainly worthwhile developing abstract and concrete views of the system. Having two specifications helped one resist the temptation to gradually decrease the level of abstraction as the specification developed. Refinement and proof would both require considerable effort, particularly as neither aspect is supported by the Toolbox.

Certain pragmatic decisions also had to be taken as to what aspects to focus on and what not to formalise. Thus, although the formal specification has helped enormously in the understanding of the system and its design, in this instance it has done little to increase confidence in correctness of the implementation.

4.8　Bibliography

[1] STEP Overview, ISO 10303, Part 1.

[2] SDAI Specification, ISO 10303, Part 22. TC184/SC4/WG7.

[3] *ibid.* Section 6 to 8.

[4] Semantic Unification Meta Model. ISO 10303.

[5] A Formal Semantics For SQL. Meira, S., Motz, M. and Tepedino, F. Intern. J. Computer Math. Vol. 34. pp. 43-63 (1990)

[6] Schenck and Wilson. Information Modelling the EXPRESS way, Oxford University Press, 1995.

[7] *ibid.* Appendix E.

[8] Analysis of the STEP Standard Data Access Interface Using Formal Methods. Botting, R.M. and Godwin, A.N. Computer Standards and Interfaces. 17(5-6), pp. 437-456, North Holland, 1995.

[9] Bicarregui J.C., An evaluation of methods for generating SQL from EXPRESS. ESPRIT 6212, Processbase, Document RAL/6212/TNR/016/4. January 1995.

[10] Bicarregui, Ritchie and Haughton, Experiences in Using Abstract Machine Notation in a GKS Case Study. FME'94: Industrial Benefit of Formal Methods, LNCS 873, Springer-Verlag, 1994.

[11] Vienna Development Method - Specification Language, Draft International Standard, ISO/IEC DIS 13817-1, 1995(E).

[12] Bicarregui, Dick and Woods, Supporting the length of formal development: form diagrams to VDM to B to C, 7th International Conference on Putting into Practice Methods and Tools for Information System Design. IBSN: 2-906082-19-9 October 1995.

[13] The CAESAR STEP Toolkit User manual (Version 1.3). Caesar Systems Limited, June 1992.

[14] The EXPRESS Language Reference Manual, ISO IS 10303-11 : 1994(E).

[15] Translating Express to SQL: A User Guide. Morris, K.C., NISTIR 90-4341, National Institute of Standards and Technology (NIST), Gaithersburg MD., 20899. USA.

[16] STEP Relational Interface, Raghaven, V., Hardwick, M., Rensselaer Polytechnic Institute, Computer Science Masters Project. (1993)

[17] Thomas D, Implementing the emerging ISO Standard STEP into a relational database, BNCOD-8, Proceedings of the 8th British national Conference on Databases.

[18] P. Clement, Internal Report on the EXPRESS to SQL Compiler. Loughborough University of Technology Technical Report. 1991.

[19] The IFAD VDM-SL Toolbox, in Woodcock and Larsen (Eds.). *FME'93: Industrial Strength Formal Methods.* Springer-Verlag, 1993.

[20] C.B. Jones C.D. Allen, D.N.Chapman. A formal definition of algol 60. Technical Report 12.105, IBM Laboratory, Hursley, Aug. 1972.

[21] D. Andrews and W. Henhapl. Pascal. In *Formal Specification and Software Development*, chapter 7, pages 175–252. Prentice-Hall, 1982.

[22] S.P.A. Lau, Derek Andrews, Anjula Garg and J.R. Pitchers. The Formal Definition of Modula-2 and Its Associated Interpreter. In L.Marshall R.Bloomfield and R. Jones, editors, *VDM '88 VDM – The Way Ahead*, pages 167–177. VDM-Europe, Springer-Verlag, September 1988.

[23] W.Henhapl C.B.Jones P.Lucas H.Bekić, D.Bjørner. A formal definition of a pl/i subset. Technical Report 25.139, IBM Laboratory, Vienna, December 1974.

[24] O.Oest (eds.) D. Bjørner. *Towards a Formal Description of Ada*, volume 98 of *Lecture Notes in Computer Science*. Springer-Verlag, 1980.

[25] J.F. Nilsson. Formal Vienna-Definition-Method models of Prolog. In J.A. Campbell, editor, *Implementations of PROLOG*, pages 281–308. Ellis Horwood Series: Artificial Intelligence, 1984.

Chapter 5

Shared Memory Synchronization

Noemie Slaats, Bart Van Assche and Albert Hoogewijs

Summary

Explicitly parallel programs consist of several threads, where each thread is executed by a different processing unit. These threads all have access to a shared memory, and communicate by writing to or reading from the shared memory. Reads and writes of different threads execute uncoordinatedly. Threads can wait for other threads by using synchronization. Although reading and writing the shared memory is similar in all shared memory systems, most shared memory systems have their own set of synchronization instructions. The semantics of the memory access and synchronization instructions together is called a *memory model*, which is usually specified informally or using a formalism specific to the memory model. We present a unified formalization of shared memory models both in traditional and in VDM notation. We also show how the Mural tool helps in writing the VDM specifications and in generating the corresponding formal theory. A proof constructed with Mural shows that even basic properties of this formal theory can be nontrivial to prove.

5.1 Introduction

A shared memory system has an address space common to all processors using the shared memory. Such a shared memory system can have one of the following implementations: a shared memory multiprocessor, a hardware distributed shared memory multiprocessor, or a network of workstations with distributed shared memory software. A shared memory multiprocessor has a physically shared memory, while in the other two systems the memory is fully distributed over the processors. In all three systems every processor has a local memory with a copy of a part of the shared memory. This memory is called a cache memory of the shared memory. To preserve the semantics of a single shared memory, these cache memories have to be kept consistent. The generic structure of a shared memory is shown in figure 5.1.

Every processor runs one thread, or actually a uniprocessor program associated with the thread. The different uniprocessor programs together are the explicitly parallel program. While running a thread, a processor issues read and write operations to the shared memory. These read and write operations are the only interaction of the processor with the shared memory. We call the sequence of operations that result from running a thread the *execution* of that thread. Since the order of the operations in the execution is derived from the order of instructions in the uniprocessor program running, we call this order the *program order* of the operations issued by the corresponding processor.

In a shared memory system without local memories, every processor has the same view of the shared memory. When duplicating or caching the contents of the shared memory in local memories, however, every processor potentially can have a different view of the shared memory. We model a processor's view of the shared memory by specifying the history of the changes applied to that view. We represent this history by the order in which operations of all processors have been observed by the current processor. We call this order the *memory order* relation. It is a partial order relation, able to model concurrent operations.

Although the memory orders are relations over more operations than the program order, there is a strong relation between both. When the memory order as observed by a processor includes the program order of the same processor, that processor obeys the *uniprocessor correctness* property. This means that a one-processor program will execute correctly on that processor.

To cooperate in a deterministic way, threads must be able to wait for one another or to synchronize. Synchronization of two or more threads is a way to guarantee an ordering between memory operations of different threads. There are two kinds of synchronization operations: low-level and high-level. *Low-level synchronization operations* are read and write operations whose ordering is guaranteed to be the same in all memory order relations. *High-level synchronization operations* are the acquire-, release- and barrier operations. They are defined in section 5.2.4.

This chapter is organized as follows: in section 5.2 we give an informal description of a shared memory synchronization model. The VDM specification associated with this model is given in section 5.3. In section 5.4 the formal theory for the memory model is discussed. To generate this formal theory the Mural tool [4] is used. In a last section we review and discuss the example.

5.2 Formal Definitions

The following information will be used to represent any operation: operation type, sequence number, processor number and set of memory addresses where the operation takes effect on. Additionally, load operations have a loaded value associated

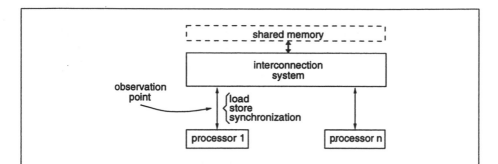

Figure 5.1: Generic structure of a shared memory system: n processors, a shared memory and inbetween an interconnection system. The interconnection system can reorder requests and can cause arbitrary delays when propagating requests from one processor to another. The shared memory itself is either physical or virtual. Program order and memory order relations over load, store and synchronization operations for a given processor are observed at the indicated observation point. for a given processor are observed at the indicated observation point.

to them, store operations have a stored value, load-modify-store operations have a loaded and a stored value, and acquire, release and barrier-operations have an identification number associated to them.

A load operation reads from memory, a store operation writes to memory, and a load-modify-store operation modifies the value at a memory location without allowing intervening operations by other processors.

Definition 1 *operation type*

An operation has one of the types in $Type = \{ns, nl, nf, ss, sl, sf, acq, rel, bar\}$. These types are respectively normal store, load, load-modify-store, synchronizing store, load, load-modify-store, acquire, release and barrier operations.

We will use the symbol $n \in \mathbf{N}$ for the *number of processors* of the memory system, $P = \{1, \ldots, n\}$ for the *set of processor numbers*, and $p \in P$ for a *processor number*. $i \in \mathbf{N}$ is the per processor *operation number*, instructions executed later having a higher operation number. Equal operation numbers for different operations on the same processor are not allowed. $j \in \mathbf{N}$ is an *identification number* for barriers and critical sections, indicating which operations belong together. An entity in the memory that can be addressed is called a *location*, and *Mem* is the set of all addressable locations. $m \in Mem$ is a *single memory location*, and $M \subset Mem$ is a *set of memory locations*, indicating which set of locations is involved in an operation. For loads, stores and load-modify-stores this is typically a singleton, and for synchronization instructions this set M is a non-empty subset of *Mem*. What is stored into a location or read from a location is called a *value*, and the set of all allowed values is called *Val*. For an overview, see table 5.1.

operation name	general form	restricted form	shorthand
normal store	(ns, i, p, M, v_s)	$(ns, i, p, \{m\}, v\_s)$	$l\_i(m, v\_s)$
normal load	(nl, i, p, M, v_l)	$(nl, i, p, \{m\}, v\_l)$	$s\_i(m, v\_l)$
normal load-modify-store	(nf, i, p, M, v_l, v_s)	$(nf, i, p, \{m\}, v\_l, v\_s)$	$f\_i(m, v\_l, v\_s)$
synchronizing store	(ss, i, p, M, v_s)	$(ss, i, p, \{m\}, v\_s)$	$sl\_i(m, v\_s)$
synchronizing load	(sl, i, p, M, v_l)	$(sl, i, p, \{m\}, v\_l)$	$ss\_i(m, v\_l)$
synchronizing load-modify-store	(sf, i, p, M, v_l, v_s)	$(sf, i, p, \{m\}, v\_l, v\_s)$	$sf\_i(m, v\_l, v\_s)$
acquire	(acq, i, p, M, j)	(acq, i, p, M, j)	$a\_i(M, j)$
release	(rel, i, p, M, j)	(rel, i, p, M, j)	$r\_i(M, j)$
barrier	(bar, i, p, M, j)	(bar, i, p, M, j)	$b\_i(M, j)$

Table 5.1: Names of the operation types, the general form of an operation tuple, the corresponding restricted form, and the abbreviation of the restricted form. The general form operates on a set of memory locations M, while the restricted form uses only one location m for load- and store-operations. Processor numbers are not specified in the restricted form: in graphs the processor number will be clear from the context.

The functions $num()$, $proc()$, $mem()$, $val\_l()$ and $val\_s()$ operate on operation tuples, and respectively return the values i, p, M, v_l and v_s.

The sets of operations of types $ns, nl, nf, ss, sl, sf, acq, rel$ and bar are called respectively S_n, L_n, F_n, S_s, L_s, F_s, Acq, Rel, and Bar. Derived sets of operation types are in table 5.2.

5.2.1   Program Order and Executions

We will use the notation $\xrightarrow{po\,p}$ for the program order relation of processor p, and $\xrightarrow{po}$ for the union of these relations. Since the individual operations already include a per-processor sequence-number $proc()$, the program order relations can be easily defined using the sequence number.

Definition 2 *program order* $\xrightarrow{po}$ *and per processor program order* $\xrightarrow{po\,p}$

The program order relation $\xrightarrow{po}$ is the relation between operations $op\_1, op\_2 \in Op$ and is defined by

$$op\_1 \xrightarrow{po} op\_2 \iff (proc(op\_1) = proc(op\_2)) \land (num(op\_1) \leq num(op\_2)).$$

On processor p, operations are executed in the order $\xrightarrow{po\,p}$, defined by

$$op\_1 \xrightarrow{po\,p} op\_2 \iff (proc(op\_1) = proc(op\_2) = p) \land (num(op\_1) \leq num(op\_2)).$$

operation set contents	formal definition
store operations	$S = S\_n \cup F\_n \cup S\_s \cup F\_s$
load operations	$L = L\_n \cup F\_n \cup L\_s \cup F\_s$
low-level synchronization operations	$Sync\_L = S\_s \cup L\_s \cup F\_s$
high-level synchronization operations	$Sync\_H = Acq \cup Rel \cup Bar$
synchronization operations	$Sync = Sync\_L \cup Sync\_H$
operations executed on processor p	$Op\_p = \{op \in Op \mid proc(op) = p\}$
operations accessing at least location set M	$Op\_M = \{op \in Op \mid M \subset mem(op)\}$
operations accessing at least location set M on processor p	$Op\_M, p = Op\_M \cap Op\_p$
operations accessing at least location m	$Op\_m = Op\_\{m\}$
operations accessing at least location m on processor p	$Op\_m, p = Op\_m \cap Op\_p$

Table 5.2: Sets of operations for specific operation types, processor number, or accessed memory locations.

Parallel Program		Executed operations	
thread 1	thread 2	processor 1	processor 2
x := 1	y := 1	$s\_1(x, 1)$	$s\_3(y, 1)$
... := y	... := x	$l\_2(y, 0)$	$l\_4(x, 0)$

Figure 5.2: A short parallel program and the operations for one possible execution of that program. It is assumed that the memory has been initialized to zero. In this example the shared memory did not process the load and store requests in program order.

For an example of a parallel program, its program order and its memory order relations, see figures 5.2 and 5.3.

From the definition of the global and per processor program order relations, we can derive the following properties:

- the per-processor program order $\overset{po\,p}{\rightarrow}$ is a total order for the operations of that processor, Op_p.

- the relation $\overset{po}{\rightarrow}$ is a partial order in the set Op.

- any order $\overset{po\,p}{\rightarrow}$ is contained in the order relation $\overset{po}{\rightarrow}$, or $\forall p\colon P \cdot \overset{po\,p}{\rightarrow} \subset \overset{po}{\rightarrow}$.

The set of all operations and the order in which they are executed contain all information, about how a program has been executed, observable by the threads. We call

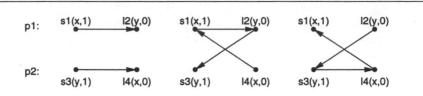

Figure 5.3: Sample global program order relation $\xrightarrow{po}$, and memory order relations $\xrightarrow{mo1}$ and $\xrightarrow{mo2}$ for processors p_1 and p_2 respectively. The relations in the graphs are the transitive reduction of the $\xrightarrow{po}$, $\xrightarrow{mo1}$ and $\xrightarrow{mo2}$ relations.

the pair of the set of operations and the program order relation of these operations an execution of the parallel program.

Definition 3 *execution E*

An execution $E = (Op, \xrightarrow{po})$ of a program consists of the set Op of operations and the order of execution $\xrightarrow{po}$ implied by the program.

5.2.2   Uniprocessor Correctness

Every processor of a multiprocessor system must obey uniprocessor correctness: when a sequential program is executed on a single processor of a multiprocessor system, the result must be the same as if the program was executed on a uniprocessor. This is achieved when all *data dependent* operations of a thread are present in the memory order relation in the same order as in program order. In its weakest form, two operations are data dependent if they access the same memory location, and either they are a store and a load operation, or they are two store operations writing different values. Executing data-dependent operations in a modified order changes either the result of one of the operations and/or the value written to memory. We will use a stronger condition than preserving data-dependences: we require that the order of any two operations referencing the same memory location is preserved.

Condition 1 *uniprocessor data dependences*

Any two operations on processor p to the same location that are ordered by program order, are ordered by the memory order relation $\xrightarrow{mo\,p}$ of that processor in the same way.

$$\forall m: Mem \cdot \forall op\_1, op\_2: Op\_m \cdot \forall p: P \cdot op\_1 \xrightarrow{po\,p} op\_2 \implies op\_1 \xrightarrow{mo\,p} op\_2$$

5.2.3   Result of a Load

Since the relation $\xrightarrow{mo\,p}$ is the order in which a processor observes the memory operations of itself and other processors, the relation $\xrightarrow{mo\,p}$ determines the result of a load

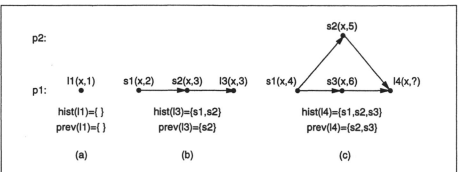

Figure 5.4: Three examples of execution sequences and their memory order relation $\stackrel{mo\_l}{\longrightarrow}$, illustrating the value condition. The first two sequences have been executed on one processor, the third on two processors. From the $\stackrel{mo\_l}{\longrightarrow}$ relation the sets $hist(l)$ and $prev(l)$ for the load l are derived, which in turn determine the result value of the load. The graphs represent the transitive reduction of the memory order relations $\stackrel{mo\_l}{\longrightarrow}$.

operation. For a load operation l, we define the set $hist(l)$ as the set of all store operations preceding l, and the set $prev(l)$ as the set of store operations immediately preceding l. When there is exactly one store operation s preceding l, the value stored by s is also the result returned by l. If there are zero, two, or more store operations preceding l, and they store zero, two, or more different values, then the result of l is undefined. For an example, see figure 5.4.

Condition 2 *value condition*

$$p \stackrel{\Delta}{=} proc(l)$$
$$hist(l) \stackrel{\Delta}{=} \{s \in S\_mem(l) \setminus \{l\} \mid s \stackrel{mo\,p}{\longrightarrow} l\}$$
$$prev(l) \stackrel{\Delta}{=} \{s \in hist(l) \mid \forall s': hist(l) \setminus \{s\} \cdot \neg(s \stackrel{mo\,p}{\longrightarrow} s')\}$$
$$\forall s: prev(l) \cdot val\_l(l) = val\_s(s)$$

The relations $\stackrel{mo\,p}{\longrightarrow}$ define the view of an individual processor of the order of memory operations. We also need the combined view of all processors of the order of the operations concerning a memory location m. We will call this relation the *access order for location* m, $\stackrel{ao}{\longrightarrow}\_m$, and its union over all memory locations the *access order relation*, $\stackrel{ao}{\longrightarrow}$.

Definition 4 *access order*
The access order $\overset{\text{ao}}{\rightarrow}\_m$ at the memory location m is the order in which operations are executed on the location m. The relation $\overset{\text{ao}}{\rightarrow}$, the access order relation, is the union of the $\overset{\text{ao}}{\rightarrow}\_m$ relations.

$$\overset{\text{ao}}{\rightarrow}\_m \triangleq \bigcup p: P \cdot \overset{\text{mo}\,p}{\rightarrow} \cap Op\_m^2$$

$$\overset{\text{ao}}{\rightarrow} \triangleq \left(\bigcup m: Mem \cdot \overset{\text{ao}}{\rightarrow}\_m\right)^*$$

Before defining the *shared memory condition*, we define *consistency of relations* and *sequential consistency of relations*.

Definition 5 *consistency of relations*
The relations $R\_1, \ldots, R\_n$ are consistent over the set A if and only if the relations $R\_1, \ldots, R\_n$ are identical when restricted to A:

$$R\_1 \cap A^2 = \ldots = R\_n \cap A^2.$$

Definition 6 *sequential consistency of relations*
The relations $R\_1, \ldots, R\_n$ are sequentially consistent over the set A if and only if they are consistent and every relation $R\_1, \ldots, R\_n$ is a total order over the set A.

While the view of operations of different processors on different memory locations can vary from processor to processor, all processors must have the same view of the order of operations on one single memory location. Additionally, combining these views must be meaningful. We call these two conditions together the *shared memory condition*.

Condition 3 *shared memory condition*

$$\forall m: Mem \cdot \{\overset{\text{mo}\,1}{\rightarrow}, \ldots, \overset{\text{mo}\,n}{\rightarrow}\} \text{ is consistent in } Op\_m$$

$$\wedge \quad \overset{\text{ao}}{\rightarrow} \text{ is a partial order.}$$

From the shared memory condition, it follows that the individual $\overset{\text{ao}}{\rightarrow}\_m$ relations are partial order relations.

5.2.4   Synchronization

In this formalization of operations and memory models, there are three types of low-level synchronization operations (synchronizing load, synchronizing store and synchronizing load-modify-store) and three types of high-level synchronizing operations (barrier, acquire and release). These operations unify the synchronization primitives used in existing memory models.

Low-level synchronization operations behave the same way as their counterparts without synchronization, except that the order of low-level synchronization operations is identical in every memory order relation.

A *barrier* is a group of barrier operations b with the same identification number $id(b)$. These individual operations execute on a set of processors $P' = \{proc(b) \mid b \in B\}$. The barrier synchronizes for the processors in P' the access to the set of memory locations $M = mem(b)$: all memory references to any of the locations M that are ordered before the barrier as observed by any of the participating processors P', are before the barrier in the memory order relations of any processor. The same holds for memory accesses ordered after the barrier. We define the relation N as the equivalence relation that holds between barrier operations of the same barrier. Typically a barrier operation is implemented by waiting until all other processors participating in the barrier arrive at their corresponding barrier operation.

A critical section has an identification number j and protects the locations of the set M by sequentializing other critical sections to any of these locations M. A critical section on processor p starts with an *acquire* operation $(acq, ?, p, M, j)$ and ends with a *release* operation $(rel, ?, p, M, j)$. Although critical sections that have at least one location in common cannot overlap, access to any of the protected variables during the execution is still possible by another processor if it does not protect these accesses with a critical section. Operations executed inside the critical section are for every memory order relation ordered between the acquire and the release.

Before we start the formalization of barrier and critical section synchronization, we introduce the relations N and N'. These relations partition the barrier operations and the acquire/release pairs. The partitioning is based on the identification number $id()$. The relation N is extended to a reflexive relation over the set Op.

Definition 7 *equivalence relations N, N'*

$$N \triangleq \{(op\_1, op\_2) \in Bar^2 \mid id(op\_1) = id(op\_2)\} \cup \{(op, op) \mid op \in Op\}$$
$$N' \triangleq \{(a, r) \in (Acq \times Rel) \mid id(a) = id(r)\}$$

Now we can express that barriers are totally ordered per memory location, and that all high- and low-level synchronization operations synchronizing a common memory location have the same ordering in all memory order relations. Also, we require that acquire-release pairs are totally ordered per memory location and neither overlap nor nest.

Condition 4 *order of synchronization operations*

$$\forall m: Mem \cdot (\overset{mo1}{\longrightarrow}/N, \overset{mo2}{\longrightarrow}/N, \ldots, \overset{mon}{\longrightarrow}/N)$$
are seq. consistent relations in $Sync\_m/N$
$$\wedge \quad \forall m: Mem \cdot (\overset{mo1}{\longrightarrow}/N', \overset{mo2}{\longrightarrow}/N', \ldots, \overset{mon}{\longrightarrow}/N')$$
are seq. consistent relations in $Sync\_m/N'$

Acquire and Release Every release requires exactly one matching acquire, but an acquire is allowed to have no matching release. In that case, the release is considered to be past the end of the execution of the thread on the processor of the acquire.

Condition 5 *correct use of acquire and release operations*

$$\forall a: Acq \cdot \forall r\_1, r\_2: Rel \cdot aN'r\_1 \wedge aN'r\_2 \Longrightarrow r\_1 = r\_2$$
$$\wedge \ \forall r: Rel \cdot \exists! \ a: Acq \cdot aN'r$$

Further, matching acquire and release operations have to reference the same set of memory locations and the acquire must be ordered before the release in the program order relation.

Condition 6 *same memory locations for matching acquire and release operations*

$$\forall a: Acq \cdot \forall r: Rel \cdot aN'r \Longrightarrow mem(a) = mem(r)$$

Condition 7 *execution order of matching acquire and release operations*

$$\forall a: Acq \cdot \forall r: Rel \cdot aN'r \Longrightarrow a \xrightarrow{po} r.$$

Also, any operation ordered by program order between the acquire and the release is for every processor also ordered by memory order between the acquire and the release.

Condition 8 *order of accesses to protected locations*

$$\forall a: Acq \cdot \forall r: Rel \cdot aN'r \Longrightarrow \forall op: Op\_mem(a) \cdot$$
$$(a \xrightarrow{po} op \xrightarrow{po} r \Longrightarrow \forall p: P \cdot a \xrightarrow{mo\,p} op \xrightarrow{mo\,p} r)$$
$$\wedge \ \forall a: Acq \cdot (\neg \exists r: Rel \cdot aN'r) \Longrightarrow \forall op: Op\_mem(a) \cdot$$
$$(a \xrightarrow{po} op \Longrightarrow \forall p: P \cdot a \xrightarrow{mo\,p} op)$$

Barriers There are two conditions specific for barriers: any operation of a barrier has to reference the same set of memory locations, and all instructions executed before a barrier are observed before that barrier by any processor, while all instructions executed after a barrier are observed after that barrier.

Condition 9 *same set of locations per barrier*

$$\forall b\_1, b\_2: Bar \cdot b\_1Nb\_2 \Longrightarrow mem(b\_1) = mem(b\_2)$$

Condition 10 *correct barrier and operation ordering*

$$\forall b\_1, b\_2 \cdot Bar. \forall p: P \cdot \forall op: Op\_mem(b\_1) \setminus \{b\_1\} \cdot$$
$$b\_1Nb\_2 \Longrightarrow (op \xrightarrow{po} b\_1 \Longrightarrow op \xrightarrow{mo\,p} b\_2)$$
$$\wedge (b\_1 \xrightarrow{po} op \Longrightarrow b\_2 \xrightarrow{mo\,p} op)$$

5.2.5 Memory Model

The following definition of a shared memory model contains the properties common to any model of a shared memory system.

Definition 8 *memory model*

A memory model *Mod* is a set of executions *E*, where every execution satisfies the general conditions 1, 2, 3, the synchronization conditions 4 to 10, and the model-specific conditions.

5.3 The VDM Specification of the Definitions

In the previous section a shared memory synchronization model is formalized in an informal way. In this section the VDM specification for all the definitions used for this formalization will be composed.

For that purpose the VDM specification support tool of Mural is used.

Mural is an interactive theorem prover and VDM specification support tool. The standard system is equipped with the theory of the VDM primitives. Because this theory is not expressive enough for our application, we added a theory for relations[1] to the parent theories of the specification.

5.3.1 Operations

The first object we have to specify is an operation. For that purpose some new types have to be declared.

A first such type, is the type to which all the terms expressing the kind of an operation can assigned to. We call this type *Type*:

Type = not yet defined.

We say that *Type* is not yet defined because there does not exist a type in the known theories, i.e. the theory of the VDM primitives and the relational theory, which we can use to specify the new type *Type*.

Because all terms that express some kind of an operation are assigned to the type *Type*, we know from section 5.2:

---

[1] This formal theory is described in appendix A

ns: *Type*

nl: *Type*

nf: *Type*

ss: *Type*

sl: *Type*

sf: *Type*

acq: *Type*

rel: *Type*

bar: *Type*

and these are the only terms of the type *Type*.

However, it is not necessary to include this information in the VDM specification. It is sufficient to wait until the VDM specification has been translated into its corresponding formal theory; and then a basic rule containing this information can be added to the set of basic rules of that theory.

In order to specify all possible operations of a particular execution of a parallel program two more types are needed. The first one is:

location = *not yet defined*.

An element of the type *location* is a memory location that can be addressed by an operation. All the allowed memory locations of a particular memory model are grouped in a set called *Mem*. This set is a constant for that memory model. Therefore its specification will be a constant of the form:

Mem: *location*-**set**.

What is stored into a memory location or read from a memory location is an element of the type *value*. This brings us to the second new type:

value = *not yet defined*.

The set of all the values that are allowed for a particular memory model is also a constant. This set is called *Val* and is specified by:

Val: *value*-**set**.

Making use of the previous defined types and constants all the possible operations can be specified.

Because the operations consist of different fields, as we can see in table 5.1, the best suited way to create these specifications is by using a composite type.

The normal store, load and load-modify-store operations

Translating the information of table 5.1, about the normal store operation to a VDM specification results in:

nstore :: *type* : *Type*
$\qquad i$: **N**
$\qquad p$: **N**$_1$
$\qquad M$: *location*-**set**
$\qquad v_s$: *value*

inv (*type*: *Type*, *M*: *location*-**set**, *v_s*: *value*) $\triangleq$
$\qquad type = ns \wedge ((M \subset Mem) \wedge (v_s \in Val))$.

The five fields of the record do not express all the information known about a normal store operation. Therefore an invariant containing the remaining information has been added. This invariant expresses that the type of a normal store operation always has to equal *ns*, and that the set of memory locations *M* has to be a subset of the allowed memory locations of the model and analogously the stored value *v_s* must be an element of the allowed values for this memory model.

The specification of the normal load operation is:

nload :: *type* : *Type*
$\qquad i$: **N**
$\qquad p$: **N**$_1$
$\qquad M$: *location*-**set**
$\qquad v_l$: *value*

inv (*type*: *Type*, *M*: *location*-**set**, *v_l*: *value*) $\triangleq$
$\qquad type = nl \wedge ((M \subset Mem) \wedge (v_l \in Val))$.

To construct the specification of a normal load-modify-store operation a record containing six fields instead of five fields is needed, because the normal load-modify-store operation first loads a value from a memory location and then stores another value to the same memory location. And of course both values have to be a member of the set of the allowed values of the memory model:

nmodify :: *type* : *Type*
$\qquad i$: **N**
$\qquad p$: **N**$_1$
$\qquad M$: *location*-**set**
$\qquad v_l$: *value*
$\qquad v_s$: *value*

inv (*type*: *Type*, *M*: *location*-**set**, *v_l*: *value*, *v_s*: *value*) $\triangleq$
$\qquad type = nf \wedge ((M \subset Mem) \wedge ((v_l \in Val) \wedge (v_s \in Val)))$.

The synchronizing store, load and load-modify-store operations
From table 5.1, it follows that the only difference between the synchronizing store (resp. load, load-modify-store) operation and the normal store (resp. load and load-modify-store) operation is the type field:

$sstore$ :: $type$: $Type$
$\quad\quad\quad\quad\; i$: $\mathbf{N}$
$\quad\quad\quad\quad\; p$: $\mathbf{N}_1$
$\quad\quad\quad , \; M$: $location$-set
$\quad\quad\quad\quad v\_s$: $value$

inv $(type\colon Type, M\colon location\text{-}set, v\_s\colon value) \triangleq$
$\quad type = ss \wedge ((M \subset Mem) \wedge (v\_s \in Val))$

$sload$ :: $type$: $Type$
$\quad\quad\quad\quad i$: $\mathbf{N}$
$\quad\quad\quad\quad p$: $\mathbf{N}_1$
$\quad\quad\quad M$: $location$-set
$\quad\quad\quad v\_l$: $value$

inv $(type\colon Type, M\colon location\text{-}set, v\_l\colon value) \triangleq$
$\quad type = sl \wedge ((M \subset Mem) \wedge (v\_l \in Val))$

$smodify$ :: $type$: $Type$
$\quad\quad\quad\quad\; i$: $\mathbf{N}$
$\quad\quad\quad\quad\; p$: $\mathbf{N}_1$
$\quad\quad\quad\; M$: $location$-set
$\quad\quad\quad\; v\_l$: $value$
$\quad\quad\quad\; v\_s$: $value$

inv $(type\colon Type, M\colon location\text{-}set, v\_l\colon value, v\_s\colon value) \triangleq$
$\quad type = sf \wedge ((M \subset Mem) \wedge ((v\_l \in Val) \wedge (v\_s \in Val)))$.

The acquire, release and barrier operations

There are three more operations left to specify. These are the acquire, release and barrier operations. They are called *high-level synchronizing* operations. Again, their specification will consist of a record, containing five fields, and an invariant explaining what properties the fields have to fulfill:

$acquire$ :: $type$: $Type$
$\quad\quad\quad\quad\; i$: $\mathbf{N}$
$\quad\quad\quad\quad\; p$: $\mathbf{N}_1$
$\quad\quad\quad\; M$: $location$-set
$\quad\quad\quad\; j$: $\mathbf{N}$

inv $(M\colon location\text{-}set, type\colon Type) \triangleq$
$\quad type = acq \wedge (M \subset Mem)$

$release$ :: $type$: $Type$
$\quad\quad\quad\quad i$: $\mathbf{N}$
$\quad\quad\quad\quad p$: $\mathbf{N}_1$
$\quad\quad\quad M$: $location$-set
$\quad\quad\quad j$: $\mathbf{N}$

inv $(type\colon Type, M\colon location\text{-}set) \triangleq$
$\quad type = rel \wedge (M \subset Mem)$

$$barrier :: type : Type$$
$$i : \mathbf{N}$$
$$p : \mathbf{N}_1$$
$$M : location\text{-set}$$
$$j : \mathbf{N}$$

inv $(type: Type, M: location\text{-set}) \triangleq$
  $type = bar \wedge (M \subset Mem).$

We still need to specify many functions before we can formalize our memory model. To make the specification of these functions a little easier some more types are defined. These new types are the union of previously declared types.
A first new type is the type *OPs* which collects all the store operations:

$OPs = nstore \mid sstore.$

Similarly we specify a type *OPl* for all load operations and a type *OPf* for all load-modify-store operations:

$OPl = nload \mid sload$

$OPf = nmodify \mid smodify.$

The type *OPsync* brings together all the elements of the type *acquire, release* and *barrier*:

$OPsync = acquire \mid release \mid barrier.$

Finally we introduce a union type that collects all kind of operations. This type is called *OP*. Making use of the previous definitions the specification of the type *OP* becomes:

$OP = OPs \mid OPl \mid OPf \mid OPsync.$

For the same reason some new types were defined, we also declare some useful functions.

5.3.2 Useful Functions

A first selected function is the function *type*. This function maps an element of the type *OP* to an element of the type *Type*; the image of a given operation under the function *type* is the type of that operation.
To which kind an operation belongs to, can be found in the first field of its corresponding record. The function associated with the first field of an operation record is the function *s-type*:

$type : OP \rightarrow Type$

$type(op) \triangleq s\text{-}type(op).$

The difference between the function *type* and the function *s-type* is: *type* is defined for all elements of the type OP and *s-type* is defined for all kinds of operations (i.e. normal load, normal store, ...) separately.

Some other useful functions are the functions *num*(), *proc*(), *mem*(), *val_l*() and *val_s*() mentioned in section 5.2. The VDM notation for these functions is similar to the previous specification:

$num : OP \rightarrow Type$

$num(op) \quad \triangleq \quad s\text{-}i(op).$

$proc : OP \rightarrow \mathbf{N}_1$

$proc(op) \quad \triangleq \quad s\text{-}p(op).$

$mem : OP \rightarrow location\text{-}\mathbf{set}$

$mem(op) \quad \triangleq \quad s\text{-}M(op).$

$val\text{-}l : OPl \mid OPf \rightarrow value$

$val\text{-}l(op) \quad \triangleq \quad s\text{-}v\_l(op).$

$val\text{-}s : OPs \mid OPf \rightarrow value$

$val\text{-}s(op) \quad \triangleq \quad s\text{-}v\_s(op).$

The last of these functions is *id* which maps a synchronizing operation to its identification number:

$id : OPsync \rightarrow \mathbf{N}$

$id(op) \quad \triangleq \quad s\text{-}j(op).$

By making use of the specifications of all these functions and types, we can specify one particular execution of a parallel program satisfying a given memory model.

5.3.3   The Program Order and Executions

Because the program order relation $\overset{po}{\rightarrow}$ depends of an execution E, the notion execution has to be specified before the program order. Once the object execution is specified the program order can be derived from this specification.

A Program Execution

A program execution describes one particular execution of a parallel program for a given memory model. The definition of an execution E given in section 5.2.1 is a tuple satisfying some restrictions. Therefore a record and an invariant will be used for the VDM specification.

At first glance it seems that there are only two fields needed in the record: a first component being the set Op of all operations that have been executed during a particular execution E and a second component being a set po of pairs of operations. This set of pairs will define the program order of the execution when its elements satisfy the following three conditions:

- not only the first but also the last component of all the pairs must be an element of the previously defined set Op;

- both components of a pair must have been executed on the same processor;

- the operation number of the first component of a pair must be less than or equal to the operation number of the second component of that pair.

However, these two components together with their restrictions are not sufficient to specify an execution. We need a third component, namely a natural number n, different from zero, declaring the number of processors used for that particular execution of the parallel program. Knowing the number of processors used, we can formulate one more condition the execution has to satisfy: i.e. every operation of Op has to be executed on a processor used for the execution.

Bringing all this information together in a record with an invariant, results in:

$Execution$ :: Op : OP-**set**
$\qquad\qquad\quad$ po : $OP \times OP$-**set**
$\qquad\qquad\quad$ n : $\mathbf{N}_1$

inv $(Op{:}\ OP\text{-}\mathbf{set}, po{:}\ OP \times OP\text{-}\mathbf{set}, n{:}\ \mathbf{N}_1) \triangleq$
$\quad \forall a{:}\ OP \cdot a \in Op \ \Rightarrow\ (proc(a) \le n) \wedge$
$\quad \forall k{:}\ OP \times OP \cdot$
$\quad k \in po \ \Leftrightarrow\ (k \in Prod(Op, Op)) \wedge$
$\quad (proc(fst(k)) = proc(snd(k)) \wedge (num(fst(k)) \le num(snd(k))))$.

The Program Order and Per Processor Program Order

The program order po is one of the three defining components of an execution E. Therefore we do not need to specify the program order explicitly: for a given execution E the program order is specified by $s\text{-}po(E)$.

The program order is defined for all the operations of an execution. The per processor order only considers those operations that are executed on one particular processor of an execution.

Similarly to the program order, the per processor order is also specified as a set of pairs with each pair of the set satisfying four conditions:

- the first three conditions are the same as the conditions for the elements of the program order;

- the fourth condition expresses that all the operations of all the pairs must be executed on the same processor p.

To specify this set of pairs we use a function $Po\text{-}p$. This function depends on two variables: a particular execution E and a processor p used for the execution E:

$Po\text{-}p$ $(p\colon \mathbf{N}_1, E\colon Execution)$ $R\colon OP \times OP\text{-}$**set**

pre $p \leq s\text{-}n(E)$

post $\forall k\colon OP \times OP \cdot k \in R \Leftrightarrow$
$\quad (k \in Prod(s\text{-}Op(E), s\text{-}Op(E))) \wedge ((proc(fst(k)) = proc(snd(k))$
$\quad \wedge proc(snd(k)) = p) \wedge (num(fst(k)) \leq num(snd(k)))).$

Knowing the VDM specification of an execution, all the instructions S_n, L_n, F_n, S_s, L_s, F_s, Acq, Rel, and Bar, which were mentioned in section 5.2, and some more can also be specified.

Sets of Operations

A first set to be specified is the set $S\text{-}n(E)$ of all normal store operations executed during a particular execution E of a parallel program. Because all normal store operations of an execution are also operations of that execution, it is obvious that the set of all normal store operations executed in E is a subset of the set $s\text{-}Op(E)$. And vice versa when a normal store operation is an element of $s\text{-}Op(E)$ then it is a normal store operation executed by E. This means that:

Sn $(E\colon Execution)$ $v\colon nstore\text{-}$**set**

post $\forall s\colon nstore \cdot s \in v \Leftrightarrow s \in s\text{-}Op(E).$

The set $Ln(E)$ (resp. $Fn(E)$) of all normal load (resp. load-modify-store) operations of E, and the set $Ss(E)$ (resp. $Ls(E)$, $Fs(E)$) of all synchronizing store (resp. load, load-modify-store) operations are specified analogously:

Ln $(E\colon Execution)$ $v\colon nload\text{-}$**set**

post $\forall l\colon nload \cdot l \in v \Leftrightarrow l \in s\text{-}Op(E)$

Fn $(E\colon Execution)$ $v\colon nmodify\text{-}$**set**

post $\forall f\colon nmodify \cdot f \in v \Leftrightarrow f \in s\text{-}Op(E)$

Ss $(E\colon Execution)$ $v\colon sstore\text{-}$**set**

post $\forall s\colon sstore \cdot s \in v \Leftrightarrow s \in s\text{-}Op(E)$

Ls (*E*: *Execution*) *v*: *sload*-**set**
post $\forall l$: *sload* $\cdot l \in v \iff l \in s\text{-}Op(E)$

Fs (*E*: *Execution*) *v*: *smodify*-**set**
post $\forall f$: *smodify* $\cdot f \in v \iff f \in s\text{-}Op(E)$.

The same can be done for the set containing all the acquire $Acq(E)$ (resp. release $Rel(E)$, barrier $Bar(E)$) operations of an execution E:

Acq (*E*: *Execution*) *v*: *acquire*-**set**
post $\forall a$: *acquire* $\cdot a \in v \iff a \in s\text{-}Op(E)$

Rel (*E*: *Execution*) *v*: *release*-**set**
post $\forall r$: *release* $\cdot r \in v \iff r \in s\text{-}Op(E)$

Bar (*E*: *Execution*) *v*: *barrier*-**set**
post $\forall b$: *barrier* $\cdot b \in v \iff b \in s\text{-}Op(E)$.

In furtherance of the next specifications, it is useful to specify the union of some previously specified sets: for example the set $S(E)$ of all store operations of an execution E and the set $L(E)$ of all load operations of E:

S : *Execution* $\to$ *OP*-**set**
$S(E) \triangleq (Sn(E) \cup Fn(E)) \cup (Ss(E) \cup Fs(E))$

L : *Execution* $\to$ *OP*-**set**
$L(E) \triangleq (Ln(E) \cup Fn(E)) \cup (Ls(E) \cup Fs(E))$.

Other sets that might be useful in the future are the set $SyncL(E)$ of all low-level synchronizing operations and the set $SyncH(E)$ of all high-level synchronizing operations:

$SyncL$: *Execution* $\to$ *OP*-**set**
$SyncL(E) \triangleq (Ss(E) \cup Ls(E)) \cup Fs(E)$

$SyncH$: *Execution* $\to$ *OP*-**set**
$SyncH(E) \triangleq (Acq(E) \cup Rel(E)) \cup Bar(E)$.

The union of the two previous sets is $Sync(E)$, the set of all synchronizing operations of a particular execution E:

Sync : *Execution* → *OP*-**set**

$Sync(E) \quad \triangleq \quad SyncL(E) \cup SyncH(E).$

All the previously declared sets group operations of the same kind. Now, instead of grouping operations of a same '*Type*', some other properties are used to classify the operations of an execution E.

For instance, the set $Op\text{-}p(E)$ brings together all the operations of an execution E executed on a same processor p; where p is a processor used for the execution E:

Op-p $(p: \mathbf{N}_1, E: \text{Execution})$ v: *OP*-**set**
pre $p \leq s\text{-}n(E)$
post $\forall op: OP \cdot op \in v \;\Leftrightarrow\; proc(op) = p \wedge (op \in s\text{-}Op(E)).$

The pre-condition of this function expresses that p needs to be a processor used for the given execution E.

$Op\text{-}M(E)$ is the set of all the operations of an execution E accessing at least a given set of memory locations M, with M a subset of all the allowed memory locations *Mem*:

Op-M $(M: \text{location-}\mathbf{set}, E: \text{Execution})$ v: *OP*-**set**
pre $M \subseteq Mem$
post $\forall op: OP \cdot op \in v \;\Leftrightarrow\; (M \subseteq mem(op)) \wedge (op \in s\text{-}Op(E)).$

The intersection of the two previous sets is called $Op\text{-}Mp(M, p, E)$:

Op-Mp : *location* × $\mathbf{N}_1$ × *Execution* → *OP*-**set**

$Op\text{-}Mp(M, p, E) \quad \triangleq \quad Op\text{-}M(M, E) \cap Op\text{-}p(p, E)$

pre $(M \subseteq Mem) \wedge (p \leq s\text{-}n(E)).$

The function $Op\text{-}m$ returns the set of all operations of an execution E accessing at least a single given memory location m. Using the function $Op\text{-}M$ its specification is straightforward:

Op-m : *location* × *Execution* → *OP*-**set**

$Op\text{-}m(m, E) \quad \triangleq \quad Op\text{-}M(\{m\}, E)$

pre $m \in Mem.$

The specification of the set $Op\text{-}mp(m, p, E)$ of all operations accessing at least a single memory location m on processor p is:

$Op\text{-}mp : location \times \mathbf{N}_1 \times Execution \rightarrow OP\text{-}\mathbf{set}$

$Op\text{-}mp(m, p, E) \;\triangleq\; Op\text{-}Mp(\{m\}, p, E)$

pre $(m \in Mem) \wedge (p \leq s\text{-}n(E))$.

For later purpose some of these sets are defined for load and synchronizing operations only:

$L\text{-}p\ (p\!:\mathbf{N}_1, E\!: Execution)\ v\!: OP\text{-}\mathbf{set}$
pre $p \leq s\text{-}n(E)$
post $\forall op\!: OP \cdot op \in v \;\Leftrightarrow\; proc(op) = p \wedge (op \in L(E))$

$L\text{-}m\ (m\!: location, E\!: Execution)\ v\!: OP\text{-}\mathbf{set}$
pre $m \in Mem$
post $\forall op\!: OP \cdot op \in v \;\Leftrightarrow\; (m \in mem(op)) \wedge (op \in L(E))$

$L\text{-}mp : location \times \mathbf{N}_1 \times Execution \rightarrow OP\text{-}\mathbf{set}$
$L\text{-}mp(m, p, E) \;\triangleq\; L\text{-}m(m, E) \cap L\text{-}p(p, E)$
pre $(m \in Mem) \wedge (p \leq s\text{-}n(E))$

$Sync\text{-}m\ (m\!: location, E\!: Execution)\ v\!: OP\text{-}\mathbf{set}$
pre $m \in Mem$
post $\forall op\!: OP \cdot op \in v \;\Leftrightarrow\; (m \in mem(op)) \wedge (op \in Sync(E))$.

Although there is not much mentioned about the memory order in the formalization, a specification of the memory order is indispensable to express the conditions a memory model has to fulfill.

5.3.4   Memory Order

Since the memory order relation is specified as a set of restrictions on a partial order relation, the only explicit information we have about the memory order $MO\text{-}p(p, E)$ is that it is a partial order:

$MO\text{-}p\ (p\!:\mathbf{N}_1, E\!: Execution)\ R\!: OP \times OP\text{-}\mathbf{set}$
pre $p \leq s\text{-}n(E)$
post $R \subseteq Prod(s\text{-}Op(E), s\text{-}Op(E)) \wedge PartOrder(R, s\text{-}Op(E))$.

More properties of this order are revealed in the following conditions.

5.3.5 Uniprocessor Correctness

The uniprocessor correctness is formalized through a property of the memory model. This property is not necessary to specify the memory model, it only expresses a property of the model. However to be sure the model satisfies this condition a basic rule, associated with the condition, will be added to the set of inference rules of the formal theory corresponding with the specification of the memory model.

The same remark can be made for all the conditions mentioned in the section 5.2.

5.3.6 The Result of a Load

Although there is no need for a specification of the value condition, some definitions appearing in this condition have to be declared:

hist $(l: OPl \mid OPf, E: Execution)$ $v: OPs \mid OPf$-**set**
pre $l \in L(E)$
post $\forall s: OPs \mid OPf \cdot s \in v \iff$
  $(s \in S(E)) \wedge ((mem(l) \subseteq mem(s)) \wedge$
  $(s \neq l \wedge (pair(s, l) \in MO\text{-}p(proc(l), E))))$.

prev $(l: OPl \mid OPf, E: Execution)$ $v: OPs \mid OPf$-**set**
pre $l \in L(E)$
post $\forall s: OPs \mid OPf \cdot s \in v$
  $\iff (s \in hist(l, E)) \wedge \forall s': OPs \mid OPf \cdot s' \in (hist(l, E) - \{s\})$
  $\Rightarrow pair(s, s') \notin MO\text{-}p(proc(l), E)$.

Also the shared memory condition introduces a new definition: the access order. To specify the definition of the access order, the access order at every memory location, *Ao-m*, has to be declared first:

Ao-m $(m: location, E: Execution)$ $R: OP \times OP$-**set**
post $\forall k: OP \times OP \cdot k \in R \iff \exists p: N_1 \cdot$
  $k \in MO\text{-}p(p, E) \wedge (k \in Prod(Op\text{-}M(\{m\}, E), Op\text{-}M(\{m\}, E)))$.

The previous result helps to specify the access order:

Ao $(E: Execution)$ $R: OP \times OP$-**set**
post $\forall k: OP \times OP \cdot k \in R \iff \exists m: location \cdot k \in Ao\text{-}m(m, E)$.

5.3.7 Synchronization Operations

To describe most conditions the memory model has to comply with, synchronization operations and some relations grouping these operations are needed. The synchronization operations have been specified before, now we still have to consider the relations.

The first relation concerns barrier operations, the second relation groups acquire and release operations which belong together:

N $(E: Execution)$ $N: OP \times OP$-**set**
post $\forall k: OP \times OP \cdot k \in N \Leftrightarrow$
$\qquad (k \in Prod(Bar(E), Bar(E))) \wedge id(fst(k)) = id(snd(k))$
$\qquad \vee (k \in Prod(s\text{-}Op(E), s\text{-}Op(E))) \wedge fst(k) = snd(k);$

N' $(E: Execution)$ $N': OP \times OP$-**set**
post $\forall k: OP \times OP \cdot k \in N'$
$\qquad \Leftrightarrow (k \in Prod(Acq(E), Rel(E))) \wedge id(fst(k)) = id(snd(k)).$

And finally our goal is reached, a memory model can be specified !

5.3.8 Memory Model

A memory model is a set of executions, therefore the type *Model*, every memory model can be assigned to is:

$Model = Execution$-**set**.

Of course all the executions which are an element of a memory model need to satisfy a few conditions. To make sure that these conditions are satisfied the set of basic rules of the formal theory corresponding to the specification of the memory model has to be extended.

5.4 A Formal Theory for Shared Memory Synchronization

5.4.1 The Formal Language

In the previous section a VDM specification for the formalization of a memory model has been presented. To determine the formal language of the formal theory corresponding to this specification, Mural comes to assist. More precisely, the translation from the specification to its corresponding formal theory happens automatically in Mural.

The automatic translation of our specification generates the demanded formal language together with a set of inference rules. However this set of inference rules is not sufficient to establish the formal theory of the considered memory model, as will be explained hereafter.

5.4.2 The Set of Inference Rules

The set of inference rules produced by Mural contains all the basic rules and some derived rules, known as proof obligations, corresponding with the translated specification. However, the specification presented in the previous section does not contain all the information available on the memory model since the ten conditions, the model has to satisfy, were not added to the specification. As mentioned before, these conditions have to be annexed to the set of basic rules.

Therefore we have to rewrite them in a more formal way:

Condition 1 *uniprocessor data dependences:*

$$E\text{: }Execution,\, m\text{: }location,\, m \in Mem,\, op1\text{: }OP,\, op2\text{: }OP,$$

$$\boxed{\text{condition 1}}\quad \frac{op1 \in Op\text{-}m(m, E),\, op2 \in Op\text{-}m(m, E),\, p\text{: }N_1,\, p \leq s\text{-}n(E)}{((op1, op2) \in Po\text{-}p(p, E)) \;\Rightarrow\; ((op1, op2) \in MO\text{-}p(p, E))}$$

Condition 2 *value condition:*

$$l\text{: }(OPl \mid OPf),\, s\text{: }(OPs \mid OPf),$$

$$\boxed{\text{condition 2}}\quad \frac{E\text{: }Execution,\, l \in L(E),\, s \in prev(l, E)}{val\text{-}l(l) = val\text{-}s(s)}$$

Condition 3 *shared memory condition.*
This condition describes two properties of the memory model. The first property expresses that the memory order relations on all the several processors must be consistent for all memory locations:

$$E\text{: }Execution,\, m\text{: }location,\, m \in Mem,\, R\text{: }(((OP \times OP)\text{-}\mathbf{set})\text{-}\mathbf{set}),$$

$$R = \{ Ri\text{: }(OP \times OP)\text{-}\mathbf{set} \mid$$

$$\boxed{\text{condition 3A}}\quad \frac{\exists p\text{: }N_1 \cdot (p \leq s\text{-}n(E)) \wedge (Ri = MO\text{-}p(p, E)) \})}{consistent\text{-}Rel(R, Op\text{-}m(m, E))}$$

The second property demands that the access order is a partial order relation:

$$\boxed{\text{condition 3B}}\quad \frac{E\text{: }Execution}{PartOrder(Ao(E),\, s\text{-}Op(E))}$$

Condition 4 *order of synchronization operations.*
The fact that barrier, acquire, release and low-level synchronization operations are totally ordered per memory location is expressed in a first rule:

$$m: location, m \in Mem, E: Execution,$$
$$R: ((((OP\text{-set}) \times (OP\text{-set}))\text{-set})\text{-set}),$$
$$R = (\{Ri: ((OP\text{-set}) \times (OP\text{-set}))\text{-set} \mid \exists p: \mathbf{N}_1 \cdot$$

$$\boxed{\text{condition 4A}}\; \frac{(p \leq s\text{-}n(E)) \wedge (Ri = QuotRel(MO\text{-}p(p, E), N(E), s\text{-}Op(E)))\})}{seq\text{-}const\text{-}Rel(R, partition(Sync\text{-}m(m, E), N(E)))}$$

A second rule involves only acquire and release operations:

$$m: location, m \in Mem, E: Execution,$$
$$R: ((((OP\text{-set}) \times (OP\text{-set}))\text{-set})\text{-set}),$$
$$R = (\{Ri: ((OP\text{-set}) \times (OP\text{-set}))\text{-set} \mid \exists p: \mathbf{N}_1 \cdot$$

$$\boxed{\text{condition 4B}}\; \frac{(p \leq s\text{-}n(E)) \wedge (Ri = QuotRel(MO\text{-}p(p, E), N'(E), s\text{-}Op(E)))\})}{seq\text{-}const\text{-}Rel(R, partition(Sync\text{-}m(m, E), N'(E)))}$$

Condition 5 *correct use of acquire and release operations.*

$$\boxed{\text{condition 5A}}\; \frac{a: acquire, E: Execution, r1: release, r2: release}{(((a, r1) \in N'(E)) \wedge ((a, r2) \in N'(E))) \;\Rightarrow\; (r1 = r2)}$$

$$\boxed{\text{condition 5B}}\; \frac{r: release, E: Execution, r \in Rel(E)}{\exists!\, a: acquire \cdot (a, r) \in N'(E)}$$

Condition 6 *same memory locations for matching acquire and release operations.*

$$\boxed{\text{condition 6}}\; \frac{a: acquire, r: release, E: Execution}{((a, r) \in N'(E)) \;\Rightarrow\; (mem(a) = mem(r))}$$

Condition 7 *execution order of matching acquire and release operations.*

$$\boxed{\text{condition 7}}\; \frac{a: acquire, r: release, E: Execution}{((a, r) \in N'(E)) \;\Rightarrow\; ((a, r) \in s\text{-}po(E))}$$

Condition 8 *order of accesses to protected locations*
The first part deals with the situation in which an acquire operation has a matching release operation:

$$\boxed{\text{condition 8A}}\; \frac{a: acquire, r: release, E: Execution}{((a, r) \in N'(E)) \;\Rightarrow}$$
$$(\forall op: OP \cdot (op \in Op\text{-}m(mem(a), E)) \;\Rightarrow$$
$$((((a, op) \in s\text{-}Op(E)) \wedge ((op, r) \in s\text{-}Op(E))) \;\Rightarrow$$
$$(\forall p: \mathbf{N}_1 \cdot (p \leq s\text{-}n(E)) \;\Rightarrow$$
$$(a, op) \in MO\text{-}p(p, E) \wedge ((op, r) \in MO\text{-}p(p, E)))))$$

The second part concerns the situation for which an acquire has no matching release:

condition 8B
$$\frac{a: acquire,\, E: Execution}{(\neg\,(\exists r: release \cdot (a, r) \in N'(E))) \Rightarrow}$$
$$(\forall op: OP \cdot (op \in Op\text{-}m(mem(a), E)) \Rightarrow$$
$$(((a, op) \in s\text{-}Op(E)) \Rightarrow$$
$$(\forall p: N_1 \cdot (p \le s\text{-}n(E)) \Rightarrow ((a, op) \in MO\text{-}p(p, E)))))$$

Condition 9   *same set of locations per barrier.*

condition 9
$$\frac{b1: barrier,\, b2: barrier,\, E: Execution}{((b1, b2) \in N(E)) \Rightarrow (mem(b1) = mem(b2))}$$

Condition 10   *correct barrier and operation ordering*

condition 10
$$\frac{b1: barrier,\, b2: barrier,\, E: Execution,\, p: N_1,\, p \le s\text{-}n(E),}{op: OP,\, op \in Op\text{-}m(mem(b1), E),\, \neg\,(b1 = op)}{((b1, b2) \in N(E)) \Rightarrow}$$
$$(((((op, b1) \in s\text{-}Op(E)) \Rightarrow ((op, b2) \in MO\text{-}p(p, E)))$$
$$\wedge$$
$$(((b1, op) \in s\text{-}Op(E)) \Rightarrow ((b2, op) \in MO\text{-}p(p, E))))$$

Everything, that was formalized previously, is captured in the formal theory except for one fact.

Type Definition

The first type specified in this text was the type *Type*. In the section 5.2 some information about this type was given. However not all this information was added to the specification because it seemed better to express it in a basic rule:

Type definition
$$\frac{t: Type}{((((t = ns) \vee (t = nl)) \vee (t = nf)) \vee}$$
$$(((t = ss) \vee (t = sl)) \vee (t = sf))) \vee$$
$$(((t = acq) \vee (t = rel)) \vee (t = bar))$$

All these basic rules together with the basic rules and formal language generated by Mural determine the formal theory of the formalized memory model.

5.4.3   A Proof

To check the usefulness of the previous formal theory, a basic property of this memory model is studied:

property po-p 1
$$\frac{p: N_1,\, p \le s\text{-}n(E),\, E: Execution}{Po\text{-}p(p, E) \subseteq s\text{-}po(E)}$$

This rule was also mentioned in section 5.2.1. It expresses that the per processor order is contained in the program order, which can be accepted intuitively.

```
from
h1      p: N₁
h2      p ≤ s-n(E)
h3      E: Execution

1       s-po(E): ((OP × OP)-set)              s-po(Execution)-formation(h3)
2       pre-Po-p(p, E)                                      folding (h2)
3       ∃R: (OP × OP)-set · post-Po-p(p, E, R)
                                              Po-p implementability(h1, h3, 2)
4       Po-p(p, E): ((OP × OP)-set)            Po-p formation(h1, h3, 2, 3)

        from
5.h1        a: (OP × OP)
5.h2        a ∈ Po-p(p, E)

        infer a ∈ s-po(E)                     lemma po-p 1(h1, h2, 5.h1, 5.h2, h3)

infer Po-p(p, E) ⊆ s-po(E)                                        ⊆-I(4, 1, 5)
```

Figure 5.5: Proof of 'property po-p 1'

Deriving the proof will show whether our intuition about the triviality of the property is valid or not. To construct the corresponding proof[2] of the rule the interactive theorem prover of Mural is used. We obtain the proof in Figure 5.5. In this proof we introduced a lemma that will be proven separately.

Lemma

The lemma introduced in the proof is as follows:

$$\boxed{\text{lemma po-p 1}} \frac{p: \mathbf{N}_1, p \leq s\text{-}n(E), a: (OP \times OP), a \in Po\text{-}p(p, E), E: Execution}{a \in s\text{-}po(E)}$$

Proving this lemma in its turn, results in the proof in Figures 5.6 and 5.7. The fact that this proof is rather long makes us revise our first impression about the triviality of the proved property.

---

[2]The inference rules, from the formal theory of the memory model, used in the proof are printed in appendix B

from
h1 $p : \mathbf{N}_1$
h2 $p \leq s\text{-}n(E)$
h3 $a : (OP \times OP)$
h4 $a \in Po\text{-}p(p, E)$
h5 $E : Execution$

1     $pre\text{-}Po\text{-}p(p, E)$ folding (h2)

2     $\exists R : (OP \times OP)\text{-}\mathbf{set} \cdot post\text{-}Po\text{-}p(p, E, R)$
                                             Po-p implementability(h1, h5, 1)

3     $post\text{-}Po\text{-}p(p, E, Po\text{-}p(p, E))$ Po-p specification(h1, h5, 1, 2)

4     $\forall k : OP \times OP \cdot (k \in Po\text{-}p(p, E)) \Leftrightarrow$
       $((k \in Prod(s\text{-}Op(E), s\text{-}Op(E))) \wedge$
       $(((proc(\mathbf{fst}\ k) = proc(\mathbf{snd}\ k)) \wedge (proc(\mathbf{snd}\ k) = p)) \wedge$
       $(num(\mathbf{fst}\ k) \leq num(\mathbf{snd}\ k))))$ unfolding (3)

5     $(a \in Po\text{-}p(p, E)) \Leftrightarrow$
       $((a \in Prod(s\text{-}Op(E), s\text{-}Op(E))) \wedge$
       $(((proc(\mathbf{fst}\ a) = proc(\mathbf{snd}\ a)) \wedge (proc(\mathbf{snd}\ a) = p)) \wedge$
       $(num(\mathbf{fst}\ a) \leq num(\mathbf{snd}\ a))))$ $\forall$-E(4, h3)

6     $(a \in Prod(s\text{-}Op(E), s\text{-}Op(E))) \wedge$
       $(((proc(\mathbf{fst}\ a) = proc(\mathbf{snd}\ a)) \wedge (proc(\mathbf{snd}\ a) = p)) \wedge$
       $(num(\mathbf{fst}\ a) \leq num(\mathbf{snd}\ a)))$ $\Leftrightarrow$ -E-left(5, h4)

7     $a \in Prod(s\text{-}Op(E), s\text{-}Op(E))$ $\wedge$-E-right(6)

8     $((proc(\mathbf{fst}\ a) = proc(\mathbf{snd}\ a)) \wedge (proc(\mathbf{snd}\ a) = p)) \wedge$
       $(num(\mathbf{fst}\ a) \leq num(\mathbf{snd}\ a))$ $\wedge$-E-left(6)

9     $num(\mathbf{fst}\ a) \leq num(\mathbf{snd}\ a)$ $\wedge$-E-left(8)

10   $(proc(\mathbf{fst}\ a) = proc(\mathbf{snd}\ a)) \wedge (proc(\mathbf{snd}\ a) = p)$ $\wedge$-E-right(8)

11   $proc(\mathbf{fst}\ a) = proc(\mathbf{snd}\ a)$ $\wedge$-E-right(10)

12   $mk\text{-}Execution(s\text{-}Op(E), s\text{-}po(E), s\text{-}n(E)) = E$
                                       Execution-introduction(h5)

13   $mk\text{-}Execution(s\text{-}Op(E), s\text{-}po(E), s\text{-}n(E)) : Execution$
                                      =-type-inherit-left(h5, 12)

14   $inv\text{-}Execution(s\text{-}Op(E), s\text{-}po(E), s\text{-}n(E))$
                                       inv-Execution-deduction(13)

15   $s\text{-}Op(E) : (OP\text{-}\mathbf{set})$ s-Op(Execution)-formation(h5)

16   $s\text{-}po(E) : ((OP \times OP)\text{-}\mathbf{set})$ s-po(Execution)-formation(h5)

17   $s\text{-}n(E) : \mathbf{N}_1$ s-n(Execution)-formation(h5)

Figure 5.6: First part of proof of 'lemma po-p 1'

18    $((\forall a \colon OP \cdot (a \in s\text{-}Op(E)) \Rightarrow (proc(a) \leq s\text{-}n(E))) \wedge$
      $(\forall k \colon OP \times OP \cdot (k \in s\text{-}po(E)) \Leftrightarrow$
      $((k \in Prod(s\text{-}Op(E), s\text{-}Op(E))) \wedge ((proc(\mathbf{fst}\ k) = proc(\mathbf{snd}\ k)) \wedge$
      $(num(\mathbf{fst}\ k) \leq num(\mathbf{snd}\ k)))))) \colon \mathbf{B}$

inv-Execution wff(15, 16, 17)

19    $inv\text{-}Execution(s\text{-}Op(E), s\text{-}po(E), s\text{-}n(E)) =$
      $((\forall a \colon OP \cdot (a \in s\text{-}Op(E)) \Rightarrow (proc(a) \leq s\text{-}n(E))) \wedge$
      $(\forall k \colon OP \times OP \cdot (k \in s\text{-}po(E)) \Leftrightarrow$
      $((k \in Prod(s\text{-}Op(E), s\text{-}Op(E))) \wedge ((proc(\mathbf{fst}\ k) = proc(\mathbf{snd}\ k)) \wedge$
      $(num(\mathbf{fst}\ k) \leq num(\mathbf{snd}\ k))))))$

inv-Execution definition(15, 16, 17, 18)

20    $(\forall a \colon OP \cdot (a \in s\text{-}Op(E)) \Rightarrow (proc(a) \leq s\text{-}n(E))) \wedge$
      $(\forall k \colon OP \times OP \cdot (k \in s\text{-}po(E)) \Leftrightarrow$
      $((k \in Prod(s\text{-}Op(E), s\text{-}Op(E))) \wedge ((proc(\mathbf{fst}\ k) = proc(\mathbf{snd}\ k)) \wedge$
      $(num(\mathbf{fst}\ k) \leq num(\mathbf{snd}\ k)))))$ =-subs-right(b)(18, 19, 14)

21    $\forall k \colon OP \times OP \cdot (k \in s\text{-}po(E)) \Leftrightarrow$
      $((k \in Prod(s\text{-}Op(E), s\text{-}Op(E))) \wedge ((proc(\mathbf{fst}\ k) = proc(\mathbf{snd}\ k)) \wedge$
      $(num(\mathbf{fst}\ k) \leq num(\mathbf{snd}\ k))))$ $\wedge$-E-left(20)

22    $(a \in s\text{-}po(E)) \Leftrightarrow$
      $((a \in Prod(s\text{-}Op(E), s\text{-}Op(E))) \wedge ((proc(\mathbf{fst}\ a) = proc(\mathbf{snd}\ a)) \wedge$
      $(num(\mathbf{fst}\ a) \leq num(\mathbf{snd}\ a))))$ $\forall$-E(21, h3)

23    $(a \in Prod(s\text{-}Op(E), s\text{-}Op(E))) \wedge ((proc(\mathbf{fst}\ a) = proc(\mathbf{snd}\ a)) \wedge$
      $(num(\mathbf{fst}\ a) \leq num(\mathbf{snd}\ a)))$ $\wedge$-I-three(7, 11, 9)

infer $a \in s\text{-}po(E)$ $\Leftrightarrow$ -E-right(22, 23)

Figure 5.7: Second part of proof of 'lemma po-p 1'

5.5   Discussion

The goal of this chapter was to prove some properties of a shared memory synchronization model in a formal way. To obtain this goal we started from the informal description of the memory model. This formalization contains all the information one has to know to compose the corresponding VDM specification. On the other hand writing down the VDM specification may help to detect some inaccuracies of the model. Having determined the VDM specification, the translation from the specification to its corresponding formal theory can be made. At this point the assistance of Mural is called in.

As mentioned before, Mural translates a VDM specification automatically to its corresponding formal theory: i.e. the system generates the formal language and the set of inference rules of the theory. The set of inference rules contains the basic rules, which define the relation between the formal language and the deduction calculus, as well as some derived rules. The derived rules are the proof obligations following from the function and constant definitions of the VDM specification. These proof obligations can be used to prove other properties of the theory before their proof has been derived. To show the correctness of the property discussed in section 5.4.3 we have made use of some proof obligations. In order to develop the proof the theorem prover available in Mural was used. This theorem prover is not at all an automatic theorem prover, it is more an interactive proof tool. This means it can give suggestions for the verification of a certain line in a proof, but most of the thinking comes from the user. However using a theorem prover is still advantageous because of the certainty one gets about the consistency of a developed proof in the considered theory.

The property we have proved, seemed to be trivial at first sight, but writing down its formal proof showed the opposite. Note that proving such theorems can be quite educative, since deriving such a proof can help the specifier to see which are the obstacles in the model's formalization to prove the property in an easier way. This information can be used to rewrite the original VDM specification as a more straightforward specification. In doing so a VDM development has been created for which a retrieve function must be defined to be sure that the new specification is a correct reification of the first. Of course, the more experience someone has, the fewer refinements he will have to write.

As a global conclusion we can state that VDM is a useful specification language. Starting from an informal text the translation to the corresponding VDM specification is straightforward. Look for example at the specification of all the different kinds of operations: to compose such a specification we only had to change the informal n-tuple, by which the operation is formalized, into a record consisting of n fields and an invariant. The invariant is required to express all the remaining information about the operation. The usefulness of a specification support tool and/or theorem prover for these kind of assignments is indisputable, even if they are only used to guarantee the consistency of the newly specified objects or derived lemmas.

5.6 Related Work

We presented a unified formalism for specifying memory models, able to represent existing memory models accurately. Since the semantics of the memory models remain unchanged when formalizing them, any program that has a defined result in the original memory model has the same result using the equivalent formalized model. Often simplifying assumptions can be made about the programs that will be executed. An assumption that holds for many parallel programs is that the parallel program is data-race free. Under this assumption, several memory models execute parallel programs in the same way. Adve and Hill present a formalization of a memory model that unifies the properties of four existing memory models for data-race free programs [1].

Our approach to memory models focuses on the result of memory operations. When implementing a shared memory, the read and write operations have to be specified in more detail than we do. The approach of Gibbons and Merritt [3] is to identify writes with a write request sent by the processor to the shared memory, and to replace read operations with a sequence of a read request sent to the memory and a read response received from the memory. A write request includes a location and a value, a read request a location, and a read response only a value. In the approach of Gibbons and Merritt, a blocking memory is a memory that refuses further requests from any processor after having received a read request and before having answered this request. In other words, the memory blocks while processing a shared-memory read.

5.7 Appendix A. A Formal Theory for Relations

5.7.1 Signature

CONSTANTS

irreflexive $\mapsto$ $(1,0)$

QuotRel $\mapsto$ $(3,0)$

total $\mapsto$ $(1,0)$

PartOrder $\mapsto$ $antisymmetric(Rel\_in([e1],[e2])) \wedge transitive(Rel\_in([e1],[e2]))$

S-TotOrder $\mapsto$ $TotOrder([e1],[e2]) \wedge irreflexive(Rel\_in([e1],[e2]))$

EquivRel $\mapsto$ $reflexive(Rel\_in([e1],[e2])) \wedge (symmetric(Rel\_in([e1],[e2])) \wedge transitive(Rel\_in([e1],[e2])))$

Rel_in $\mapsto$ $(2,0)$

TotOrder $\mapsto$ $PartOrder([e1],[e2]) \wedge total(Rel\_in([e1],[e2]))$

transitive $\mapsto$ $(1,0)$

reflexive $\mapsto$ $(1,0)$

partition $\mapsto$ $(2,0)$

equiv-class $\mapsto$ $(3,0)$

seq-const-Rel $\mapsto$ $(2,0)$

S-PartOrder $\mapsto$ $PartOrder([e1],[e2]) \wedge irreflexive(Rel\_in([e1],[e2]))$

antisymmetric $\mapsto$ $(1, 0)$

Prod $\mapsto$ $(2, 0)$

symmetric $\mapsto$ $(1, 0)$

5.7.2   Axioms

antisymmetric-def
$$\frac{R: ((X \times X)\text{-set})}{antisymmetric(R) = (\forall a1: X \cdot \forall a2: X \cdot}$$
$$((((a1, a2)) \in R) \land (((a2, a1)) \in R)) \Rightarrow (a1 = a2))$$

equiv-class-def
$$\frac{a: X, \, Q: ((X \times X)\text{-set}), \, A: (X\text{-set}), \, EquivRel(Q, A), \, a \in A}{equiv\text{-}class(a, Q, A) = (\{a': X \mid ((a, a')) \in Rel\_in(Q, A)\})}$$

irreflexive-def
$$\frac{A: (X\text{-set}), \, R: ((X \times X)\text{-set})}{irreflexive(Rel\_in(R, A)) =}$$
$$(\forall a: X \cdot (a \in A) \Rightarrow (\neg (((a, a)) \in R)))$$

partition-def
$$\frac{Q: ((X \times X)\text{-set}), \, A: (X\text{-set}) \, EquivRel(Q, A)}{partition(A, Q) = (\{S[a]: X\text{-set} \mid \exists a: X \cdot}$$
$$(a \in A) \land (S[a] = equiv\text{-}class(a, Q, A))\})}$$

Prod-def
$$\frac{A: (X\text{-set}), \, B: (Y\text{-set})}{Prod(A, B) = (\{k: X \times Y \mid (\mathbf{fst} \ k \in A) \land (\mathbf{snd} \ k \in B)\})}$$

Prod-form
$$\frac{A: (X\text{-set}), \, B: (Y\text{-set})}{Prod(A, B): ((X \times Y)\text{-set})}$$

QuotRel-def
$$\frac{R: ((X \times X)\text{-set}), \, Q: ((X \times X)\text{-set}), \, A: (X\text{-set}), \, EquivRel(Q, A)}{QuotRel(R, Q, A) =}$$
$$(\{S: (X\text{-set}) \times (X\text{-set}) \mid \exists a1: X \cdot \exists a2: X \cdot}$$
$$((a1 \in A) \land (a2 \in A))$$
$$\land$$
$$(((\mathbf{fst} \ S = equiv\text{-}class(a1, Q, A)) \land (\mathbf{snd} \ S = equiv\text{-}class(a2, Q, A)))$$
$$\land$$
$$(((a1, a2)) \in R))\})$$

reflexive-def
$$\frac{A: (X\text{-set}), \, R: ((X \times X)\text{-set})}{reflexive(Rel\_in(R, A)) = (\forall a: X \cdot (a \in A) \Rightarrow (((a, a)) \in R))}$$

Rel_in-def
$$\frac{A: (X\text{-set}), \, R: ((X \times X)\text{-set})}{Rel\_in(R, A) = (\{k: X \times X \mid k \in (R \cap Prod(A, A))\})}$$

seq-const-Rel-def

$$\frac{R: (((X \times X)\text{-set})\text{-set}), A: (X\text{-set})}{\begin{array}{c} seq\text{-}const\text{-}Rel(R, A) = \\ (\exists S: (X \times X)\text{-set} \cdot \\ TotOrder(S, A) \\ \wedge \\ (\forall Ri: (X \times X)\text{-set} \cdot (Ri \in R) \Rightarrow (S = (Ri \cap Prod(A, A)))))\end{array}}$$

symmetric-def

$$\frac{R: ((X \times X)\text{-set})}{\begin{array}{c} symmetric(R) = \\ (\forall a1: X \cdot \forall a2: X \cdot (((a1, a2)) \in R) \Rightarrow (((a2, a1)) \in R))\end{array}}$$

total-def

$$\frac{A: (X\text{-set}), R: ((X \times X)\text{-set})}{\begin{array}{c} total(Rel\_in(R, A)) = \\ (\forall a1: X \cdot \forall a2: X \cdot ((a1 \in A) \wedge (a2 \in A)) \\ \Rightarrow \\ (((((a1, a2)) \in R) \vee (((a2, a1)) \in R)) \vee (a1 = a2)))\end{array}}$$

transitive-def

$$\frac{R: ((X \times X)\text{-set})}{\begin{array}{c} transitive(R) = \\ (\forall a1: X \cdot \forall a2: X \cdot \forall a3: X \cdot \\ ((((a1, a2)) \in R) \wedge (((a2, a3)) \in R)) \Rightarrow (((a1, a3)) \in R))\end{array}}$$

5.8 Appendix B. Some Rules Used in the Proof

5.8.1 Axioms

Execution-introduction

$$\frac{t: Execution}{mk\text{-}Execution(s\text{-}Op(t), s\text{-}po(t), s\text{-}n(t)) = t}$$

inv-Execution definition

$$\frac{\begin{array}{c} Op: (OP\text{-set}), po: ((OP \times OP)\text{-set}), n: \mathbf{N_1}, \\ ((\forall a: OP \cdot (a \in Op) \Rightarrow (proc(a) \le n)) \\ \wedge \\ (\forall k: OP \times OP \cdot (k \in po) \Leftrightarrow \\ ((k \in Prod(Op, Op)) \wedge ((proc(\mathbf{fst}\ k) = proc(\mathbf{snd}\ k)) \\ \wedge(num(\mathbf{fst}\ k) \le num(\mathbf{snd}\ k)))))): \mathbf{B}\end{array}}{\begin{array}{c} inv\text{-}Execution(Op, po, n) = \\ ((\forall a: OP \cdot (a \in Op) \Rightarrow (proc(a) \le n)) \\ \wedge \\ (\forall k: OP \times OP \cdot (k \in po) \Leftrightarrow \\ ((k \in Prod(Op, Op)) \wedge ((proc(\mathbf{fst}\ k) = proc(\mathbf{snd}\ k)) \\ \wedge(num(\mathbf{fst}\ k) \le num(\mathbf{snd}\ k))))))\end{array}}$$

inv-Execution-deduction

$$\frac{mk\text{-}Execution(e1, e2, e3): Execution}{inv\text{-}Execution(e1, e2, e3)}$$

$$\boxed{\text{Po-p formation}}\ \frac{p\colon \mathbf{N}_1,\, E\colon \textit{Execution},\, \textit{pre-Po-p}(p, E),\ \exists R\colon (OP \times OP)\text{-}\mathbf{set} \cdot \textit{post-Po-p}(p, E, R)}{\textit{Po-p}(p, E)\colon ((OP \times OP)\text{-}\mathbf{set})}$$

$$\boxed{\text{Po-p specification}}\ \frac{p\colon \mathbf{N}_1,\, E\colon \textit{Execution},\, \textit{pre-Po-p}(p, E),\ \exists R\colon (OP \times OP)\text{-}\mathbf{set} \cdot \textit{post-Po-p}(p, E, R)}{\textit{post-Po-p}(p, E, \textit{Po-p}(p, E))}$$

$$\boxed{\text{s-n(Execution)-defn}}\ \frac{\textit{mk-Execution}(e1, e2, e3)\colon \textit{Execution}}{\textit{s-n}(\textit{mk-Execution}(e1, e2, e3)) = e3}$$

$$\boxed{\text{s-Op(Execution)-defn}}\ \frac{\textit{mk-Execution}(e1, e2, e3)\colon \textit{Execution}}{\textit{s-Op}(\textit{mk-Execution}(e1, e2, e3)) = e1}$$

$$\boxed{\text{s-po(Execution)-formation}}\ \frac{t\colon \textit{Execution}}{\textit{s-po}(t)\colon ((OP \times OP)\text{-}\mathbf{set})}$$

5.8.2   Proof Obligations

$$\boxed{\text{inv-Execution wff}}\ \frac{Op\colon (OP\text{-}\mathbf{set}),\, po\colon ((OP \times OP)\text{-}\mathbf{set}),\, n\colon \mathbf{N}_1}{((\forall a\colon OP \cdot (a \in Op)\ \Rightarrow\ (proc(a) \leq n))}$$

$$\wedge$$

$$(\forall k\colon OP \times OP \cdot (k \in po)\ \Leftrightarrow$$
$$((k \in \textit{Prod}(Op, Op)) \wedge ((proc(\mathbf{fst}\ k) = proc(\mathbf{snd}\ k)) \wedge$$
$$(num(\mathbf{fst}\ k) \leq num(\mathbf{snd}\ k))))))\colon \mathbf{B}$$

$$\boxed{\text{Po-p implementability}}\ \frac{p\colon \mathbf{N}_1,\, E\colon \textit{Execution},\, \textit{pre-Po-p}(p, E)}{\exists R\colon (OP \times OP)\text{-}\mathbf{set} \cdot \textit{post-Po-p}(p, E, R)}$$

5.9   Bibliography

[1]   S. V. Adve and M. D. Hill. A unified formalization of four shared-memory models. *IEEE Transactions on Parallel and Distributed Systems*, 4(6):613–624, June 1993.

[2]   J.C. Bicarregui, J.S. Fitzgerald, P.A. Lindsay, R. Moore, and B. Ritchie. *Proof in VDM: a practitioners guide*, Springer-Verlag London Limited 1994.

[3]   Phillip B. Gibbons and Michael Merritt. Specifying nonblocking shared memories. In *4th Annual ACM Symposium on Parallel Algorithms and Architectures (SPAA)*, 1992.

[4]   C.B. Jones, K.D. Jones, P.A. Lindsay, and R. Moore. Mural: *a formal development support system*, Springer-Verlag London Limited 1991.

Chapter 6

On the Verification of VDM Specification and Refinement with PVS

Sten Agerholm, Juan Bicarregui and Savi Maharaj

Summary

This chapter describes using the PVS system as a tool to support VDM-SL. It is possible to translate from VDM-SL into the PVS specification language in a very easy and direct manner, thus enabling the use of PVS for typechecking and verifying properties of VDM-SL specifications and refinements. The translation is described in detail and illustrated with examples. The drawbacks of the translation are that it must be done manually (though automation may be possible), and that the "shallow embedding" technique which is used does not accurately capture the proof rules of VDM-SL. The benefits come from the facts that the portion of VDM-SL which can be represented is substantial and that it is a great advantage to be able to use the powerful PVS proof-checker. A variety of examples of verifications using PVS are described in the chapter.

6.1 Introduction

The PVS system[13], developed at SRI Menlo Park, in California, combines an expressive specification language with a powerful theorem-proving tool in which interactive proof is tightly integrated with many automatic procedures which speed up routine parts of proof development. The combination makes for a user-friendly system which is easy to learn and to use for doing non-trivial theorem-proving. The specification language is based on classical higher-order logic, enriched with a type system based on Church's simple theory of types with extensions for subtyping and dependent types. The result is an expressive language which has much in common with formal notations such as VDM-SL. A system of parameterized theories provides structuring for developments and extensive libraries add definitions of many useful mathematical constructs similar to those used in VDM-SL.

The striking, if superficial, similarity between VDM-SL and the PVS specification language means that a significant portion of VDM-SL may be represented very directly in PVS. This gives rise to an informal "shallow embedding" [10] of a substantial portion of VDM-SL. The embedding makes use of the parameterized theories of PVS to represent VDM-SL specifications and refinement relationships between pairs of specifications. The result is a simple and direct means of harnessing the power of the PVS proof-checker for proving validation conditions and proof obligations arising from specifications and refinements. The embedding also provides automatic generation of some proof obligations which can be made to arise as *type-checking constraints* (TCCs) in PVS. The drawbacks of the method are that translation must (at present) be performed manually, and that the proof rules of VDM-SL are not accurately captured because of differences between the logics of VDM-SL and PVS. The latter fact implies that what we are doing would be more accurately described as VDM-*style* specification.

Using this approach outlined above, we have hand-translated a number of VDM-SL specifications and refinements into the PVS logic, and used the prover to check various properties of these specifications. This process resulted in the detection of several errors in some of these specifications. In this chapter we describe one medium-sized example which illustrates most of the aspects of our approach. The structure of the chapter is as follows. In Section 6.2 we briefly describe the PVS system. This is followed in Section 6.3 by an informal presentation of the translation from VDM-SL to the PVS specification language. Section 6.4 complements Section 6.3 by illustrating through the use of an example how a specification as a whole is represented as a PVS theory. In this section we also discuss using the PVS proof-checker to typecheck the example specification and to prove various validation conditions about it. In Section 6.5 we turn to the subject of refinement, showing how the example of Section 6.4 can be represented in PVS as a refinement of a more abstract specification, and how the PVS proof-checker was used to discharge all the resulting proof obligations. In the final sections we discuss the validity of our informal translation from VDM-SL to PVS, make some observations about what was learned during this exercise, and present our conclusions.

6.2   The PVS System

The PVS system is produced by a team of researchers at SRI International, in California. The philosophy behind the system is that it should provide a high degree of support for requirements specification, since errors at this initial stage are considered to be the most costly. However, the system itself is general purpose and lends itself to a variety of applications [13], including verifications of algorithms and hardware systems and embeddings of other logics.

The foundation of the system is the expressive PVS Specification Language. This is based on classical higher-order logic, enhanced with a rich system of types including subtyping, dependent types and recursive types. Specifications may be structured using a system of parameterized theories. Various aspects of the syntax of the PVS specification language will be explained where they arise in the chapter.

The PVS specification language is supported by a collection of tools including a type checker and an interactive proof checker. The tools run under emacs which provides a basic user interface. Typechecking in PVS is undecidable and generally results in the generation of proof obligations called *type-checking constraints* (TCCs). TCCs may be proved by invoking a powerful tactic called tcp or, if this tactic fails, by use of the PVS proof-checker.

One of the main attractions of the PVS proof-checker is that basic proof commands are tightly integrated with powerful decision procedures and tactics. The tactics may be combined in various ways to form proof strategies. Some of the most commonly used tactics embody simple proof rules (splitting conjunctions and disjunctions, instantiating quantifiers, skolemizing, etc). Others implement sophisticated decision procedures. Examples are the tactic PROP for propositional simplification and the all-powerful tactic GRIND, which subsumes PROP and does much more. Other tactics such as HIDE allow management of the proof state.

The version of PVS referred to in this chapter is the "alpha-plus" release available in June 1996.

6.3 From VDM-SL to the Higher Order Logic of PVS

A large subset of VDM-SL can be translated into a higher order logic such as the PVS specification language. This section describes such a translation in sufficient detail to support manual translations, though more formality might be required in order to support an implementation of the translation process. The translation method may be viewed as a (very) shallow embedding of VDM-SL in PVS. The syntax of VDM-SL constructs is not embedded: we work with the "semantics" of the constructs directly. Therefore it can be argued that the translation is not safe (in a logical sense). This is a disadvantage of shallow embeddings in general, though some shallow embeddings are more safe than others. The translation of VDM-SL to PVS is relatively safe in this sense since PVS and VDM-SL share many concepts and constructs.

One of the differences between VDM-SL and PVS is that a VDM-SL expression can be undefined; there is one common undefined element to all types, which can be viewed as sets. For example, an expression is undefined if a divisor is zero, if a finite sequence is applied to an index outside its indices, or if a pattern match in a let expression fails. Most of such situations are handled implicitly by restrictions on the translation of various constructs, in combination with type checking in PVS. For instance, PVS itself generates type checking conditions to capture division by zero. A related factor is that PVS does not support partial functions. All VDM-SL functions are translated to PVS functions and PVS generates an obligation stating that a given function must be total. Partial functions are discussed in more depth in Section 6.6.

Below we discuss how various constructs of VDM-SL specifications can be translated. We show VDM-SL expressions in the ASCII notation supported by the IFAD VDM-SL Toolbox.

6.3.1   Basic Types, the Product Type and Type Invariants

Boolean and number types can be viewed as sets and translated directly to the corresponding types in PVS. It is not necessary to edit arithmetic expressions and logical connectives since they have the same symbols and names in PVS. Specially, the connectives and and or are used as "and-also" and "or-else" in both the Toolbox version of VDM-SL and PVS. Hence, it is allowed to write "P(x) and x/x = 1" if one can prove the automatically generated condition "P(x) IMPLIES x /= 0".

Restricted quantifications are translated to quantifications over PVS subtypes. Hence, a universal quantification like forall x in set s & P[x] can be translated to forall (x:(s)): P[x]. Note that the & is replaced with : and we insert brackets around the binding.

In VDM-SL it is possible to specify a subtype of a type by writing a predicate that the elements of the subtype must always satisfy. This predicate is called an invariant. As an example consider the definition of a type of positive reals:

```
Realp = real
inv r == r >= 0
```

This introduces a new constant inv_Realp implicitly, which equals the invariant predicate. The definition is translated to PVS as follows:

```
inv_Realp(r:real) : bool = r >= 0
Realp: TYPE = (inv_Realp)
```

The type Realp is defined as a subtype of the built-in type real.

The product type of VDM-SL can be translated directly to the product type of PVS. VDM-SL tuples are written using a constant mk_, e.g. mk_(1,2,3). This constant could be ignored in the translation, but instead we have introduced and usually use a dummy constant mk_, defined as the identity function. The only way to split a tuple in VDM-SL is using pattern matching on mk_, e.g. in a let expression like let mk_(x,y,z) = t in e. The translation of pattern matching is discussed in more detail in Section 6.3.6.

6.3.2   Record Types

VDM-SL records are translated directly to records in PVS. There is only a slight difference in syntax. PVS does not automatically introduce a constructor function mk_A as in VDM-SL for a record definition called A, but the function is easy to define. Below, we first give an example of how to translate a standard record type definition and then give a more complicated example where an invariant is also specified.

Standard Records

We consider a simple example, which defines a record of points in the two-dimensional positive real plane. The VDM-SL definition of the record type is (Realp was introduced above):

```
Point:: x: Realp
        y: Realp
```

This is translated to PVS as follows:

```
Point: TYPE = [# x: Realp, y: Realp #]
```

In both cases, field selectors x and y are introduced implicitly. Unfortunately, PVS does not support the VDM-SL notation for field selection, which is the standard one using a dot and the field name, e.g. p.x for some point p. Instead fields are viewed as functions that can be applied to records. Thus the VDM-SL expression p.x translates to the PVS expression x(p). The PVS notation is less convenient, e.g. a nested field selection as in r.a.b.c translates to c(b(a(r))).

In VDM-SL each new record definition generates a new "make" function for building elements of the record. In order to allow a direct translation of such expressions to the same expressions in PVS, the constructor function is defined along with a record definition. The constructor for points is:

```
mk_Point(a:Realp,b:Realp) : Point = (# x:= a, y:= b #)
```

In VDM-SL such make constructors are also used for pattern matching in function definitions and in let expressions but this is not possible in PVS. Instead we use Hilbert's choice operator (choose), as described in Section 6.3.6.

VDM-SL also provides an is_ test function for records, which is sometimes used to test where elements of union types come from. Since we do not support union types properly (see Section 6.3.4) we shall ignore this constant.

Records with Invariants

Sometimes a VDM-SL record definition is written with an invariant. For instance, an equivalent way of defining the point record above would be the following definition

```
Point:: x: real
         y: real
inv mk_Point(x,y) == x >= 0 and y >= 0
```

where an invariant is used to specify that we are only interested in the positive part
of the two-dimensional real plane. We translate this as follows:

```
inv_Point(x:real,y:real) : bool = x >= 0 and y >= 0
```

```
Point: TYPE = {p: [# x:real, y:real #] | inv_Point(x(p),y(p))}
```

```
mk_Point(z:(inv_Point)) : Point = (# x:= x(z), y:= y(z) #)
```

Note that we restrict the arguments of `mk_Point`. For instance, the following definition does not work

```
mk_Point(a:real,b:real) : Point = (# x:= a, y:= b #)
```

since we cannot prove that this yields a point for all valid arguments.

There is one small semantic difference between VDM-SL records and the above
representation in PVS. In VDM-SL it is allowed to write `mk_Point(1,-1)` though
this will not have type `Point`. The only use of such a (kind of) junk term would be in
`inv_Point(mk_Point(1,-1))`, which would equal false. In the PVS representation,
this invariant expression is written as `inv_Point(1,-1)`.

6.3.3   Sequences, Sets and Maps

In this section, we briefly consider the translation of finite sequences, finite sets and
finite maps. Invariants on these types are treated much like in the previous section
on records.

Finite Sets

A type of finite sets is provided in the PVS `finite_sets` library. The type is defined
as a subtype of the set type, which represents sets as predicates. Most operations
on sets exist, or can be defined easily. One annoying factor is that for instance set
membership, set union and set intersection are all prefix operations in PVS. E.g.
one must write `member(x,s)` for the VDM-SL expression "`x in set s`". Moreover,
user-defined constants must be prefix and one cannot define new symbols. PVS
supports only a simple and restricted syntax of expressions.

Finite Sequences

VDM-SL finite sequences can be represented as finite sequences or as finite lists in
PVS. The difference is that finite sequences are represented as functions and finite

lists as an abstract datatype. There is more support for finite lists, so we have usually chosen this type as the representation. An advantage of sequences is that indexing is just function application. However, with both representations one must be careful since indexing of sequences starts from one in VDM-SL and from zero in PVS. The safest thing to do is therefore to define new indexing operations in PVS and use these for the translation.

Finite Maps

PVS does not support finite maps, so an appropriate theory must be derived from scratch. In doing this, one could probably benefit from the paper on finite maps in HOL by Collins and Syme [12], who have implemented their work in a HOL library. However, many operations on finite maps are not supported in this library, so an extended theory of finite maps must be worked out.

As a start one could just axiomatize maps in PVS, e.g. by introducing maps as an uninterpreted subtype of the function type, with a few appropriate definitions (and axioms). In fact, for the examples very little support was needed.

A representation of maps using functions has advantages. Map application will just be function application and map modification can be translated to PVS with expressions. For example, the VDM-SL map modification m ++ { 1 |-> 2, 2 |-> 3 }, where a map m from numbers to numbers is modified to send 1 to 2 and 2 to 3, translates to m with [1 |-> 2, 2 |-> 3].

6.3.4 Union Types

In VDM-SL, the union of two or more types corresponds to the set union of the types. Thus, the union type is a non-disjoint union, if two types have a common element this will be just one element in the union type. Higher order logics do not support non-disjoint unions, but support disjoint sums (unions) or abstract datatypes as in PVS. In general, a VDM-SL union type cannot be translated easily to a PVS datatype. However, if the component types of the union are disjoint then this is partly possible. The translation is only satisfactory when the component types are quote types; these correspond to singleton sets.

Union of Disjoint Types

The union of disjoint types can be represented as a new datatype with constructor names for the different types. This representation is not perfect, the component types does not become subtypes of the union type as in VDM-SL. For example this means that the operators defined on the individual types are not inherited as in VDM-SL, where the dynamic type checking ensures that arguments of operators have the right types. In the special case where all components of the union type are new types, it might be possible to define the union type first and then define each

of the component type as subtypes of this. Such tricks would not be easy to employ
in an automatic translation.

Enumerated Types

An enumerated type is a union of quote types, which is written using the following
ASCII syntax in VDM-SL: ABC = <A>|<B>|<C>. This can be translated almost
directly to PVS, with some minor syntax changes: ABC: TYPE = {A,B,C}. PVS
does not support identifiers enclosed in < and >.

6.3.5   Function Definitions

Total functions are translated directly to PVS functions. As mentioned before,
partial functions cannot be translated in this way. As we shall see in Section 6.6,
it is possible to encode some partial functions as total functions in PVS by using
subtypes to represent their domains of definition. Other formalizations are also
possible (see e.g. [2, 1]). Polymorphic functions are not considered at the moment.

Standard explicit function definitions, which are function definitions that do not
have postconditions, can be translated directly to PVS, if they are not recursive. A
precondition will be translated to a subtype predicate. If functions are recursive we
must demonstrate that they are total functions in PVS. It is up to the translator
to specify an appropriate measure, which is decreased in each recursive call, for the
termination proof. Moreover, VDM-SL supports mutual recursive function definitions which would not be easy to translate. The example specifications used only
few recursive definitions and these were very simple.

Implicit function definitions, which are specified using pre- and postconditions only
and have no function body, can be represented using the choice operator. Almost
equivalently, one can also use function specification, which is a way of defining
partially specified functions; it is only specified on a subset of a type how a function
behaves, and this is specified by an "underdetermined" relation, not an equation
[18, 15].

Implicit Definition

Let us first consider the following semi-abstract example of an implicit function
definition in VDM-SL:

```
f(x:real,y:real) z:Point
pre p[x,y]
post q[x,y,z]
```

where the variables in square brackets may occur free in the precondition p and the
postcondition q. This translates to the following PVS definitions:

```
pre_f(x:real,y:real) : bool = p[x,y]
```

```
post_f(t:(pre_f))(z:Point) : bool = let (x,y) = t in q[x,y,z]

f: FUNCTION[t:(pre_f) -> (post_f(t))]
```

The precondition is translated to a predicate on the arguments of the function and the postcondition is translated to a binary relation on the arguments and the result. The function itself is defined as an uninterpreted constant using a dependent function type: given arguments t satisfying the precondition it returns a result satisfying the postcondition, or more precisely, a result related to t by the postcondition. This relation may be underdetermined, i.e. it may specify a range of possible values for a given input, but the function will always return a fixed value in this range. If the precondition is not satisfied the result is an arbitrary value.

As a result of an uninterpreted constant definition, the PVS type checker generates an existence condition, which says that we must prove there exists a value in the specified type. Hence, above we must prove there exists a function from the precondition to the postcondition. In general, proving this condition can be non-trivial, since one must usually provide a witness, i.e. a function of the specified form. (For instance, it would be difficult to prove that there exists a square root function.)

Explicit Definition

Explicit definitions of recursive functions can be problematic for automatic translation since a translator must insert a well-founded measure for proofs of termination. This is easy enough when the recursion is simple, which it is for primitive recursive functions over numbers and abstract datatypes, but for more general recursive functions this can be hard. PVS has some strategies for proving termination in simple cases.

An explicit function definition has no postcondition but instead a direct definition, and perhaps a precondition. Let us consider a standard example of a primitive recursive function on the natural numbers:

```
fac: nat -> nat
fac(n) == if n = 0 then 1 else n * fac(n-1)
pre 0<=n
```

This translates to the following PVS definitions:

```
pre_fac(n:nat) : bool = n >= 0

fac(n:(pre_fac)) : recursive nat =
  if n = 0 then 1 else n * fac(n-1) endif
  measure (lambda (n:(pre_fac)): n)
```

Note that we have inserted "recursive" and "measure", which are part of the syntax for recursive function definitions in PVS. The measure is used to generate conditions for termination of recursive calls. (The precondition is redundant above, it is included for illustration.)

6.3.6   Pattern Matching

Pattern matching plays an important role in VDM-SL specifications. It is used frequently to get access to the values at fields of a record, and it is the only way to get access to the values of the components of a tuple. We can represent a successful pattern matching but not a failing one, since we do not represent undefined expressions. However, undefined expressions are either avoided due to type checking, or else represented by arbitrary values, i.e. values of a certain type that we do not know anything about.

Pattern Matching in Let Expressions

Here are some examples which use a record type A with three fields a, b and c. Assuming x, y and z are variables, the following VDM-SL let expression

```
let mk_(x,y,z) = e1 in e2[x,y,z]
```

can be translated to exactly the same term in PVS, except that the tuple constructor mk_ must be omitted for the expression to parse. The following VDM-SL let expression with a pattern match on the record type A

```
let mk_A(x,y,z) = e1 in e2[x,y,z]
```

can be translated to the following PVS term:

```
let x = a(e1), y = b(e1), z = c(e1) in e2[x,y,z]
```

The field selector functions are used to destruct the expression. This corresponds to the way that PVS itself represents pattern matching on tuples (using project functions). If one of the variables in the VDM-SL expression was the don't care pattern, written as an minus sign -, then we could just replace this with a new variable. We do not allow constants in patterns in let expressions, since they do not make much sense (they are however allowed in VDM-SL).

The following VDM-SL "let-be-such-that" expression

```
let mk_A(x,y,z) in set s be st b[x,y,z] in e[x,y,z]
```

can be translated to

```
let v = (choose ({w:(s) | let x = a(w), y = b(w), z = c(w)
                          in b[x,y,z]}))
in
   let x = a(v), y = b(v), z = c(v) in e[x,y,z]
```

where we use the choice operator, **choose**, to represent the looseness in the VDM-SL specification. Don't care patterns are translated as suggested above, by introducing new variables. We allow constants and other values in let-be-st expressions. For instance, we can translate

```
let mk_A(x,y,0) in set s be st b[x,y] in e[x,y]
```

into the PVS term

```
let
  v = (choose ({w:(s) | let x = a(w), y = b(w), n = c(w)
                        in n = 0 and b[x,y]}))
in
  let x = a(v), y = b(v) in e[x,y]
```

where we include a test in the body of the **choose**.

Pattern Matching in Cases Expressions

The following VDM-SL cases expression

```
cases e:
  mk_A(0,-,z) -> e1,
  mk_A(x,1,z) -> e2,
  others      -> e3
end
```

can be translated to the following conditional expression in PVS:

```
cond
  a(e) = 0 -> let z = c(e) in e1,
  b(e) = 1 -> let x = a(e), z = c(e) in e2,
  else      -> e3
endcond
```

PVS's built-in cases expression only works on abstract datatypes.

Pattern Matching in Function Definitions

Pattern matching can be used on arguments in a function definition, where the patterns are typically variables (or don't care patterns which are translated to new variables). We can treat this by inventing a new variable using the function definition and then extending the body with a let expression to represent the pattern match. This approach is also used in the formal semantics of VDM-SL.

6.3.7   State and Operations

A VDM-SL specification may contain a state definition, which specifies a number
of variable names for elements of the state space. The state space is known to
operations and nowhere else. The state definition is essentially a record definition
and is therefore represented as a record type in PVS. Operations are represented
as state transformations, i.e. functions which, in addition to the operation's input
values, take the initial state as an argument and return the output state as a result
(and possibly an explicit result value). Hence, operation definitions can be translated
in a similar way as functions.

The body of operation definitions may contain assignments and sequential compo-
sitions. Assignments are translated to PVS with expressions and sequential com-
positions are represented using let expressions. In this chapter we do not consider
conditions (which should be easy) and while loops (which probably could be translated to recursive functions). More exotic features such as exception handling are
also excluded from consideration.

Assume we have the following state definition in VDM-SL:

```
state ST of
        x: real
        y: real
        z: real
end
```

This can be translated to:

```
ST: TYPE = [# x: real, y: real, z: real #]
mk_ST(x:real,y:real,z:real): ST = (# x:=x, y:=y, z:=z #)
```

Now assume we have the sequence:

```
x:=5; y:=3; z:=1
```

This can be translated to

```
lambda (s:ST):
  let s1 = s  with [x:=5],
      s2 = s1 with [y:=3],
      s3 = s2 with [z:=1]
  in s3
```

or simply to

```
lambda (s:st): s with [x:=5, y:=3, z:=1]
```

since the assignments are independent in this example.

6.4 A Specification Example: MSMIE

The Multiprocessor Shared-Memory Information Exchange (MSMIE) is a protocol for "inter-processor communications in distributed, microprocessor-based nuclear safety systems" [17], which has been used in the embedded software of Westinghouse nuclear systems designs.

The protocol uses multiple buffering to ensure that no "data-tearing" occurs as separate processors communicate via some shared memory. In other words, data should never be overwritten by one process while it is still being read by another. One important requirement is that neither writing nor reading processes should have to wait for a buffer to become available; another is that recent information should be passed, via the buffers, from writers to readers. The example has previously been analyzed using CCS in [11] and using VDM and B in [9]. In common with these analyses, we shall be working with a simplified system in which it is assumed that information is being passed from a single "slave" processor to several "master" processors. Thus, there are several reading processors, "masters", but only one writing, "slave" process.

The information exchange is realised by a system with three buffers. At any time, one buffer is available for writing, one for reading, and the third is either between a write and a read and hence contains the most recently written information, or between a read and a write and so is idle.

The status of each buffer is recorded by a flag which can take one of four values:

s - "assigned to slave" This buffer is reserved for writing. It may actually be being written at the moment or just marked as available for writing.

n - "newest" This buffer has just been written and contains the latest information. It is not being read at the moment.

m - "assigned to master" This buffer is being read by one or more processors.

i - "idle" This buffer is not being read or written and does not contain the latest data.

The names of the master processors that are currently reading are also stored in the state.

The VDM specification of [8] and [9] is concerned with various "data models" of MSMIE: the state of the device is modelled but not the slave and master processors nor the dynamic evolution of the system as they access the buffers in parallel. This analysis concerns only the operations which modify the buffer status flags. In the system as a whole, these operations are protected by a system of semaphores which allows each operation uninterrupted access to the state, and thus their behaviour is purely sequential.

There are three such operations:

slave This operation is executed when a write finishes. The buffer that was being written is given the status "newest" thereby replacing any other buffer with this status.

acquire This is executed when a read begins. The new reader name (passed as a parameter) is added to the set of readers and status flags are updated as appropriate.

release This is executed when a read ends. The given reader name is removed from the set of readers and status flags are updated as appropriate.

The precise description of these operations is left to the formal specification in the following section.

We note, in passing, that the MSMIE protocol has the the undesirable property that it is possible for information flow from slave to master to be held up indefinitely. This problem is dealt with in the original paper [17] by the use of timing constraints. The paper [11] suggests an improvement to the protocol in which the problem is avoided by the use of a fourth buffer. This improved protocol is quite intricate, and is modelled in [8] by using non-standard extensions to VDM which provide a more concise means of expression than standard VDM-SL. In this report we restrict ourselves to standard VDM-SL specifications and so do not treat the improved MSMIE protocol.

The paper [8] explores several ways of specifying the MSMIE system in VDM with varying degrees of abstraction. These specifications can be translated more or less "as is" into PVS, which can then be used to carry out proof obligations. The specifications can be written in such a way that some of the proof obligations are automatically generated by PVS, though it is still necessary to type in others by hand.

The VDM specifications of MSMIE which we show are in VDM-SL and therefore differ slightly from those in [8]. They were developed with the help of the IFAD VDM-SL Toolbox [14].

6.4.1   The VDM Specification

The specification uses an auxiliary function called *count*, which counts the number of occurrences of a given item in a sequence.

functions

$count[@T] : @T \times @T^* \to \mathbf{N}$

$count\ (s, ss) \triangleq$
    cases ss :
        $[] \to 0,$
        others $\to$ if hd $ss = s$
            then $1 + count[@T]\ (s, \text{tl } ss)$
            else $count[@T]\ (s, \text{tl } ss)$
    end

The possible values of the status flags are given via an enumerated type; the type of the names of master processes is deferred.

types

$Status = \text{S} \mid \text{M} \mid \text{N} \mid \text{I};$

$MName = \text{token}$

The state records the status of each of the three buffers, and the names of all currently reading master processes. These are represented by, respectively, a sequence of status values and a set of master names. The invariant captures constraints on the possible states that are reachable: there is exactly one buffer assigned to the writing slave process; at most one buffer is currently being read, and at most one holds newest data that is not being read; the set of readers is empty precisely when no buffer is being read. In the initial state, one buffer is assigned to the slave and the other two buffers are marked as idle.

state Σ of
    $b : Status^*$
    $ms : MName\text{-set}$
    inv mk-Σ $(b, ms) \triangleq$
        len $b = 3 \wedge$
        $count[Status]\ (\text{S}, b) = 1 \wedge$
        $count[Status]\ (\text{M}, b) \in \{0, 1\} \wedge$
        $count[Status]\ (\text{N}, b) \in \{0, 1\} \wedge$
        $(count[Status]\ (\text{M}, b) = 0 \iff ms = \{\})$
    init $s \triangleq s = $ mk-Σ $([\text{S}, \text{I}, \text{I}], \{\})$
end

The *slave* operation is executed when a slave process completes writing. The buffer that has just been written, previously of status S, is given the status N reflecting that it now contains the newest data. This buffer replaces any other buffer with the N status. The operation also selects one of the available buffers and assigns to it status S, making it the new buffer available for writing.

operations

slave ()
ext wr $b : (Status^*)$
pre true
post $\forall i \in \{1, 2, 3\} \cdot$
$$(\overleftarrow{b}(i) = \text{S} \Rightarrow b(i) = \text{N}) \wedge$$
$$(\overleftarrow{b}(i) = \text{M} \Rightarrow b(i) = \text{M}) ;$$

The *acquire* operation is executed when a master process is about to begin reading. The new reader's name, passed as a parameter, is added to the set of active readers, and status flags are updated as necessary. If there is already a buffer being read, then the new reader also begins to read that buffer and no status changes are needed. Otherwise it reads the buffer with the newest data, status N, and the status of that buffer is changed to M.

acq $(l : MName)$
ext wr $b : (Status^*)$
    wr $ms : (MName\text{-set})$
pre $(\neg (l \in ms)) \wedge$
    $(\exists i \in \{1, 2, 3\} \cdot b(i) = \text{N} \vee b(i) = \text{M})$
post $ms = \overleftarrow{ms} \cup \{l\} \wedge$
    $\forall i \in \{1, 2, 3\} \cdot$
        if $\overleftarrow{b}(i) = \text{N} \wedge \overleftarrow{ms} = \{\}$
        then $b(i) = \text{M}$
        else $b(i) = \overleftarrow{b}(i) ;$

The release operation takes place when a master process has finished reading. The master's name is removed from the set of readers and buffer flags reassigned as appropriate. If there are still other masters reading then the status flags do not need to be changed. Otherwise, the buffer that has just been relinquished must have its status flag reassigned. There are two possibilities. If there is some other buffer which was written while the read was taking place, and therefore has status N, then the released buffer no longer contains the newest data and must have its status set to I. Otherwise, it still contains the freshest data and must have its status reset to N.

rel $(l : MName)$
ext wr $b : (Status^*)$
    wr $ms : (MName\text{-set})$
pre $l \in ms$

post $ms = \overleftarrow{ms} \setminus \{l\} \wedge$
 $\quad \forall i \in \{1, 2, 3\} \cdot$
 $\qquad$ if $\overleftarrow{b}(i) = M \wedge ms = \{\}$
 $\qquad$ then $b(i) \in \{N, I\} \wedge count[Status](N, b) = 1$
 $\qquad$ else $b(i) = \overleftarrow{b}(i)$

6.4.2 PVS Translation

The VDM specification is represented as a PVS theory called msmie_sigma2. The theory is parameterized over a non-empty type of master names.

```
msmie_sigma2[MName : TYPE+] : THEORY
```

```
  BEGIN
```

The theory begins by importing another theory containing definitions of functions on lists. The "count" function is defined within this imported theory.

```
  IMPORTING list_funs
```

As in VDM, the possible values of the status flags are represented by an enumerated type.

```
  Status : TYPE = {Slave,Master,Newest,Idle}
```

The state and invariant of the VDM specification are represented by a single (dependent) type in PVS. The definition is best understood in two parts. First, the state is represented as a record containing two fields: a list, b of Status values, and a set of master names, ms. The set of valid states is then represented by forming the subtype, sigma2, of all such records which satisfy the invariant.

```
  sigma2 : TYPE =
  {x : [# b  : list[Status],
           ms : setof[MName] #] |

  ((length (b(x)) = 3) AND
   (count (Slave,b(x)) = 1) AND
   member(count(Master,b(x)),{x:nat|x=0 OR x=1}) AND
   member(count(Newest,b(x)),{x:nat|x=0 OR x=1}) AND
   ((count (Master,b(x)) = 0) <=> (ms(x) = emptyset)))}
```

The initial state is defined as a record containing appropriate values and its type is explicitly constrained to be sigma2. When this definition is typechecked, PVS will automatically generate as a type-checking constraint (TCC) the condition that the

initial state satisfies the invariant. We shall look more closely at these TCCs in the
next section.

```
initial_sigma2 : sigma2 =
  (# b := (: Slave, Idle, Idle :), ms := emptyset #)
```

For each operation, the precondition is represented as a predicate over the valid
states (sigma2). The postcondition is represented as a predicate over pairs of valid
states. The operation is then defined as a function which maps each value from the
subtype defined by the precondition to some unspecified valid state which, when
paired with the input value, satisfies the postcondition. Typechecking such a definition will cause PVS to generate a TCC stating that a suitable value for the post
state does indeed exist. In other words, we are asked to show that the specified
operation is *feasible*.

Our first example is the slave operation. The definitions of the pre- and postconditions resemble very closely the original VDM specification. One difference is that
there is no analogue in PVS to the frames in VDM, so that the fact that the variable
ms has read-only status in the VDM specification must be explicitly stated in the
PVS postcondition.

```
pre_slave  : [sigma2 -> bool] = LAMBDA (st:sigma2) :
   true

post_slave : [(pre_slave),sigma2 -> bool] =
   LAMBDA (st:(pre_slave),st2:sigma2) :
     ((FORALL (i:{x:nat| x=0 OR x=1 OR x=2}) :
        (nth(b(st),i) = Slave IMPLIES nth(b(st2),i) = Newest)
        AND
        (nth(b(st),i) = Master IMPLIES nth(b(st2),i) = Master))
      AND
      (ms(st2) = ms(st)))
```

The slave operation is then defined using the PVS choice operator choose. Our use
of choose leads to a rather different interpretation of looseness from that adopted
in VDM-SL. We defer discussion of this point until Section 6.6.3.

```
slave : [(pre_slave) -> sigma2] =
        LAMBDA (st:(pre_slave)) :
            choose({st2:sigma2 | post_slave(st,st2)})
```

The specification of acquire is done similar. First the precondition and postcondition
are defined as predicates.

```
pre_acq : [MName ->[sigma2 -> bool]] =
  LAMBDA (l:MName)(st:sigma2) :
```

```
(NOT member(l,ms(st))) AND
(EXISTS (i:{x:nat| x=0 OR x=1 OR x=2}) :
    (nth(b(st),i) = Newest OR nth(b(st),i) = Master))

post_acq : [l:MName -> [(pre_acq(l)),sigma2 -> bool]]  =
        LAMBDA (l:MName)(st:(pre_acq(l)),st2:sigma2) :
            (ms(st2) = union(ms(st),singleton(l))) AND
            (FORALL (i:{x:nat| x=0 OR x=1 OR x=2}) :
                IF nth(b(st),i) = Newest AND ms(st) = emptyset
                THEN nth(b(st2),i) = Master
                ELSE nth(b(st2),i) = nth(b(st),i)
                ENDIF)
```

Next, the acquire operation is defined as a function which, when given a master name l and a state belonging to the type (`pre_acq(l)`), returns a nondeterministically chosen state in sigma2 such that the two states together satisfy the postcondition `post_acq(l)`

```
acq : [l:MName, (pre_acq(l)) -> sigma2] =
        LAMBDA (l:MName, st:(pre_acq(l))) :
            choose({st2:sigma2 | post_acq(l)(st,st2)})
```

The specification of the release operation is similar to that of acquire and is not described here.

6.4.3 Typechecking Constraints

When the theory `msmie_sigma2` is typechecked by PVS, a number of typechecking constraints (TCCs) are generated. These must be proved in order to demonstrate that the theory is well-typed. Simple TCCs can be handled by invoking an automatic TCC-prover, `tcp`, but more difficult ones must be proved interactively by the user. In the case of the theory `msmie_sigma2`, there are only 4 TCCs which are too difficult for `tcp` to prove. Interestingly, these TCCs correspond to the satisfiability proof obligations for the specification. We are required to show that the initial state satisfies the invariant, and that each of the three operations is feasible.

Showing that the Initial State Satisfies the Invariant

The first TCC generated for `msmie_sigma2` is shown below. It results from the fact that we have explicitly stated that the initial state, `initial_sigma2`, is of type `sigma2`; we are required to prove that `initial_sigma2` satisfies the predicate which defines the subtype `sigma2`. In other words, we must show that the initial state satisfies the invariant. The proof is too difficult for `tcp`, but can be done quickly using the interactive prover. The main goal, which consists of a conjunction of 5 formulae, is split, making each conjunct into a separate subgoal. Each of these is

then proved by repeatedly expanding definitions until a statement is obtained which
PVS recognises to be trivially true.

```
initial_sigma2_TCC1: OBLIGATION
  ((length[Status]((: Slave, Idle, Idle :)) = 3)
      AND (count[Status](Slave, (: Slave, Idle, Idle :)) = 1)
        AND
      member[nat](count[Status](Master, (: Slave, Idle, Idle :)),
                  {x: nat | x = 0 OR x = 1})
          AND
        member[nat](count[Status](Newest, (: Slave, Idle, Idle :)),
                    {x: nat | x = 0 OR x = 1})
            AND
          ((count[Status](Master, (: Slave, Idle, Idle :)) = 0)
              <=> (emptyset[MName] = emptyset[MName]))));
```

Showing that the Operations Are Feasible

To specify the operations we used the nondeterministic choice operator of PVS. For
this to be correctly typed, PVS requires us to demonstrate that there exist possible
candidates for the nondeterministically chosen values. In other words, we must show
that each operation is feasible.

We show the statement of this proof obligation for the acquire operation. Given
any master name 1, and any state st within the type defined by the precondition,
(pre_acq(1)), we must prove that the set of all states, st2, satisfying the postcondition post_acq(1)(st,st2) is nonempty.

```
acq_TCC1: OBLIGATION
        (FORALL (l: MName, st: (pre_acq(l))):
           nonempty?[sigma2]({st2: sigma2 | post_acq(l)(st, st2)}));
```

This TCC has been proved interactively using PVS. The proof is unsurprising but
not trivial: the user must supply a suitable candidate for the nondeterministic choice
and then verify that all the various conditions imposed by the postcondition and
the invariant are satisfied.

We describe only the main highlights of the proof. After skolemizing, expanding
definitions, and making some hidden hypotheses explicit, we are in a position where
we may supply a possible candidate for the value that is nondeterministically chosen. This is done using the tactic INST, which is given two arguments: an integer
representing the appropriate subgoal and a value for instantiation consisting of a
record representing the state after the operation is carried out. In this case, the
postcondition of the acquire operation happens to be very explicit so the calculation
of the post state simply reflects the postcondition. Note that identifiers such as
st!1 are skolem variables generated by PVS.

```
(INST -8
  "(# ms := union(ms(st!1), singleton(l!1)),
     b := (: IF nth(b(st!1), 0) = Newest AND ms(st!1) = emptyset
              THEN Master ELSE nth(b(st!1), 0) ENDIF,
            IF nth(b(st!1), 1) = Newest AND ms(st!1) = emptyset
              THEN Master ELSE nth(b(st!1), 1) ENDIF ,
            IF nth(b(st!1), 2) = Newest AND ms(st!1) = emptyset
              THEN Master ELSE nth(b(st!1), 2) ENDIF :) #)")
```

This gives us two subgoals: we must show that the witness satisfies both the post-condition and the invariant. We shall not describe these proofs in detail because they are lengthy and not particularly instructive. Briefly, each subgoal consisted of a conjunction which was split to give several new subgoals. These subgoals were then proved by case analysis (splitting the hypotheses), rewriting and simplifying each individual case, and then using a decision procedure or some general tactic such as GRIND to either verify the conclusion or discover a contradiction within the hypotheses. Much use was made of the HIDE command to hide irrelevant formulae and hence speed up the workings of the tactics.

Using a proof approach similar to that described above, we were able to show that the release operation is also feasible. The slave operation should have been similarly easy to handle, but, unfortunately, we were unable to complete the proof because of a bug in the PVS system concerning equality. In certain situations arising after a lengthy sequence of tactics, it seems that the system fails to recognise goals which are simply instances of the reflexivity of equality. This is a known bug and will, hopefully, be corrected in future versions of PVS.

6.4.4 Some Validation Conditions

In both the VDM and PVS specifications of the slave operation, the postconditions explicit specify what happens to those buffers which have status Slave or Master, but do not describe the effect on buffers which have status Newest or Idle. However, in conjunction with the invariant (and the frame in the VDM version) the postcondition ensures that no other Newest buffer remains, exactly one new Slave buffer is chosen, and no new Master buffers are added. This fact was stated as a validation condition in [8], and we have verified it using PVS. We show its statement in both VDM and PVS notations.

$$\forall\, i \in \{1,2,3\} \cdot (\overleftarrow{b}\,(i) \in \{\text{N}, \text{I}\} \;\Rightarrow\; b\,(i) \in \{\text{I}, \text{S}\})$$

```
slave_prop : CONJECTURE
   (FORALL (i:{x:nat| x=0 OR x=1 OR x=2}) :
      member(nth(b(st),i), {x:Status|x=Newest OR x=Idle})
      IMPLIES
      member(nth(b(slave(st)),i), {x:Status|x=Idle OR x=Slave}))
```

Our PVS proof of this statement required about 500 tactics and is difficult to follow intuitively, although neither its structure nor any of the individual steps is particularly sophisticated. After some initial preparation including skolemization, definition expansion, and adding some simple lemmas, the tactic PROP is invoked. This has the effect of splitting the many disjunctions among the hypotheses and thereby breaking the top goal down into about 200 subgoals. The majority of these were proved easily by some definition expansion, simplification, rewriting, and use of the tactic GRIND to detect contradictions among the hypotheses of the subgoal. Of the 54 subgoals which remained, 36 were proved by simply using GRIND. For the remaining subgoals, further case analysis was used to split each one into smaller subgoals which were then proved by GRIND.

The lemmas stated below were required later in order to prove a refinement proof obligation. We present them as validation conditions since they are reasonable properties to require of the MSMIE system. Their proofs were carried out interactively and required about 15 tactics each.

```
slave_prop2 : LEMMA
   (FORALL (st,st2:sigma2) :
       post_slave(st,st2) IMPLIES count(Newest,b(st2)) = 1)

slave_prop3 : LEMMA
   (FORALL (st,st2:sigma2) :
       post_slave(st,st2) IMPLIES
         count(Master,b(st)) = count(Master,b(st2)))
```

6.5   Representing Refinement

The states of the MSMIE system may be described more abstractly by ignoring the identity of individual buffers and distinguishing only the possible combinations of buffers which satisfy the invariant. The two binary choices in the invariant concerning the number of buffers assigned to Master and Newest mean that there are four such combinations: (Slave, Idle, Idle), (Slave, Idle, Newest), (Slave, Idle, Master), and (Slave, Newest, Master).

6.5.1   The VDM Specification

In VDM, the possible status combinations are represented by giving a new enumerated type comprising four tokens.

types

   $Status1 =$ SII | SIN | SIM | SNM

The state simply records which combination is current and the invariant and initial state are the "images under retrieval" of the concrete ones given previously.

state $\Sigma1$ of
  $bs : Status1$
  $ms : MName$-set

  inv mk-$\Sigma1\,(bs, ms)$ $\triangleq$
  $\quad ms = \{\} \;\Leftrightarrow\; bs \in \{\text{SII}, \text{SIN}\}$

  init $s \triangleq s = $ mk-$\Sigma1\,(\text{SII}, \{\})$
end

The operations are similar to those given in the previous specifications. In particular, the postconditions rely on the same case distinctions.

operations

$slave\,()$
ext wr $bs : Status1$
  rd $ms : (MName$-set$)$

pre true
post $(\overleftarrow{bs} \in \{\text{SII}, \text{SIN}\} \;\Rightarrow\; bs = \text{SIN}) \wedge$
$\quad\;\; (\overleftarrow{bs} \in \{\text{SIM}, \text{SNM}\} \;\Rightarrow\; bs = \text{SNM})$;

$acq\,(l : MName)$
ext wr $bs : Status1$
  wr $ms : (MName$-set$)$
pre $(\neg\,(l \in ms)) \wedge (\neg\,(bs = \text{SII}))$
post $ms = \overleftarrow{ms} \cup \{l\} \wedge$
$\quad$ if $\overleftarrow{ms} = \{\}$
$\quad$ then $bs = \underleftarrow{\text{SIM}}$
$\quad$ else $bs = \overleftarrow{bs}$;

$rel\,(l : MName)$
ext wr $bs : Status1$
  wr $ms : (MName$-set$)$
pre $l \in ms$
post $ms = \overleftarrow{ms} \setminus \{l\} \wedge$
$\quad$ if $ms = \{\}$
$\quad$ then $bs = \underleftarrow{\text{SIN}}$
$\quad$ else $bs = \overleftarrow{bs}$

6.5.2 The PVS Specification

We have formalised the more abstract specification as a theory in PVS. The techniques used are the same as for the concrete specification. The TCCs generated

by typechecking are also similar, but they are easier to prove because this is a less
elaborate specification.

```
msmie_sigma1[MName : TYPE+] : THEORY

  BEGIN

  Status1 : TYPE = {SII,SIN,SIM,SNM}

  sigma1 : TYPE =
   {x : [# bs : Status1,
          ms : setof[MName] #] |
    (member(bs(x),{x:Status1|x=SII OR x=SIN}) <=> ms(x) = emptyset)}

  initial_sigma1 : sigma1 =
     (# bs := SII, ms := emptyset #)


  pre_slave  : [sigma1 -> bool] = LAMBDA (st:sigma1) :
     true

  post_slave : [(pre_slave),sigma1 -> bool] =
     LAMBDA (st:(pre_slave),st2:sigma1) :
       ((member(bs(st),{x:Status1|x=SII OR x=SIN}) IMPLIES
            bs(st2) = SIN)
        AND
        (member(bs(st),{x:Status1|x=SIM OR x=SNM}) IMPLIES
            bs(st2)´ = SNM))
        AND
        (ms(st2) = ms(st))

  slave : [(pre_slave) -> sigma1] =
     LAMBDA (st:(pre_slave)) :
        choose({st2:sigma1 | post_slave(st,st2)})

  pre_acq : [MName -> [sigma1 -> bool]] =
     LAMBDA (l:MName)(st:sigma1) :
        (NOT member(l,ms(st))) AND (bs(st) /= SII)

  post_acq : [l:MName -> [(pre_acq(l)),sigma1 -> bool]] =
             LAMBDA (l:MName)(st:(pre_acq(l)),st2:sigma1) :
                ((ms(st2) = union(ms(st),singleton(l)))) AND
                 (IF
                       ms(st) = emptyset
                  THEN
```

```
                    bs(st2) = SIM
              ELSE
                    bs(st2) = bs(st)
              ENDIF)

acq : [l:MName, (pre_acq(l)) -> sigma1] =
        LAMBDA (l:MName, st:(pre_acq(l))) :
              choose({st2:sigma1 | post_acq(l)(st,st2)})
```

The specification of the release operation is not shown.

```
END msmie_sigma1
```

6.5.3 The Refinement Relationship

We formalise, as a PVS theory, the statement that sigma2 is a refinement of sigma1. The refinement relationship is modelled by a theory which imports the theories representing the concrete and abstract specifications. The proof obligations that pertain to refinement must be typed in by hand; they are not automatically generated by the system. They are declared to be CONJECTURES in the theory, as described below and then PVS is used to prove them.

```
sigma1_sigma2[MName : TYPE+] : THEORY

  BEGIN

  IMPORTING msmie_sigma1[MName], msmie_sigma2[MName]
```

First, we define the "retrieve" operation mapping concrete states to abstract ones. The definition is given by cases, and is much the same as that given in [8]. Typechecking generates a TCC stating that the retrieved state does indeed satisfy the invariant of sigma1. This is proved automatically by tcp.

```
retr2_1 : [sigma2 -> sigma1] = LAMBDA (st:sigma2) :
  (# bs :=
          LET cc : [nat,nat] =
              (count(Newest,b(st)),count(Master,b(st)))
          IN
            IF    cc = (0,0) THEN SII
            ELSIF cc = (1,0) THEN SIN
            ELSIF cc = (0,1) THEN SIM
            ELSE                  SNM
            ENDIF,
      ms := ms(st) #)
```

Next we typed in the various proof obligations required to demonstrate that `sigma2` is a refinement of `sigma1`. All of these have been verified using PVS. We shall indicate how difficult it was to carry out each verification.

Showing adequacy was a relatively non-trivial task, taking a few hours to complete. The proof itself is conceptually simple: we consider each of the possible values of the system status in the abstract specification, and supply a suitable value for the concrete state in each case. For each of these we must then show two things: that it is the value returned by the , and that it satisfies the invariant of sigma2. The first can be proved almost automatically by expanding some definitions and invoking the tactic `GRIND`. To prove the second we must use the invariant of the abstract state. The entire proof script for adequacy is about 130 lines long.

```
adeq2_1 : CONJECTURE
  (FORALL (st1:sigma1) :
     (EXISTS (st2:sigma2) : retr2_1(st2) = st1))
```

Next we proved that the maps the concrete initial state to the abstract initial state. This was very simple: after expanding one definition, the "grind" tactic completed the proof.

```
init2_1 : CONJECTURE
  (retr2_1 (initial_sigma2) = initial_sigma1)
```

Next was the domain rule for the slave operation. This is trivial and was proved automatically by "grind".

```
slave_dom2_1 : CONJECTURE
  (FORALL (st2:sigma2) :
     (pre_slave (retr2_1(st2))) IMPLIES pre_slave(st2))
```

To prove the result rule for slave we first added the lemmas `slave_prop1` and `slave_prop2` which were validation conditions in the theory `msmie_sigma2`. Next, we used the tactic `TYPEPRED` to make the invariant of `sigma2` visible to the prover. Once this preparation was in place, the `GRIND` tactic completed the proof.

```
slave_result2_1 : CONJECTURE
  (FORALL (st2_:((pre_slave:[sigma2->bool])),st2:sigma2) :
     ((pre_slave (retr2_1(st2_)) AND (post_slave(st2_,st2)))
      IMPLIES
      (post_slave (retr2_1(st2_),retr2_1(st2)))))
```

The domain rule for acq required a proof about 30 tactics long as well as a lemma about the `count` function. The proof structure is as follows: first definitions were expanded, the lemma was added, hidden type information was made visible, and the proof was split into two subgoals; then the `GRIND` tactic was called upon to complete the proof.

```
acq_dom2_1 : CONJECTURE
   (FORALL (st2:sigma2) : (FORALL (l:MName) :
      (pre_acq (l)(retr2_1(st2))) IMPLIES pre_acq(l)(st2)))
```

The result rule for acq required a complicated, interactive proof comprising hundreds of tactics which took several days to complete.

```
acq_result2_1 : CONJECTURE
   (FORALL (l:MName) :
   (FORALL (st2_:(pre_acq(l):[sigma2->bool]),st2:sigma2) :
      ((pre_acq (l)(retr2_1(st2_)) AND (post_acq(l)(st2_,st2)))
      IMPLIES
      (post_acq (l)(retr2_1(st2_),retr2_1(st2)))))))
```

The domain rule for the release operation was proved automatically by GRIND.

```
rel_dom2_1 : CONJECTURE
   (FORALL (st2:sigma2) : (FORALL (l:MName) :
      (pre_rel (l)(retr2_1(st2))) IMPLIES pre_rel(l)(st2)))
```

The result rule for this operation required a complex, interactive proof very similar to that of the result rule for acq.

```
rel_result2_1 : CONJECTURE
   (FORALL (l:MName) :
   (FORALL (st2_:(pre_rel(l):[sigma2->bool]),st2:sigma2) :
      ((pre_rel (l)(retr2_1(st2_)) AND (post_rel(l)(st2_,st2)))
      IMPLIES
      (post_rel (l)(retr2_1(st2_),retr2_1(st2)))))))

END sigma1_sigma2
```

6.6 Discussion

In this section we note various observations made during our experiments. These include some points about the PVS system, as well as a discussion of some differences between the logics of VDM-SL and the PVS specification language.

6.6.1 Using the PVS System

PVS facilitates proofs at a fairly non-tedious level, due to the integrated decision procedures and rewriting techniques. Low level proof hacking using for instance associativity and commutation properties of arithmetic operations is usually not necessary. Of course, the real difficult side of theorem proving is still difficult, for instance, understanding the application (and formalizing it correctly), inventing proofs, and generating suitable lemmas. However, we were impressed by the fact that we were actually able to prove all (but one) of the proof obligations, including refinement proof obligations, for the MSMIE example. This augers well for the usability of the system for further applications.

In all of our examples we made use of the TCC mechanism of PVS to obtain some automatic proof obligation generation. This results in TCCs which are, in general, too complicated to be solved by the PVS command "typecheck-prove", which is good at automatically finding proofs of simple TCCs. Unfortunately, in the present implementation of PVS it is impossible to prevent this command from embarking on time-consuming attempts to prove all existing TCCS for the current theory, even though the user may know that certain ones are too difficult to be solved. A more flexible version of "typecheck-prove", or perhaps simply a time limit to its operation, would be welcome.

One may like or dislike the PVS Emacs interface. Though all of the authors were used to Emacs, we disliked some of its features relating to PVS. For instance, we found that the way in which buffers popped up and destroyed existing Emacs windows was confusing and irritating. We also felt that the quite frequent switching between buffers that we had to do became somewhat of a bottleneck. Moreover, the interface was unreliable and it was often necessary to restart PVS when Emacs ended up in a state where you could not execute important PVS commands.

6.6.2   Partiality in VDM and PVS

The most notable difference between the specification languages of PVS and VDM is that PVS deals only in total functions. In practice, much of the language flexibility of partial functions in LPF can be captured in PVS by the use of subtypes and dependent types to express the domain of definition of a function. A good example is the *nth* function on lists which is defined recursively in PVS as follows:

```
nth(l, (n:nat | n < length(l))): RECURSIVE nat =
   IF n = 0 THEN car(l) ELSE nth(cdr(l), n-1) ENDIF
   MEASURE length(l)
```

As the following examples show, this function may be used freely when writing specifications: the fact that it is partial imposes no special syntactic constraints. For example we can write:

```
ex1:nat = nth((: 1, 3 , 2 :), 1)

ex2:nat = nth((: 1, 3 , 2 :), 4)
```

Correctness is maintained by typechecking. The first example causes no problems. However, the second example results in the false TCC

```
4 < length[nat]((: 1, 3, 2 :))
```

An example of a use of partial functions which is possible in LPF but not in PVS involves the subp function, due to Cliff Jones. In PVS it may be defined as follows[1].

```
subp(i:nat,j:nat | i >= j): RECURSIVE nat =
  IF i=j THEN 0 ELSE 1 + subp(i,j+1) ENDIF
  MEASURE abs(i-j)
```

When applied to natural numbers i and j, where i > j, this function returns the difference i-j. This property can be formalised and proved in both PVS and LPF. However, the following property which is also true of subp in LPF, cannot be proved in PVS — in fact, it cannot even be typechecked.

```
subp_lemma : CONJECTURE
  FORALL (i,j:nat) : (subp(i,j) = i - j) OR (subp(j,i) = j - i)
```

Attempting to typecheck this results in the false TCC:

```
subp_lemma_TCC1: OBLIGATION (FORALL (i, j: nat): i >= j);
```

Fortunately, the present example does not contain any construction where this distinction is significant.

6.6.3 Looseness in VDM and PVS

Another semantic difference between VDM and our translation to PVS is in the interpretation of expressions whose values are not fully determined.

In VDM, looseness in function definitions is interpreted as underspecification, that is to say, every invocation of a function with the same argument will return the same result; whereas looseness in operation definitions is understood to be genuine non-determinism, so separate invocations of a loosely specified operation can yield different results even if called with the same arguments and in the same state [16]. The motivation for this distinction is that, in an implementation, the result of an operation may depend on some state not being modelled in the abstraction, whereas a function should be declarative however it is implemented.

For example, for functions f and g:

$$f(x) = \text{let } y \text{ be st } y > x \text{ in } y \text{ end}$$
$$g(x) = \text{let } y \text{ be st } y > x \text{ in } y \text{ end}$$

we can always be certain that $f(x) = f(x)$, but $f(x) = g(x)$ may not necessarily hold in a refinement.

PVS, on the other hand, takes a more constrained interpretation of looseness: all occurrences of the same choice expression must yield the same result wherever they

---

[1]This definition is due to Klaus Havelund

occur. So, if we make the corresponding definitions in PVS,

```
f(x) = choose({y:nat | y > x})
g(x) = choose({y:nat | y > x})
```

then we always have `f(x) = g(x)` also.

The VDM interpretation of loose functions is appropriate in the context of a development employing the "design by contract" paradigm. Underspecification represents the deferral of a design decision concerning the choice of a fully determined implementation. Thus looseness can be removed during refinement and the resulting behaviour will be no worse from the caller's point of view than that of the loose function. However, this interpretation of looseness has severe implications for reasoning as it prohibits the indiscriminate substitution of equals. We cannot make the simple chain of equalities:

$$f(x) = \text{let } y \text{ be st } y > x \text{ in } y \text{ end} = g(x)$$

Rather, each occurrence of a loose expression must in some way be tagged in order that it is possible to determine which occurrence is being referred to when it occurs in proofs. It also means that beta-reduction can only be undertaken when the argument is fully determined [16].

The PVS interpretation of looseness yields simpler proofs since we can be sure that identical expressions will have equal value irrespective of how they arise. However, this interpretation of looseness defies compositionality in refinement as if the same choice expression occurs in two separate parts of a specification, they must both be treated similarly in any subsequent refinement.

In the present example, we have interpreted implicit operations by use of PVS choice operator. In the case where there is some genuine choice, as in *slave*, this is not strictly correct. With this interpretation we could prove properties of the specification which are not necessarily preserved by an implementation.

These differences in the semantics raise methodological questions about the use of such constructions in practice. Though partiality and looseness are both extremely useful, they should be used with caution particularly in circumstances where there is disagreement as to their interpretation.

6.6.4   Errors in Example Specifications

The translation into PVS did not reveal any errors in the MSMIE specification. However, a number of errors were found in two other realistic VDM-SL specifications (not shown here) which were translated into PVS by Agerholm. A third specification, also translated by Agerholm, was not found to contain any errors.

The errors themselves are not major and should perhaps mainly be read as small and funny, but also worrying, examples of the errors that people make in writing formal specifications (and programs). They may be divided into three categories: (1) those that were pointed out directly during the proof of a type checking condition, (2) those that probably could have been found easily by testing specifications, (3) other errors, some of which are quite subtle, e.g. due to parentheses problems. What the errors teach us is that in specification debugging one can benefit from working with specifications in a formal way. However, other alternatives for validation such as testing could have found some of the errors as well. For detailed discussion of the errors that were found, the reader is referred to [3].

6.7 Conclusion

The VDM-SL style of specification and refinement fits well with the PVS specification language. As a result we were able to use a very direct embedding of VDM in PVS (for example, logical formulae in VDM are represented by those of PVS), which means that the proof capabilities of the PVS system are available directly to the VDM user. This is not always the case where a deeper, more indirect embedding is required, forcing the user to navigate through layers of definitions. A shallow embedding is very desirable in a closed system like PVS, though it is less important in open systems such as HOL and Isabelle where a programming language is available to automate the deep embedding process.

At present the translation from VDM-SL to PVS, and the generation of refinement proof obligations must both be done manually. As well as being inconvenient, these manual processes are opportunities for the introduction of errors. It is possible to automate the translation step outside of PVS, generating PVS theories from VDM-SL specifications. However, the closed nature of the PVS system makes it difficult to achieve a close integration with other tools supporting VDM-SL such as can be achieved with other more open systems [4, 3]. This leads to the disadvantage that a VDM-SL user who wishes to use PVS for proofs must master the PVS notation and become, in effect, a PVS user as well.

Because of the difficulties described in the previous paragraph, as well as the semantic differences between PVS and VDM-SL described in Section 6, we do not view PVS as a satisfactory proof tool for VDM-SL. However, the ease with which VDM-SL *style* may be transported to PVS means that this style may be a useful approach for VDM-SL users wishing to experiment with PVS.

The authors are all convinced of the need for and the benefits to be derived from the use of tools to support VDM specification. The extensive type-checking done by the PVS system contributes greatly to our confidence in the correctness of the specifications and refinements. For example, we can be certain that functions are applied only to arguments within their domain.[2] We also derived confidence from the proof process. Although this is somewhat muted by reports of bugs in the PVS prover, the advantages of mechanical support for proof compared to making proofs by hand almost certainly outweighs the possibility of the system constructing an

---

[2]A similar kind of facility, called a proof obligation generator, is currently being developed for the IFAD VDM-SL Toolbox [6].

erroneous proof.

The PVS prover was sufficiently fast and powerful to make it feasible to do proofs of the size shown in this chapter, though the time required to do this is considerable and so proof for "real-world" applications remains an expensive activity. On the other hand, the proofs which were undertaken, though not mathematically sophisticated, involved such elaborate case analyses that it is unlikely that they would be successfully carried out without the help of tools.

Further work needs to be carried out in order to discover the implications as far as refinements are concerned of the different approaches to looseness taken in VDM-SL and PVS. It would also be interesting to see how the approach scales up to larger, more "real-world" applications which might provide a more exacting test of the capabilities of the PVS system. Finally, the authors are interested in a comparison between PVS and the new VDM proof tool based on Isabelle which is currently under development at IFAD.

Acknowledgments

Sten Agerholm would like to thank Peter Gorm Larsen for his support and interest in the work reported here. Agerholm's work was funded by the Danish Research Councils. Savi Maharaj wishes to thank the European Research Consortium in Informatics and Mathematics for funding her stay at the Rutherford Appleton Laboratory where her work was carried out.

6.8 Bibliography

[1] S. Agerholm. *A HOL Basis for Reasoning about Functional Programs*. PhD thesis, BRICS, Department of Computer Science, University of Aarhus, 1994. Available as Technical Report RS-94-44.

[2] S. Agerholm. LCF examples in HOL. In *The Computer Journal*, 38(2), 1995.

[3] S. Agerholm. Translating Specifications in VDM-SL to PVS. In *Proceedings of the 9th International Conference on Theorem Proving in Higher Order Logics (TPHOL '96)*, Springer-Verlag LNCS 1125, 1996.

[4] S. Agerholm and J. Frost. An Isabelle-based Theorem Prover for VDM-SL. In *Proceedings of the 10th International Conference on Theorem Proving in Higher Order Logics (TPHOLs'97)*, Springer-Verlag LNCS, 1997.

[5] S. Agerholm and J. Frost. Towards an Integrated CASE and Theorem Proving Tool for VDM-SL. In *FME'97*, Springer-Verlag LNCS, 1997.

[6] B. Aichernig and P. G. Larsen. A Proof Obligation Generator for VDM-SL. In *FME'97*, Springer-Verlag LNCS, 1997.

[7] D.J. Andrews and M. Bruun et al. Information Technology — Programming Languages, their environments and system software interfaces — Vienna Development Method-Specification Language Part 1: Base language. ISO Draft International Standard: 13817-1, 1995.

[8] J.C. Bicarregui. A Model-Oriented Analysis of a Communications Protocol. Technical report RAL-93-099, Rutherford Appleton Laboratory, 1993.

[9] J.C. Bicarregui and B. Ritchie. Invariants, Frames and Postconditions: a comparison of the VDM and B notations. In *Proceeding of Formal Methods Europe '93*, Springer-Verlag LNCS 670, 1993. Also in *IEEE Transaction on Software Engineering*, 21(2), 1995.

[10] R. J. Boulton and A. D. Gordon *et al.* Experience with Embedding Hardware Description Languages in HOL. In *Theorem Provers in Circuit Design: Theory, Practice and Experience: Proceedings of the IFIP TC10/WG 10.2 International Conference*, North-Holland, IFIP Transactions A-10, 1992.

[11] G. Bruns and S. Anderson. The Formalization and Analysis of a Communications Protocol. In *Formal Aspects of Computing*, 6(1), Springer, 1994.

[12] G. Collins and D. Syme. A theory of finite maps. In *Proceedings of the 8th International Workshop on Higher Order Logic Theorem Proving and its Applications*, Springer-Verlag LNCS 971, September 1995.

[13] J. Crow, S. Owre *et al. A Tutorial Introduction to PVS*. Computer Science Laboratory, SRI International, Menlo Park, CA, February 1993.

[14] R. Elmstrøm, P.G. Larsen, and P.B. Lassen. The IFAD VDM-SL Toolbox: A practical approach to formal specifications. In *ACM Sigplan Notices* 29(9), 1994

[15] P.G. Larsen. *Towards Proof Rules for VDM-SL*. PhD thesis, Technical University of Denmark, Department of Computer Science, March 1995. ID-TR:1995-160.

[16] Peter G. Larsen and Bo S. Hansen. Semantics of Underdetermined Expressions. In *Formal Aspects of Computing*, 8(1), 1996.

[17] L.L. Santoline *et al.* Multiprocessor Shared-Memory Information Exchange. In *IEEE Transactions on Nuclear Science,* 36(1), 1989.

[18] H. Sondergaard and P. Sestoft. Non-determinism in functional languages. In *The Computer Journal*, 35(5), 1992.

Chapter 7

Supporting Proof in VDM-SL using Isabelle

Sten Agerholm and Jacob Frost

Summary

This chapter describes the construction of a theorem proving component of a prototype integrated CASE and theorem proving tool which combines the benefits of a general-purpose theorem prover called Isabelle with those of a commercial software development environment for VDM-SL—the IFAD VDM-SL Toolbox. The integrated tool supports proof in the notation of the CASE tool by handling "difficult" constructs such as patterns and cases expressions in a novel way using reversible transformations. Hence, it gives the user a consistent view on the modeling, the model analysis and the proof processes as both pragmatic testing and formal proof is supported in one notation. The chapter illustrates the use of the theorem prover on two examples where automation of proof support is a key issue and a challenge due to the three-valued nature of the Logic of Partial Functions (LPF) underlying VDM-SL.

7.1 Introduction

A large part of industry's reluctance towards theorem proving is caused by the "take it or leave it" approach that has been taken when presenting the technology to industry. The focus has traditionally been on fully verified systems, and the theorem prover has been the starting point of discussion. We suggest instead taking a more pragmatic starting point, such as a CASE tool, and step by step "upgrading" this tool with support for proofs. More light-weight use of theorem provers is to "debug" specifications by proving various consistency conditions, such as type checking conditions in PVS [20] and type checker generated proof obligations in the IFAD VDM-SL Toolbox [5]. More heavy-weight use is, for example, to prove refinements of specifications.

This chapter presents the first steps towards building an industrial-strength proof support tool for VDM-SL using this CASE tool oriented approach. Our starting point is the IFAD VDM-SL Toolbox [17, 8, 11], which is a commercial software development environment that supports a range of development activities, including various static checks, specification level execution and debugging and code generation to C++. We try to combine the benefits of this toolset with the benefits of the generic theorem prover Isabelle[1] [18]. We do not build the theorem prover from scratch since this is a far too time consuming task, and systems like Isabelle are designed to allow fast construction of theorem provers for new logics. The chapter focuses both on the construction of a theorem prover for VDM-SL in Isabelle, called VDM-LPF, and on the integration of this "proof engine" with the IFAD VDM-SL Toolbox in a way that gives the user a consistent view on the specification and the proof process. Our intended use of the combined tool is mainly for proving type consistency proof obligations. Experiments have already shown this to be a powerful approach to debug specifications [2] and to prove safety properties for operations in state-based systems. However, it will also be possible to prove general correctness requirements of specifications.

The first attempt to build proof support for VDM-SL was in the Mural project [13, 6], and these results have been an important starting point for this work, in particular the book [6]. However, our combined tool extends the subset of VDM-SL supported in Mural with (at least) let expressions, cases expressions, patterns, enumerated expressions, quote types and the character type. Difficult constructs like patterns and cases expressions are handled using reversible transformations and special-purpose derived proof rules that mimic the original expressions.

LPF

The "Logic of Partial Functions" (LPF) is a well-established basis for reasoning about VDM-SL specifications [12, 13, 6]. Consequently we have chosen to base the theorem prover component of our system on LPF.

LPF is designed specifically to cope with "undefined values" resulting from partiality of functions. Logics such as first-order classical logic are two-valued in the sense that formulas are either true or false. In contrast, LPF is three-valued, allowing formulas also to be undefined. Because many of the connectives are non-strict, a formula can be defined even though its subformulas are undefined. For example, the formula e1 or e2 is true whenever one of its subformulas e1 or e2 is true even if the other is undefined. To be false both subformulas must be false. In the remaining situations the disjunction is undefined.

---

[1]A generic theorem prover provides a logical framework in which new logics can be formulated. A new logic is called an instantiation, or an object-logic.

The definition of LPF means that it has many nice properties. For example, both disjunction and conjunction behave symmetrically. In fact, all inference rules valid in LPF are also valid in classical logic. However, the opposite is not true. Most noticeably, the law of the excluded middle e or not e does not hold due to the third value representing undefinedness.

Isabelle

Isabelle [18] is a generic theorem proving system which can be instantiated to support reasoning in new so-called *object-logics* by extending its *meta-logic*. The language of the meta-logic is typed lambda-calculus. The syntax of an object-logic is implemented by extending this language with new types and constants. The inference rules of an object-logic are implemented by extending the meta-logic with corresponding meta-axioms. Object-level natural deduction proofs can be carried out as meta-level proofs using different forms of resolution to apply rules.

The Isabelle system contains a range of useful features. For example, it provides unknowns, which are essentially free variables that can be instantiated gradually during a proof by higher-order unification. It also provides syntax annotations, syntax declarations and several translation mechanisms that are useful for handling concrete syntax. In addition, it has a tactic language and generic packages to write powerful proof procedures for object logics with little effort.

Organization of this Chapter

We first give an overview of our approach to build an integrated CASE and theorem proving tool in Section 7.2. The following three sections, Section 7.3 to Section 7.5, describe the Isabelle instantiation: syntax, proof theory and proof support (tactics). Section 7.6 and Section 7.7 concern the integration, respectively the transformation of expressions to fit into the subset supported by Isabelle and the generation of "representations" of specifications as Isabelle theories. Section 7.8 presents future work and Section 7.9 the conclusions. This chapter collects material from the two papers [3, 4].

7.2 Overview of Approach

The overall idea of the integrated system is that a user writes a VDM-SL specification using the IFAD VDM-SL Toolbox to syntax check, type check and possibly validate the specification. When the user wants to prove a property entered by hand or a proof obligation generated by the type checker, he can start the Proof Support Tool (PST), generate axioms from a specification and load these into a VDM-SL instantiation of Isabelle. The PST will then provide a Graphical User Interface (GUI) to Isabelle through which proofs can be conducted and managed in a flexible way. This system architecture is illustrated in Figure 7.1. We call this a two-layered

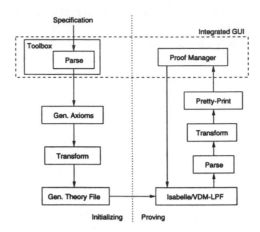

Figure 7.1: Overview of system architecture.

architecture in the sense that the theorem prover is the bottom layer, the "proof engine", and the proof support tool and its graphical user interface are the top layer. In between the layers, transformation, parsing and pretty-printing occur.

7.2.1   Reading of Figure 7.1

The left hand side of Figure 7.1 concerns initializing the proof support tool for a specification. The specification is written and then syntax and type checked using the Toolbox. It must be type checked because axioms are generated on basis of this assumption (see Section 7.7). The resulting abstract syntax tree representation of the specification is communicated to the proof support tool (via a file link). From the syntax tree, axioms are generated as proof rules whose hypotheses are stated using abstract syntax for VDM-SL and type judgements. The expression parts of axioms are then transformed to a subset of VDM-SL. This subset does not contain for instance patterns and cases expressions. Finally, the transformed axioms are printed together with signature information for new constants to an Isabelle theory file.

The theory file generated as above is read into an instantiation of Isabelle, called Isabelle/VDM-LPF, which contains a proof theory for the VDM-SL subset. The right hand side of Figure 7.1 illustrates how proofs of theorems and proof obligations are conducted by sending commands to Isabelle via the PST graphical user interface. Such commands could tell Isabelle to start a new proof or to apply some tactic in an on-going backwards proof. Proof states in backwards proofs are represented as proof rules in Isabelle and the Toolbox parser has been extended to read Isabelle's notation for these. After parsing proof states to abstract syntax, a transformation function is applied, which reintroduces for instance patterns and cases expressions.

Finally, a VDM-SL ASCII pretty-printer produces concrete syntax which can be displayed to the user. Both the generation of axioms, the transformation and the pretty-printing are specified in VDM-SL itself. The underlying "programs" work by executing specifications using the Toolbox.

7.3 Syntax

Isabelle is a generic theorem prover which provides distinguishing features for embedding new logics (syntax and proof rules) and reasoning in these logics. Isabelle has a meta-logic, an intuitionistic higher order logic based on typed lambda-calculus, in which constructs of new logics become constants, primitive proof rules become (meta-) axioms, and derived rules become (meta-) theorems. Moreover, it provides a few, but powerful tactics for applying these rules, based on different kinds of resolution and generic packages for writing proof search procedures for new logics (see Section 7.5).

When embedding a language such as VDM-SL in Isabelle, two sometimes conflicting criteria must be met. Firstly, the language should allow smooth reasoning using features of Isabelle. Secondly, it should provide a user-friendly and familiar notation. These two goals are achieved by implementing an abstract and a concrete syntax and by relating these using automatic translations.

Syntax issues are described in more detail in the Appendix. Here, we just illustrate on some examples that, with our definitions, Isabelle is able to print and parse exactly the VDM-SL concrete syntax such as the following[2]:

```
[3,1,2]
{x + 1 | x in set {1,2,3} & x >= 2}
forall x:nat, y:nat & x + y = y + x
let x = 5, y = x + 6, z = 7 in y + z
if n = 0 then 1 elseif n = 1 then 2 elseif n < 10 then 9 else n
mk_(x,5,z).#2 + mk_(1,2,3,4).#3 = 8
```

As illustrated in the last line, Isabelle's syntax handling features support something as exotic as arbitrary-length tuples and generalized projections.

7.4 Proof System of VDM-LPF

The proof system for VDM-SL axiomatized in Isabelle has been developed with minor modifications from that presented in the book [6], where LPF is used as the basis. In addition to primitive and derived rules for propositional and predicate LPF, the book contains a large number of rules for datatypes such as natural numbers, sets, sequences, maps, etc. As in many other formulations of LPF, these rules are

---

[2]Throughout this chapter we use ASCII syntax for VDM-SL in order to highlight the similarity between the syntax used by the IFAD Toolbox and the Isabelle instantiation.

formulated as natural deduction rules. This fits well with the choice of Isabelle which supports natural deduction style proof particularly well.

The following two subsections describe part of the VDM-SL proof system and its implementation in Isabelle. The axiomatization of, for example, datatypes is not discussed since we do not contribute to the presentation in [6].

7.4.1 Proof Rules

The proof system of LPF contains most of the standard rules of propositional and predicate logic. However, it is a three-valued logic so it does not provide the law of excluded middle, and some rules have additional typing assumptions, for example, in order to ensure that equality is defined.

Most of the rules of the Isabelle instantiation are taken from [6]. The adaptation consists mostly of changing the syntax. For example, consider the rules:

$$\frac{\quad}{\text{true}} \qquad \frac{P;\ Q}{P \wedge Q} \qquad \frac{P \vee Q;\ P \vdash R;\ Q \vdash R}{R}$$

$$\frac{x : A \vdash_x \neg P(x)}{\neg(\exists x \cdot : A \cdot P(x))} \qquad \frac{b : A;\ a = b;\ P(b)}{P(a)}$$

These rules are translated into the following Isabelle axioms:

```
true_intr        "true"
and_intr         "[| P; Q |] ==> P and Q"
or_elim          "[| P or Q; P ==> R; Q ==> R |] ==> R"
not_exists_intr  "(!!x.x:A ==> not P(x)) ==> not (exists x:A & P(x))"
eq_subs_left     "[| a=b; P(b); b:A |] ==> P(a)"
```

In these axioms, ==> represents meta-implication while [| and |] enclose a list of assumptions separated by ;. Note that variable subscripts for locally bound variables in sequents are handled using meta-quantification !!. Apart from using the concrete ASCII syntax of VDM-LPF (see Appendix), these examples illustrate how the horizontal line and turnstile in the original rules are represented as meta-implication.

In some cases, the order of assumptions is changed to make the rules work better with Isabelle's resolution tactics, which often use unification on the first assumption to instantiate variables. In particular, type assumptions are often moved from the front of the assumption list to the back, since these do not typically contain any important information for restricting the application of rules. An example of this is the last substitution rule above.

7.4.2 Combining Natural Deduction and Sequent Style Proof

In order to formalize proof rules as meta-level axioms in Isabelle it is necessary to define a judgement relating object-level formulas to meta-level formulas in Isabelle's higher-order logic. In the LPF variant used here, there is no distinction between expressions and formulas. Hence, expressions (and formulas) are represented as lambda-calculus terms of type `ex`. In Isabelle meta-level formulas are terms of type `prop`. Consequently, the standard judgement relating object-level expressions to meta-level formulas is the following lifting constant:

```
TRUE' :: ex => prop   ("(_)" 5)
```

The concrete syntax associated with this constant in brackets specifies that `TRUE'` will not occur explicitly in (meta-) axioms representing proof rules (5 is a precedence). Hence, `TRUE'` was invisible in the proof rules presented above.

The standard judgement `TRUE'` is sufficient for implementing a natural deduction system for LPF. However, in order to automate proving in VDM-LPF, it is advantageous to be able to conduct (or simulate) sequent calculus style backward proof. In classical logic this can be done by representing multiple conclusions as negated assumptions. This issue is a consequence of the law of excluded middle. However, LPF is a three-valued logic and does not satisfy this law. Instead, we have therefore declared an additional judgement for this purpose:

```
FALSE' :: ex => prop   ("FALSE _" 5)
```

In this case the concrete syntax requires an object-level formula to be preceded by `FALSE` (specified in brackets). The idea is that this judgement acts as a kind of non-strict negation with respect to the third value of LPF. This form of negation, which can only occur at the outermost level, allows multiple conclusions to be represented as a "negated" assumptions. This is discussed further in Section 7.5.

There are two new rules for the `FALSE` judgement:

```
FALSE_dup    "(FALSE P ==> P) ==> P"
FALSE_contr  "[| FALSE P; P |] ==> Q"
```

The first rule allows a conclusion to be duplicated as a negated assumption using `FALSE`, while the second rule is a contradiction-like rule. Together these rules imply that `FALSE` behaves as desired.

The inclusion of the additional judgement `FALSE` to represent multiple conclusions has interesting consequences for the proof system. For example, the primitive rule

```
(!! y.y:A ==> def P(y)) ==> def exists x:A & P(x)
```

becomes derivable, and it is no longer necessary or useful. This is fortunate since the rule appears to be hard to apply properly, especially in automatic backwards proof. An automatic proof of the rule is given in Section 7.5.2.

Soundness

We are confident, but have not formally proved, that the modifications of the proof system discussed above are sound. We base this confidence on Cheng's thesis [7], who has proved essentially this result for VDM-SL without datatypes. Cheng formulates both a sequent calculus and a natural deduction proof system for predicate LPF with equality and non-strict connectives[3]. Among other things, he proves that these proof systems are equivalent in terms of what can be derived. However, he does not consider datatypes like those of VDM-LPF. Hence, we should eventually extend Cheng's work to ensure that the VDM-SL datatype extensions of LPF do not violate soundness. We have done some preliminary work on this.

7.5   Proof Tactics

Isabelle's built-in tactics can be used immediately with VDM-LPF for fine-grained proof. However, it is advantageous to build special-purpose tactics exploiting the **FALSE** judgement as well as tactics for doing automatic proof search. This section describes such basic tactics as well as proof search tactics.

7.5.1   Basic Tactics

In many cases Isabelle's standard resolution tactics are suitable for applying the rules of VDM-LPF directly. For example, consider a proof state with the following subgoal:

```
1.   Q and P ==> P or Q
```

The conclusion of this goal can be broken down using the standard resolution tactic `resolve_tac` with the or-introduction rule `or_intr_left`, which will apply this rule to the conclusion in a backward fashion. This can be written using Isabelle's useful shorthand `br`, where b stands for **by**:

```
- br or_intr_left 1;   (* same as: by(resolve_tac [or_intr_left] 1) *)
1.   Q and P ==> P
```

In a similar fashion the assumption of the subgoal can be broken down, this time using `eresolve_tac` to apply the and-elimination rule `and_elim` in a forward fashion on the assumption of the subgoal:

```
- be and_elim 1;   (* same as: by (eresolve_tac [and_elim] 1) *)
1.   [| Q; P |] ==> P
```

Finally, the remaining subgoal can be solved using `assume_tac` which simulates proof by assumption in natural deduction:

```
- ba 1;   (* same as: by (assume_tac 1) *)
No subgoals!
```

---

[3]The connectives, in particular definedness (for "true or false"), in our variant of LPF are all strict.

In addition to the above tactics, Isabelle has a few other basic resolution tactics for applying natural deduction rules (see [18]).

There are a few situations where the above tactics are not suitable for applying the rules of VDM-LPF. For example, consider the following subgoal where a multiple conclusion is represented as an assumption using the `FALSE` judgement:

```
1.   [| P and Q; FALSE P or Q |] ==> R
```

In this case `resolve_tac` cannot be used directly to apply `or_intr` to (part of) the conclusion `P or Q`, since it is represented as an assumption. Instead we have developed variants of the standard resolution tactics, which can be used in such situations. The names of these are obtained by just adding an additional prime on standard names, as in `resolve_tac'`. These tactics use the proof rules for the `FALSE` judgement to allow a rule to be applied to conclusions represented in assumptions using `FALSE`. In addition to these, a VDM-LPF variant of `assume_tac`, called `assume_tac'`, allows one step proofs of subgoals like:

```
[| P |] ==> P
[| P; FALSE P |] ==> R
[| P; not P |] ==> R
```

The first case is just ordinary proof by assumption, the next covers the situation where a conclusion appears in the assumptions due to `FALSE`, while the last case deals with the situation where a proof branch is ended by an application of the primitive LPF contradiction rule `[| P; not P |] ==> Q`.

7.5.2   Proof Search Tactics

Isabelle also provides a generic classical reasoning package for automating larger parts of proofs than supported by the tactics above. However, VDM-LPF is not classical and therefore it seems hard to use this package. Classical laws are used for simulating sequents using natural deduction. Instead we have implemented a new package designed specifically for VDM-LPF. This package combines ideas from Cheng's thesis on LPF [7] with ideas and code from the classical reasoning package. As in Isabelle, the aim of this is to provide a practical tool and less emphasis is put on completeness issues.

The proof search tactics in the packages are based on the same basic idea: do sequent calculus style backward proofs using suitable rules to break assumptions and conclusions of subgoals gradually down, until the conclusion is provable from an assumption. In other words, natural deduction introduction rules are applied as right sequent style rules, while elimination rules are applied as left rules. Our package handles multiple conclusions using `FALSE` and by working as if using the primed versions of the tactics. Rules for both `FALSE` and strict negation `not` are required by the package. In contrast, the Isabelle classical reasoning package does not make such a distinction since it uses just classical negation to represent multiple conclusions (this is not possible in non-classical logics).

Rules applied by the tactics are organized in rule sets and are supplied directly as arguments of the tactics. As in Isabelle's classical reasoner, a rule set is constructed by dividing rules into groups of introduction rules, elimination rules, etc. For each of these groups, the rules are further divided into safe and hazardous rules. Roughly speaking, the idea is that a safe rule can always be attempted blindly, while a hazardous rule might, for example, sidetrack the search (thus requiring backtracking) or cause the search to loop. The search tactics generally try safe rules before the hazardous ones.

In most cases, the grouping is fairly straightforward, for example, consider the following rules for disjunction:

```
or_intr_left   "P ==> P or Q"
or_intr_right  "Q ==> P or Q"
or_intr        "[| FALSE P ==> Q |] ==> P or Q";
or_elim        "[| P or Q; P==>R; Q==>R |] ==> R"
not_or_intr    "[| not P; not Q |] ==> not (P or Q)"
not_or_elim    "[| not (P or Q); [| not P; not Q |] ==> R |] ==> R"
```

The first two rules are hazardous introduction rules, since they force a choice between the two disjuncts. In contrast the third is a safe introduction rule using FALSE to represent the two possible conclusions. The fourth rule is just the standard elimination rule for disjunction. In addition to these, rules explaining how negation behaves when combined with disjunction are needed. This is the purpose of the last two rules. The reason why these are needed is that it is not possible to give general rules for negation. These conjunction-like introduction and elimination rules are both safe. The rule set `prop_lpfs` for propositional VDM-LPF contains all the above rules, except the hazardous introduction rules which are replaced by the single safe one.

In order to illustrate how the search strategy described above can be used to find proofs, a sketch of a small proof following this strategy is shown below:

```
1.  not (Q and P) ==> not P or not Q

- br or_intr 1;
1. [|  not (Q and P); FALSE  not P |] ==>  not Q

- be not_and_elim 1;
1. [| FALSE  not P;  not Q |] ==>  not Q
2. [| FALSE  not P;  not P |] ==>  not Q

- ba' 1; ba' 1;  (* same as: by (assume_tac' 1) *)
No subgoals!
```

The tactic `lpf_fast_tac` combines the strategy above and depth first search with backtracking at suitable points (e.g. if more than one unsafe rule is applicable). This is probably the most used tactic in the package. For example, when invoked as `lpf_fast_tac prop_lpfs 1`, this tactic proves the above theorem in one step.

Other similar tactics support safe steps only to be carried out (`lpf_safe_tac`), support the restriction of the depth of proofs (`lpf_depth_tac`), etc. So far these tactics have been used to prove (in one step) essentially all of the 120 derived propositional and predicate logic rules mentioned in [6].

Before we consider a "real" case study, we end this subsection by considering a simple example where the assumption of the rule is itself a generalized rule:

```
val [asm] =
goal Pred.thy "(!!y.y:A ==> def P(y)) ==> def exists x:A & P(x)";
by (lpf_fast_tac (exists_lpfs addDs [asm]) 1);
qed "def_exists_inh";
```

This situation is handled by adding the assumption to `exists_lpfs`, which contains a number of rules about the exists quantifier and is one of the intermediate rule sets used to build the theory of predicate VDM-LPF. Hence, the proof search tactics provide a universal strategy which also works for most proofs about quantifiers as long as a sufficient quantifier rule set is supplied as an argument to guide the search. Moreover, this example shows that `lpf_fast_tac` can be used to prove a quantifier rule which is primitive in LPF (see Section 7.4.2).

7.5.3 Gateway Example

This section illustrates how the VDM-LPF instantiation works on an example VDM-SL specification of a trusted gateway (provided by John Fitzgerald). Though the example is small, it is inspired by an industrial case study on formal methods [10, 14]. Strictly speaking, we do not support reasoning about the specification itself, but about an axiomatization of the specification which is automatically generated as described in Section 7.7. The details of the axiomatization are not important for this section.

In the following we first present excerpts from a specification of the trusted gateway and then illustrate the use of our proof tactics to prove invariant and safety properties. We use ASCII syntax for both the Toolbox's and Isabelle's VDM-SL since it is an important point that they are the same.

A Trusted Gateway

A trusted gateway connects an input port to two output ports, which are a high- and a low-security port (see Figure 7.2). The purpose of the gateway is to prevent accidental disclosure of classified or sensitive information on the low-security port. The trusted gateway reads messages from the input port into an internal block where it analyzes them according to two categories of high- and low-classification strings. It must send messages containing only low-classification strings to the low-security port and all other messages to the high-security port.

In VDM-SL we can model a trusted gateway as the following record type:

Figure 7.2: A Trusted Gateway

```
Gateway:: input: Port
          highOutput: Port
          lowOutput: Port
          high: Category
          low: Category
          block: Message
 inv g == (forall msg in set elems g.highOutput &
              classification(msg,g.high,g.low) = <HIGH>) and
          (forall msg in set elems g.lowOutput &
              classification(msg,g.high,g.low) = <LOW>) and
          g.high inter g.low = {}
```

This type has an invariant which specifies correct behaviour of gateways, i.e. all messages on the high-security output port must be classified as high, all messages on the low-security output port must be classified as low, and the two categories of high- and low-classification should not have any strings in common. A message is modeled as a sequence of strings, a port as a sequence of messages, and a category as a set of strings.

The different operations on the gateway are modeled as functions acting on elements of type `Gateway`. These include a function for loading an element into the internal block, a function for analyzing the contents of the block and a function for emptying the block. For illustration, the specification of the analyze function is shown:

```
Analyze: Gateway -> Gateway
Analyze(g) ==
  if classification(g.block,g.high,g.low) = <HIGH>
  then mk_Gateway(g.input,
                  g.highOutput ^ [g.block],
                  g.lowOutput,
                  g.high,g.low,g.block)
  else mk_Gateway(g.input,
                  g.highOutput,
                  g.lowOutput ^ [g.block],
                  g.high,g.low,g.block);
```

This function copies messages from the internal block to the appropriate output port, depending on the result returned by the classification function. The definition of the classification function is central:

```
classification: String * Category * Category -> (<HIGH> | <LOW>)
classification(s,high,low) ==
```

```
if contains_category(s,high)
then <HIGH>
elseif contains_category(s,low)
then <LOW>
else <HIGH>
```

Note that the order of the if-conditions is important, and messages that contain neither high nor low classified strings are classified as high for security reasons.

Invariant Properties

In order to be well-formed, functions such as **Analyze** must respect the invariant of their result type. For **Analyze**, this means that its body must yield a gateway assuming that its argument is a gateway. This is stated as follows in Isabelle:

```
g : Gateway ==>
if classification@(g.block, g.high, g.low) = <HIGH> then
  mk_Gateway(g.input, g.highOutput ^ [g.block], g.lowOutput,
    g.high, g.low, g.block)
else
  mk_Gateway(g.input, g.highOutput, g.lowOutput ^ [g.block],
    g.high, g.low, g.block) :
Gateway
```

Note that essentially the same ASCII syntax is supported by Isabelle here and by the VDM-SL Toolbox in the previous section, but object-level application in VDM-LPF is written using @ instead of the usual juxtaposition (discussed further in Section 7.7.1). Also note that postfix field selection is supported in Isabelle by declarations such as

```
block' :: ex => ex  ("_.block" ...)
high'  :: ex => ex  ("_.high" ...)
```

produced by the axiomatization. The above statement, which is generated automatically using the proof obligation generator described in [5], has been proved in VDM-LPF. However, due to lack of space it is not possible to show the entire interactive proof here. Instead some central steps in the proof are discussed.

The first obvious step is to use case analysis on the conditional expression. Due to the third value in VDM-LPF, we get three subgoals, the two obvious ones and another which says that the test condition must be true or false (it could potentially be undefined in some cases). Here we concentrate on the subgoal corresponding to the first branch of the conditional:

```
[| g : Gateway; classification@(g.block,g.high,g.low) = <HIGH> |] ==>
mk_Gateway
  (g.input, g.highOutput^[g.block], g.lowOutput, g.high,
   g.low, g.block) :
Gateway
```

To prove this, we first unfold the type definition of `Gateway` in the assumptions and the conclusion, then we prove some trivial type judgement subgoals automatically, and what we obtain is the subgoal:

```
[| classification@(g.block,g.high,g.low) = <HIGH>; g.input : Port;
   g.highOutput : Port; g.lowOutput : Port; g.high : Category;
   g.low : Category; g.block : Message;
   (forall m in set elems g.highOutput &
       classification@(m,g.high,g.low) = <HIGH>) and
   (forall m in set elems g.lowOutput &
       classification@(m,g.high,g.low) = <LOW>) and
   g.high inter g.low = {} |] ==>
(forall m in set elems (g.highOutput^[g.block]) &
    classification@(m,g.high,g.low) = <HIGH>) and
(forall m in set elems g.lowOutput &
    classification@(m,g.high,g.low) = <LOW>) and
g.high inter g.low = {}
```

The hardest part is clearly to prove the first conjunct of the conclusion, the other two follow trivially from the assumptions. One tactic `lpf_fast_tac` proves the above subgoal:

```
by (lpf_fast_tac
    (prop_lpfs addIs [foralls_lemma] addEs [Port_elim]) 1);
```

Its rule set argument for guiding the proof search contains proof rules for propositional reasoning, a suitable lemma for the difficult conjunct and a single rule for type checking ports. The lemma states how to break the quantification according to the sequence concatenation, and it is proved from various properties about sets, sequences and of course the set-bounded universal quantifier.

Safety Property

The safety property for a trusted gateway states that all messages on the low security output port are given a low security classification:

```
g : Gateway ==>
forall m in set elems g.lowOutput &
  classification@(m, g.high, g.low) = <LOW>
```

This has a single tactic proof:

```
by (lpf_fast_tac
    (prop_lpfs addEs [Gateway_elim] addDs [inv_Gateway_dest]) 1);
```

The rule set argument supports propositional reasoning, unfolding of the gateway type assumption and unfolding of the resulting gateway invariant. Inspecting the property more closely, it is not surprising that the proof turned out to be that simple, since the safety property is essentially a part of the invariant. Thus the real challenge is to prove that the invariant on `Gateway` is preserved.

7.6 Transformations

We have now completed the description of the VDM-SL proof engine based on Isabelle. The following two sections concern aspects related to the integration of this proof tool with the IFAD VDM-SL Toolbox.

As already noted, the proof tool supports a subset of VDM-SL, since VDM-SL was designed for writing large specifications in industry with constructs that are not designed for embedding in a theorem prover. This section describes how we treat some of the complex constructs by transforming expressions down to expanded expressions in the subset that has been formalized in Isabelle.

Throughout this section we use a record type R of the following form:

```
R :: a:T1
     b:T2
     c:T3
```

7.6.1 Pattern Matching

We represent pattern matching by transforming patterns to combinations of if and let expressions where a boolean condition for matching is expressed using an existential quantification. The user of the system does not see these expanded forms since the expansion is reversed before showing output from Isabelle to the user (after this has been parsed by the Toolbox parser).

In this section we illustrate how to treat patterns in let, quantified and comprehension expressions. In the presentation, we just use expression templates, but the transformation does work for real specifications, see Section 7.7.

Let Expressions

The VDM-LPF instantiation of Isabelle supports only simple let expressions of the form

```
let x = e1, y = e2[x], z = e3[x,y] in expr
```

where x, y and z are variables. Note that the first variable of the let expression may be used in the second expression, etc.

However, a VDM-SL let expression may contain general patterns in addition to variables. Consider a let expression of the form

```
let mk_R(x,-,z) = e1,
    mk_((e),y) = e2
in body
```

Here, x, z and y are pattern variables, - is the don't care pattern and (e) is a value pattern, i.e. the expression e is evaluated. The expression e1 must be a record of type R for the first pattern to match, and for the second pattern to match, e2 must be a tuple with two components where the first component is equal to the value of e. If one of the patterns does not match, then the expression is undefined.

The above expression is transformed to an equivalent expanded expression containing if expressions, existential quantifiers and simple let expressions:

```
let new = e1 in
if (exists x:T1, z:T3, dc:T2 & mk_R(x,dc,z) = new) then
  let x = new.a, z = new.c in
  let new2 = e2 in
  if (exists y:Ty & mk_(e,y) = new2) then
    let y = new2.#2 in body
  else undefined
else undefined
```

This expression lies within the VDM subset formalized in Isabelle; undefined is a constant symbol defined with no rules and represents a divergence from [6]. The variables new, new2 and dc must be new identifiers generated by the transformation (see Section 7.7). The & ends a binding list and corresponds to "such that". The selector #2 takes the second component of a tuple. The type information on, for example, y in the second exists is available in the Toolbox abstract syntax tree after type checking. Note that we illustrate the transformation on concrete syntax due to readability, but it is really performed on the abstract syntax tree.

Quantified Expressions

Patterns in quantified expressions are represented using an existential quantifier and an implication => Consider for example

```
forall mk_(mk_R(x,-,z),(e)) in set s & expr[x,z]
```

which is transformed to:

```
forall new in set s &
  (exists x:T1, z:T3, dc:T2 & mk_(mk_R(x,dc,z),e) = new) =>
  let x = new.#1.a, z = new.#1.c in expr[x,z]
```

For existential quantification we must replace implication by conjunction.

Comprehensions

Set, map, and sequence comprehensions can all be treated in the same way. For example the set comprehension

```
{expr[x,z] | mk_(mk_R(x,-,z),(e)) in set s & p[x,z]}
```

is transformed to:

```
{let x = new.#1.a, z = new.#1.c in expr[x,z] | new in set s &
 exists
    x:T1, z:T3, dc:T2 & mk_(mk_R(x,dc,z),e) = new and p[x,z]}
```

This is also illustrated in the example in Section 7.7.

7.6.2 Cases Expressions

Cases expressions are not supported in the instantiation of Isabelle. VDM-SL cases expressions are transformed to certain combinations of if and simple let expressions, in a way somewhat similar to let expressions with patterns. However, to the user these combinations appear to be cases expressions since the transformation to expanded expressions is reversed before expressions are displayed. Moreover, there are proof rules which make the if-let combinations appear to be cases expressions.

Consider the following example which uses the same patterns that were used above:

```
cases expr:
  mk_R(x,-,z) -> e1,
  mk_((e),y) -> e2,
  others -> e3
end
```

This is transformed to the following expression:

```
let new = expr in
if (exists x:T1, z:T3, dc:T2 & mk_R(x,dc,z) = new) then
  let x = new.a, z = new.c in e1
elseif (exists y:Ty & mk_(e,y) = new) then
  let y = new.#2 in e2
else e3
```

One difference between the expanded forms of let and cases expressions is the use of undefined else branches in if expressions used to represent let expressions.

A number of proof rules has been derived to make the expanded forms mimic cases expressions, i.e. these rules can be applied on let-if combinations in such a way that it appears to the user that these are real cases expression (due to reverse transformation):

```
cases_match
  "[| P(e); e:A; e1(e):B |] ==>
  (let x = e in if P(x) then e1(x) else e2(x)) = e1(e)"
cases_not_match
  "[| not P(e); e:A; e2(e):B |] ==>
  (let x = e in if P(x) then e1(x) else e2(x)) =
  (let x = e in e2(x))"
cases_form_sqt
```

```
"[| def P(e); e:A;
    [| P(e) |] ==>  e1(e):B;
    [| not P(e) |] ==> let x = e in e2(x):B |] ==>
 (let x = e in if P(x) then e1(x) else e2(x)) : B"
```

Let us explain why these proof rules mimic cases expressions from the viewpoint of a user. For simplicity we consider a slightly different example than above. Suppose we are doing a proof where we would like to reduce a cases expression of the form:

```
cases ex:
  mk_(n,m,m) -> n+m,
  mk_(n,-,n) -> n,
  others     -> 0
end
```

Further, suppose that we expect the first pattern to not match. We would then use the proof rule `cases_not_match` to reduce the cases expression. In conducting a proof this rule would be instantiated to:

```
"[| not exists n:nat, m:nat & mk_(n,m,m) = ex; ex:A;
    if (exists n:nat, dc:nat & mk_(n,dc,n) = ex) then n
    else 0:B |] ==>
 (let new = ex in
  if (exists n:nat, m:nat & mk_(n,m,m) = new) then
    let n = new.#1,
        m = new.#2 in n+m
  elseif (exists n:nat, dc:nat & mk_(n,dc,n) = new) then
    let n = new.#1 in n
  else 0) =
 (let new = ex in
  if (exists n:nat, dc:nat & mk_(n,dc,n) = new) then n else 0)"
```

Isabelle would typically do this instantiation and the necessary β-reductions automatically, a user just tells it to apply the rule (by providing the name of the rule). It is important to realize that the left-hand side of the equality is the expanded form of the original cases expression and that the right-hand side of the equality is still a cases expression, namely:

```
cases ex:
  mk_(n,-,n) -> n,
  others     -> 0
end
```

Hence, the first cases expression above reduces to a cases expression where the first pattern has been thrown away, if this pattern does not match. Note that the if-then-else structure of the derived cases rules works because

```
if b1 then e1
elseif b2 then e2
```

```
else e3
```

is just syntactic sugar for

```
if b1 then e1
else if b2 then e2
     else e3
```

7.7 Generating Axioms: An Example

In order to support reasoning about specifications, we automatically generate axioms stated as proof rules which formalize the meaning of the definitions in a specification. These axioms are stated in Toolbox abstract syntax extended with a construction for proof rules, type judgements and subtypes. Once the axioms have been transformed to the Isabelle subset, they can be read into Isabelle and then used in proofs. We shall not go into the details here of the specification of the axiom generator, which was done in VDM-SL and developed using the Toolbox itself, as it is straightforward and based on [6]. Note that in addition to axioms for specifications, Isabelle needs the signatures of new constants. These are also straightforward to generate, again the specification of this was done in VDM-SL using the Toolbox.

In this section we illustrate the working of the axiom (and signature) generator on a small example, which is adapted from an example of a forthcoming book on VDM-SL [9] and inspired by a real industrial system. The example concerns an alarm paging system for a chemical plant. A safety requirement of the system is that for any period of time and any possible alarm code (and location) there must be an expert with the required qualifications to deal with the alarm on duty according to a certain plan.

The specification below is stated in the expression (or functional) subset of VDM-SL, but we could as well have used a state to model the plant and defined some of the functions as implicit operations on the state (using preconditions and postconditions). The approach to state definitions and implicit operations is (also) borrowed from the Mural project. A state definition is treated in essentially the same way as a record and implicit operations are treated as functions on the state which take the state as an extra argument and result.

7.7.1 Type Definitions

We shall model the chemical plant as a record type whose invariant specifies the safety requirement:

```
Plant :: plan   : Plan
         alarms : set of Alarm
inv mk_Plant(plan,alarms) ==
    forall per in set dom plan, alarm in set alarms &
```

```
QualificationsOK(alarm,plan(per));
```

The record has two fields, containing a plan and a set of alarms respectively. The function `QualificationsOK` defines the safety requirement and will be specified later.

A plan is simply a map from periods to sets of experts:

```
Plan = map Period to set of Expert
inv plan == forall exs in set rng plan & exs <> {};

Period = token;
```

The invariant says that there should always be at least one expert associated with any period. The data type of periods is left unspecified (using the `token` type which just denotes an infinite set with equality).

An expert has an ID and a set of qualifications:

```
Expert :: expertid : ExpertId
          quali    : set of Qualification
inv mk_Expert(-,q) == q <> {};

ExpertId = token;

Qualification = <Elec> | <Mech> | <Chem> | <Chief>;
```

Qualifications are modeled as an enumeration type. An expert must have at least one qualification.

The datatype of alarms is modeled as a record type with two fields, one for the alarm codes and one for the location of the alarms:

```
Alarm :: code : AlarmCode
         loc  : Location;

AlarmCode = <A> | <B> | <C>;

Location = <P1> | <P2> | <P3> | <P4> | <P5> | <P6> | <P7>
```

A function is clearly needed to specify which qualifications are required for the different alarms, this is done below.

We shall now consider the signature of new constants and axioms generated for these type definitions. We cannot include all axioms in this chapter. Axioms are generated by executing a shell script `genax` with the file name of our specification `alarm.vdm` as an argument. The result is a file `alarm.thy` which contains the Isabelle theory file for the specification. This is ready to be loaded into the Isabelle/VDM-LPF instantiation, which is started by executing the binary `vdmlpf` in a shell.

The theory file starts with the signature of new constants. For a record type, like `Plant` used for illustration in the following, a record constructor function is introduced:

```
mk_Plant :: [ex,ex] => ex
```

This means that `mk_Plant` is a function in the Isabelle meta-logic, which takes two expressions as arguments, corresponding to the two fields, and yields an expression as a result, corresponding to a record with these two field values. The field selectors of the record type are defined in both an abstract and a concrete syntax version which allows the concrete syntax to support VDM-SL field selection using a postfix notation:

```
plan' :: ex => ex    ("_.plan" ...)
alarms' :: ex => ex    ("_.alarms" ...)
```

The primes are used on constants of the abstract syntax by convention. The parenthesis on the right specifies a priority grammar for the postfix notation, we shall not go into details here. For a record type with an invariant, the signature of the invariant function must also be included:

```
inv_Plant :: ex
```

In contrast to the constructor and selector functions this is represented as an object-logic function. A special object-logic application operator is defined in VDM-LPF and written using an @. The invariant function could be represented as a meta-logic function but there are technical reasons for not doing this. VDM-SL map application and sequence indexing have to be represented in the object-logic, since maps and sequences are object logic values. And the application of invariant functions, as well as many other functions, is not distinguished from these first forms of applications in the abstract syntax tree of the IFAD Toolbox. Hence, different translations of such equivalently represented constructs would be difficult.

After the signature declarations the generated axioms are stated as proof rules. The definition axiom for the invariant function is stated as follows:

```
inv_Plant_defn
  "inv_Plant@(mk_Plant(plan, alarms)) ==
   forall per in set dom plan, alarm in set alarms &
     QualificationsOK@(alarm, plan@(per))"
```

This is stated as a simple meta-equality rewrite rule. A number of formation and definition axioms are introduced for record types. For the record constructor function, the following two axioms are needed:

```
mk_Plant_form
  "[| gax41 : Plan; gax42 : set of Alarm;
      inv_Plant@(mk_Plant(gax41, gax42)) |] ==>
   mk_Plant(gax41, gax42) : Plant"

mk_Plant_defn
  "gax5 : Plant ==> mk_Plant(gax5.plan, gax5.alarms) = gax5"
```

The **gax** variables may look strange, they are automatically indexed by the axiom generator. Each field selector of a record type yields two similar axioms:

```
plan_Plant_form
  "gax5 : Plant ==> gax5.plan : Plan"

plan_Plant_defn
  "[| gax41 : Plan; gax42 : set of Alarm |] ==>
   mk_Plant(gax41, gax42).plan = gax41"
```

Many typing hypotheses appear in order to ensure definedness of object equality =. Basic type definitions like the definition of **Plan** and **AlarmCode** yield fewer axioms. Hence, for **Plan** just two definition axioms are generated:

```
inv_Plan_defn
  "inv_Plan@(plan) == forall exs in set rng plan & exs <> {}"

Plan_defn
  "Plan ==
   << gax1 : map Period to set of Expert & inv_Plan@(gax1) >>"
```

The latter defines **Plan** as a subtype of a map type, restricted using the invariant of **Plan**. The **AlarmCode** definition just yields one axiom

```
AlarmCode_defn
  "AlarmCode == <A> | <B> | <C>"
```

but as a side effect axioms are also generated for each of the quote types, for example:

```
A_axiom
  "<A> : <A>"

A_singleton
  "gax47 : <A> ==> gax47 = <A>"

A_B_disjoint
  "<A> <> <B>"
```

Disjointness axioms are needed for all pairs of quotes. In VDM-SL, the notation <A> is used for both a quote type and its one element. This can be supported in Isabelle since the corresponding constants of the meta-logic have different meta-types. Ambiguities are resolved by the Isabelle type checker.

7.7.2   Function Definitions

We shall now continue the example from above by specifying a few functions. As already noted we need a function to map alarm codes and locations to qualifications required of experts. We also need a function to specify the safety requirement, and a function to page a set of experts to handle a specific alarm.

However, consider first a simpler function that tests whether a given expert is on duty in a certain period:

```
OnDuty: Expert * Period * Plant -> bool
OnDuty(ex,per,plant) ==
  ex in set plant.plan(per)
pre per in set dom plant.plan;
```

This function has as precondition that the period is valid, i.e. it is covered by the plan. This ensures that the map application in the body of the function is defined.

All functions of specifications are represented as object-logic functions, just like invariants. Hence, the signature of OnDuty is simply:

```
OnDuty :: ex
```

The signature of the precondition function pre_OnDuty is the same.

A function definition like this, with a precondition and in the explicit style, results in two axioms, one defining the precondition and one defining the function:

```
pre_OnDuty_defn
  "pre_OnDuty@(ex, per, plant) == per in set dom plant.plan"

OnDuty_defn
  "[| ex : Expert; per : Period; plant : Plant;
      pre_OnDuty@(ex, per, plant) |] ==>
   OnDuty@(ex, per, plant) = ex in set plant.plan@(per)"
```

Strictly speaking the latter should include a type judgement in the hypotheses saying that the body of the function is well-typed, in order to ensure that the LPF equality is defined. However, as mentioned in Section 7.2, we assume that the specifications have been checked using the Toolbox type checker (extended with proof obligations), and for convenience we shall therefore omit this condition. Note that we could include the condition as a hypothesis, prove the hypothesis once and for all, and then derive the above axiom. This integration could be taken further in a very tightly integrated system where the Toolbox type checker could be integrated even more with the proof process to "prove" type judgements arising in proofs.

The following function interprets alarms:

```
AlarmQualifications: Alarm -> set of Qualification
AlarmQualifications(alarm) ==
  cases alarm:
    mk_Alarm(<A>,-)   -> {<Mech>},
    mk_Alarm(<B>,loc) ->
        if loc in set {<P1>,<P3>,<P7>}
        then {<Chief>,<Elec>,<Chem>}
        else {<Elec>},
```

```
    others -> {<Chief>}
  end;
```

Alarms with code <A> require a mechanic, regardless of the location (specified using a "don't care" pattern). Alarms with code <B> at the locations <P1>, <P3> and <P7> are more serious, they require three qualifications, including a chief. <B> alarms at other locations require an electrician. The pattern variable loc is bound to the value of the location field of <B> alarms. Finally, all other alarms require a chief (e.g. for inspecting the situation).

The axiomatization of this definition is straightforward of course, it just yields one axiom. However, the interesting aspect of the definition is the cases expression in the function body, which is translated to nested let and if expressions:

```
AlarmQualifications_defn
  "alarm : Alarm ==>
   AlarmQualifications@(alarm) =
   (let tf21 = alarm in
    if exists dc22 : Location & mk_Alarm(<A>,dc22) = tf21 then
      {<Mech>}
    elseif exists loc : Location & mk_Alarm(<B>,loc) = tf23 then
      let loc = tf23.loc in
      if loc in set {<P1>, <P3>, <P7>} then
        {<Chief>, <Elec>, <Chem>}
      else {<Elec>}
    else {<Chief>})"
```

The variables tf are generated automatically during the transformation. Again, as discussed above, a type judgement for the function body should strictly speaking be included in the hypotheses.

We can now define the safety requirement, which was stated in the invariant of Plant, using the function:

```
QualificationsOK: Alarm * set of Expert -> bool
QualificationsOK(alarm,exs) ==
  let reqquali = AlarmQualifications(alarm) in
    forall quali in set reqquali &
      exists ex in set exs & quali in set ex.quali
```

The axiomatization is obvious:

```
QualificationsOK_defn
  "[| alarm : Alarm; exs : set of Expert |] ==>
   QualificationsOK@(alarm, exs) =
   (let reqquali = AlarmQualifications@(alarm) in
    forall quali in set reqquali &
      exists ex in set exs & quali in set ex.quali)"
```

Again, this is in principle a derived axiom.

The function definitions above are all stated in the explicit style, which means that an algorithm is given for calculating the results. VDM-SL also supports an implicit style, where the result is just specified by a postcondition. The following function definition is in the implicit style:

```
Page(a:Alarm,per:Period,plant:Plant) r:set of Expert
pre per in set dom plant.plan and
    a in set plant.alarms
post r subset plant.plan(per) and
    AlarmQualifications(a) subset
        dunion {quali | mk_Expert(-,quali) in set r};
```

This function uses the plan of a plant to page a set of experts for a given alarm and period. A valid implementation of this function could just calculate all experts on duty for a certain period, regardless of the alarm, but a better implementation would probably try to minimize the set in some way.

Implicit function definitions yield four axioms, two defining the preconditions and postcondition respectively, and one definition and one formation axiom for the new function:

```
pre_Page_defn
  "pre_Page@(a, per, plant) ==
   per in set dom plant.plan and a in set plant.alarms"

post_Page_defn
  "post_Page@(a, per, plant, r) ==
   r subset plant.plan@(per) and
   AlarmQualifications@(a) subset
   dunion {let quali = tf31.quali in quali | tf31 in set r &
     exists quali : set of Qualification, dc32 : ExpertId &
       mk_Expert(dc32, quali) = tf31 and true}"

Page_defn
  "[| a : Alarm; per : Period; plant : Plant;
     pre_Page@(a, per, plant) |] ==>
   post_Page@(a, per, plant, Page@(a, per, plant))"

Page_form
  "[| a : Alarm; per : Period; plant : Plant;
     pre_Page@(a, per, plant) |] ==>
   Page@(a, per, plant) : set of Expert"
```

Note that the body of the postcondition is expanded slightly in order to treat the pattern in the set comprehension expression. The Toolbox parser inserts true when there is no restriction predicate in a comprehension expression. The Toolbox type checker ensures that the third axiom makes sense by generating a satisfiability proof obligation. Hence, also axioms for implicit functions are generated on the assumption that specifications are type correct.

7.8   Future Work

Although the current system can be used to reason about VDM-SL specifications, it can clearly be improved in many ways. Some future work and improvements are discussed briefly below.

Proof Rules

The proof system still needs work to be truly practical. Many of the rules for the different VDM-SL datatypes seem quite ad hoc and more work is needed here. Although often ignored, it is a major task to develop well-organized and powerful proof rules for datatypes like those of VDM-SL. Moreover, such proof rules should be organized in rule sets for the proof search tactics (if possible). This is also a major and important task.

Tactics

The current version of VDM-LPF does not provide a simplifier. Unfortunately it does not seem easy to instantiate Isabelle's generic simplifier to support reasoning about equality in VDM-LPF, since in order to do this we must justify that we can identify the VDM-LPF object-level equality with Isabelle's meta-level equality. If we cannot use Isabelle's simplifier, a special-purpose VDM-LPF simplifier should be constructed.

In addition, it might be useful to construct a number of special purpose tactics, for example, for reasoning about arithmetic and for proving trivial type conditions, which tend to clutter up proofs.

Compatibility

VDM-LPF is meant to be used to reason about VDM-SL and to be integrated with existing tools. A natural question is whether or not all these are compatible, and if not, what should then be changed. For example, is the proof system used sound with respect to the ISO standard (static and dynamic) semantics of VDM-SL? Although no inconsistencies have been found in the proof system itself, preliminary investigations suggest that there might be a problem with compatibility. For example, it is currently possible to derive **true or 1** as a theorem in the proof system, but according to the semantics of VDM-SL this is undefined. Since the semantics of VDM-SL is defined by an ISO standard it is perhaps most tempting to try to modify the proof system to exclude theorems as the one above. However, the result might be a proof system which is not suited for practical reasoning. This compatibility issue requires further attention.

Natural Deduction versus Sequent Calculus

The current instantiation is based on a natural deduction formulation of LPF. However, there are indications suggesting that a sequent calculus formulation of LPF might be a better foundation, in particular for automating proofs.

Status of the Current Prototype

The current prototype does not completely integrate the Toolbox and the theorem prover Isabelle, since the proof manager and the graphical user interface have not been implemented. However, it does provide the bits and pieces to support the integration. One shell script generates and transforms axioms, another parses, reverse transforms and pretty-prints Isabelle proof states. Proofs are presently conducted by interacting with Isabelle directly, which is feasible since the Isabelle instantiation supports a subset of the ISO standard for VDM-SL ASCII notation.

By exploiting transformations, we are able to treat essentially the full functional subset of VDM-SL. We have not considered, for instance, constructs like let-be-such-that expressions and union patterns, whose underdetermined semantics destroys reflexivity of equality [15]. As in Mural, we can treat state definitions and implicit operations. However, we have not yet considered explicit operations and statements, which form an imperative subset of VDM-SL, but already existing work on formalizing Hoare logic in the HOL theorem prover may be useful here [1]. Features of VDM-SL like exception handling have not been considered either.

7.9 Conclusion

In this chapter we have described the implementation of some central aspects of a proof support tool for VDM-SL based on Isabelle and how this tool has been integrated with the IFAD VDM-SL Toolbox. In particular we have illustrated the formalization of existing LPF proof rules in Isabelle and new facilities for automating proof search, which automatically proved essentially all of the 120 propositional and predicate logic derived rules listed in [6]. We feel that our experiments have shown Isabelle to be a very useful tool for quickly building specialized proof support for new and even non-standard logics such as VDM-LPF. Moreover, Isabelle is relatively easy to adapt to VDM-SL and to integrate with the IFAD VDM-SL Toolbox.

VDM-LPF supports only a subset of VDM-SL, and it is a major challenge to build proof support for the full VDM-SL standard. The language was designed for writing large specifications in industry, and this is reflected in both its syntax and its data types. On the syntax side, it supports pattern matching in for example let and quantifier expressions, and it has constructs such as cases expressions, again with patterns, which are difficult to represent in a theorem prover. On the data type side, it has non-disjoint unions, record types with postfix field selection, and arbitrary-length tuples that are not equivalent to nested pairs. Moreover, the underlying logic of VDM-SL is the non-classical three-valued Logic of Partial Functions, which makes traditional classical approaches to, for example, proof search infeasible.

We are able to handle difficult constructs of VDM-SL by transforming these to expanded expressions in the VDM-LPF subset. However, the user needs never realize the transformations while writing proofs, since we can reverse transformations and provide a collection of derived proof rules which mimic the original expressions, though these actually work on expanded expressions. The transformations are dependent on the abstract syntax tree representation of expressions in the Toolbox, and would not be possible in Isabelle.

As a further consequence of the fact that the Isabelle instantiation supports the VDM-SL standard, we can use the Toolbox parser to read output from Isabelle. It has only been slightly modified to read proof rules, type judgements and subtypes, which are not part of the VDM-SL standard. Similarly, an ASCII pretty-printer for VDM-SL can be used to print abstract syntax both after it has been transformed to a subset understood by Isabelle and after Isabelle output has been parsed and reverse transformed to the original abstract syntax. Hence, no major changes or additions were needed to the IFAD Toolbox, in order to build the present prototype of an integrated system. Finally, as another consequence, the Isabelle instantiation can be used directly to reason in a subset of VDM-SL.

A main feature of the integrated CASE and theorem proving tool is that testing and proof for specification validation can be employed at the same time. All facilities of the IFAD VDM-SL Toolbox are available while conducting proofs. Moreover, the user always works in the notation provided by the Toolbox and is not limited by restrictions on syntax imposed by the proof component. Furthermore, it is possible to support industrial requirements like proof management, automation and version control, which typically are not well-addressed in theorem provers, outside the theorem prover in the proof support tool.

A generic framework like Isabelle allows quick implementation of powerful theorem provers through reuse. However, we have seen some limitations to reuse when dealing with a three-valued logic like VDM-LPF. In particular, the generic simplifier and classical reasoning package appear not to be easy to use with VDM-LPF. However, in our implementation of a special purpose reasoning package we were able to reuse many idea and even code from the existing package.

Acknowledgments

We would like to thank Peter Gorm Larsen for useful discussions concerning this work. Bernhard Aichernig and Peter Gorm Larsen commented on early drafts of this chapter. The work was financially supported by the Danish Research Councils.

7.10 Bibliography

[1] S. Agerholm. Mechanizing program verification in HOL. In *Proceedings of the 1991 International Workshop on the HOL Theorem Proving System and Its Applications*. IEEE Computer Society Press, 1992. A full version is in Technical Report IR-111, University of Aarhus, Department of Computer Science, Denmark.

[2] S. Agerholm. Translating specifications in VDM-SL to PVS. In J. von Wright, J. Grundy, and J. Harrison, editors, *Proceedings of the 9th International Conference on Theorem Proving in Higher Order Logics (TPHOLs'96)*, volume 1125 of *Lecture Notes in Computer Science*. Springer-Verlag, 1996.

[3] S. Agerholm and J. Frost. An Isabelle-based theorem prover for VDM-SL. In *Proceedings of the 10th International Conference on Theorem Proving in Higher Order Logics (TPHOLs'97)*, LNCS. Springer-Verlag, August 1997.

[4] S. Agerholm and J. Frost. Towards an integrated CASE and theorem proving tool for VDM-SL. In *FME'97*, LNCS. Springer-Verlag, September 1997.

[5] B. Aichernig and P. G. Larsen. A proof obligation generator for VDM-SL. In *FME'97*, LNCS. Springer-Verlag, September 1997.

[6] J. C. Bicarregui, J. S. Fitzgerald, P. A. Lindsay, R. Moore, and B. Ritchie. *Proof in VDM: A Practitioner's Guide*. FACIT. Springer-Verlag, 1994.

[7] J. H. Cheng. A logic for partial functions. Ph.D. Thesis UMCS-86-7-1, Department of Computer Science, University of Manchester, Manchester M13 9PL, England, 1986.

[8] R. Elmstrøm, P. G. Larsen, and P. B. Lassen. The IFAD VDM-SL Toolbox: A practical approach to formal specifications. *ACM Sigplan Notices*, 29(9):77–80, September 1994.

[9] J. Fitzgerald and P. G. Larsen. *Modelling Systems: Practical Tools and Techniques*. Camdridge University Press, The Edinburgh Building, Cambridge CB2 2RU, UK, 1997. To appear.

[10] J. Fitzgerald, P. G. Larsen, T. Brookes, and M. Green. *Applications of Formal Methods, edited by M.G. Hinchey and J.P. Bowen*, chapter 14. Developing a Security-critical System using Formal and Convential Methods, pages 333–356. Prentice-Hall International Series in Computer Science, 1995.

[11] IFAD World Wide Web page. http://www.ifad.dk.

[12] C. B. Jones. *Systematic Software Development using VDM*. Prentice-Hall International Series in Computer Science. Prentice-Hall, 1986.

[13] C. B. Jones, K. D. Jones, P. A. Lindsay, and R. Moore. *Mural: A Formal Development Support System*. Springer-Verlag, 1991.

[14] P. G. Larsen, J. Fitzgerald, and T. Brookes. Applying Formal Specification in Industry. *IEEE Software*, 13(3):48–56, May 1996.

[15] P. G. Larsen and B. S. Hansen. Semantics for underdetermined expressions. *Formal Aspects of Computing*, 8(1):47–66, January 1996.

[16] P. G. Larsen, B. S. Hansen, et al. Information technology — Programming languages, their environments and system software interfaces — Vienna Development Method — Specification Language — Part 1: Base language. International Standard, ISO/IEC 13817-1, December 1996.

[17] P. Mukherjee. Computer-aided validation of formal specifications. *Software Engineering Journal*, pages 133–140, July 1995.

[18] L. C. Paulson. *Isabelle: A Generic Theorem Prover*, volume 828 of *Lecture Notes in Computer Science*. Springer-Verlag, 1994.

[19] F. Pfenning and C. Elliott. Higher-order abstract syntax. In *Proceedings of the SIGPLAN'88 Conference on Programming Language Design and Implementation*, pages 199 – 208, Atlanta, Georgia, June 1988.

[20] PVS World Wide Web page. `http://www.csl.sri.com/pvs/overview.html`.

7.11   VDM-SL Syntax in Isabelle

This appendix describes the formalization of VDM-SL syntax in Isabelle, using an abstract and a concrete syntax and translations between them.

Abstract Syntax

We first provide a flavour of the core abstract syntax which is used internally in Isabelle for reasoning. It is a higher-order abstract syntax [19] in order to ensure smooth and elegant handling of bound variables. This means that object-level variables are identified with meta-level variables of a particular type. Meta-abstraction is used to represent variable binding, and substitution for bound variables is expressed using meta-function application. Isabelle's β-conversion handles the variable capturing problem. Moreover, typical side-conditions involving free variables are handled using universal meta-quantification and meta-application.

The abstract syntax has two central categories, one of expressions and one of types. Consequently Isabelle's typed lambda-calculus is extended with two new types **ex** and **ty** respectively. These types are logical in the sense that they are meant to be reasoned about, and new constants of these types are equipped with a standard prefix syntax.

Expressions and types of VDM-SL are represented in Isabelle using constants with result type **ex** and **ty**. Some examples of such constants are

```
not'     :: ex => ex
forall'  :: [ty,ex => ex] => ex
eq'      :: [ex,ex] => ex
natty'   :: ty
succ'    :: ex => ex
```

These constants correspond to negation, universal quantification, equality, the type of natural numbers and the successor function. The constant for universal quantification is an example of a higher-order constant because it takes a function as its second argument. Using such constants as above it is possible to write expressions in a simple prefix form in the abstract syntax. The constants are primed in order to distinguish them from constants of the concrete syntax. The following example is a boolean expression which states that adding one is not the identity function for any natural number:

```
forall'(natty',%x.not'(eq'(x,succ'(x))))
```

This example illustrates how meta-abstraction % is used to express variable binding at the object-level.

Concrete Syntax

The purpose of the concrete syntax is to provide a user-friendly and familiar notation for presentation, while the role of the abstract syntax presented above was to support reasoning internally in Isabelle. The concrete syntax is based on the ISO standard of the VDM-SL ASCII notation [16]. This makes Isabelle/VDM-LPF relatively easy to use as a stand-alone tool for people who have experience with VDM-SL (and proof). Furthermore, it provides a standardized text-based format for exchanging data with other software components, such as the IFAD VDM-SL Toolbox.

The VDM-SL syntax standard is expressed as a context free grammar with additional operator precedence rules to remove ambiguities. The concrete syntax of VDM-LPF is expressed as a priority grammar, i.e as a grammar where the nonterminal symbols are decorated with integer priorities [18]. This priority grammar is constructed by a systematic and fairly straightforward translation of productions and operator precedence rules into priority grammar productions. In most cases the base form of the priority grammar productions comes directly from the corresponding production in the VDM-SL grammar, while the priorities of the production are constructed from the corresponding operator precedences. Some simple examples of such priority grammar productions are:

$$ex^{(250)} \leftarrow \text{not } ex^{(250)}$$
$$ex^{(310)} \leftarrow ex^{(310)} = ex^{(311)}$$

The structure of the above productions matches the corresponding declarations of the abstract syntax. Consequently, in such cases the concrete syntax is implemented in Isabelle simply by adding a syntax annotation to the relevant constant declaration of the abstract syntax. The constant declarations corresponding to the two productions above are

```
not' :: ex => ex  ("(2not _/)" [250] 250)
eq'  :: [ex,ex] => ex  ("(_ = /_)" [310,311] 310)
```

where the types correspond to nonterminals of the productions. The syntax annotation in brackets consists of two parts: a quoted mixfix template followed by an optional priority part. The mixfix template describes the terminals and contains other printing and parsing directives (see [18]).

However, not all of the concrete syntax can be handled by adding syntax annotations to the constant declarations for the abstract syntax. In cases such as multiple binding quantifiers, set comprehensions, if-then-elseif expressions, enumerated sequences, etc., the structure of the concrete syntax differs from that of the abstract syntax. Such situations are handled using separate syntax declarations which declare a special kind of constants. These constants only serve a syntactic purpose and are never used internally for reasoning. The syntax declarations below are those needed for multiple binder universal quantifications:

```
""       :: tbind => tbinds  ("_")
tbinds_ :: [tbind,tbinds] => tbinds  ("(_,/ _)")
tbind_  :: [idt,ty] => tbind  ("(_ :/ _)")
forall_ :: [tbinds,ex] => ex  ("(2forall/ _ &/ _)" [100,100] 100)
```

Unlike when using syntax annotations, the relationship to the abstract syntax is not established automatically in such separate syntax declarations. Instead translations are defined to relate the abstract and the concrete syntax, as discussed in the following section.

Translations

A simple example of a translation is the expansion of the special notation for not equal <> in the concrete syntax to negated equality in the abstract syntax. This is implemented using Isabelle's macro mechanism. A macro is essentially a rewrite rule which works on Isabelle's abstract syntax trees. In this case the macro is

```
"x <> y" == "not x = y"
```

This translation means that not equal will behave just as a negated equality in proofs. Another deliberate consequence is that any negated equality will be presented using the more readable not equal notation. In other words the original formatting is not always retained, but instead the implementation tries to improve it whenever possible.

Another more complicated example is that of universal quantification with multiple type bindings. In VDM-LPF such a quantifier is viewed simply as a syntactic shorthand for a number of nested single binding quantifiers. The translation between the concrete external first-order representation and the internal higher-order abstract representation is implemented using a mixture of macros and print translations. However, these are too complex to be included here. During parsing, the effect of these macros and translations is that concrete syntax such as

```
forall x:nat, y:nat & x = y
```

is automatically translated to the following abstract syntax:

```
forall'(nat,%x.forall'(nat,%y.eq'(x,y)))
```

Similarly, during printing, the abstract form is translated to the concrete form. Constants such as tbind_ and forall_ of the previous section do not occur explicitly here, since they are only used in the standard first-order syntax trees corresponding to the concrete syntax. However, they are used in the relevant macros and translations. Other variable binding constructs are handled in a similar fashion to universal quantification.

Index